the TRIUMPH of the AIRHEADS
and the RETREAT from COMMONSENSE

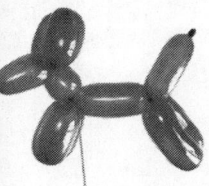

SHELLEY GARE

the TRIUMPH of the AIRHEADS
and the RETREAT from COMMONSENSE

Published jointly by
Park Street Press, a division of ACP Magazines Ltd (ABN 18 053 273 546) and
Media 21 Publishing Pty Ltd (ABN 82 090 635 073)

ACP Magazines Ltd
54 Park Street, Sydney, GPO Box 4088, Sydney, NSW 1028

Media21 Publishing Pty Ltd
30 Bay Street, Double Bay, NSW 2028
Tel: (02) 9362 1800 Fax: (02) 9362 9500
Email: m21@media21.com.au
Website: www.media21publishing.com

© Copyright Shelley Gare 2006
© Copyright Park Street Press 2006
© Copyright Media21 Publishing Pty Ltd 2006

First published, 2006. Reprinted 2007

Some material in this book has appeared before in essays and columns written by the author and published in various journals. There are footnotes throughout this book and the work of others is always acknowledged. If any person feels their work has not been adequately acknowledged, we would ask you to contact the publishers so this can be rectified for future editions.

National Library of Australia Cataloguing-in-Publication entry

Gare, Shelley.
The triumph of the airheads : and the retreat from commonsense.

ISBN 1 876624 54 X.

1. Social influence. 2. Commonsense reasoning – Social aspects - Australia.
3. Australia - Intellectual life. I. Title.

303.320994

All rights reserved. This publication is copyright. No part of it may be reproduced or transmitted in any form without the prior written permission of the publishers.

Designer: Sharon McGrath
Cover illustration: Greg Bakes
Back cover photograph: Greg Barrett
Colour reproduction: Clayton Lloyd, Flawless Imaging
Printed by: McPhersons Printing Group
Sales: Stephen Balme Email: stephen@media21.com.au

FOR CHRISSIE (1953–2006)

CONTENTS

FOREWORD 8

1. WHY I COMES BEFORE U 13
   Dumbing down and going up

2. THE UNBEARABLE LITENESS OF BEING 27
   The end of seriousness

3. POWER, MONEY AND ISAAC NEWTON 45
   What Mme de Pompadour knew that economic rationalists don't

4. SALUTE THE RICH 65
   Money makes airheads of all of us

5. THE NEW F-WORD 83
   Empowering the inner ditz

6. THE WORLD IS MY OYSTER SHELL 101
   How to buy a life

7. HOW TO EDUCATE A GOLDFISH 125
   Ignorance is an airhead's best friend

8. MANAGEMENT FOR AIRHEADS 153
   Hot air rises

9. ACCOUNTABLE (OR NOT) 181
   Numbers are an airhead's second-best friend

10. THE SOMETHING-NOTHING PROBLEM 209
    From woo-woo to guru: who stole our brains?

11. STUFF HAPPENS 235
    Can an airhead have ethics?

12. A SENSE OF THE RIDICULOUS 263
    How to, like, stay sane

ACKNOWLEDGEMENTS 280
ENDNOTES 282

FOREWORD

A teacher at an elite primary school made a casual aside to me one day. He was talking about disappointed parents; the ones who insist their child should have done better in the exams or have been made a prefect or cricket captain, but the school got it wrong. These parents, often rich and powerful, are a phenomenon of our time. The teacher explained in a matter-of-fact way that he and his colleagues call it the David Jones syndrome. What these parents often really mean, he said, is that they want a different child: "It's as if they've gone into DJs and they wanted a Miele but they got a Simpson."

I can't help feeling as if someone has taken a pinch of my heart every time I think about that story. I don't know what kind of materialistic parent would not want to love their child more than their child's exam results. What parent is so desperate for status that their child has to be a status symbol, too? I don't know what kind of competitive, airheaded world we've created where such attitudes are so common that teachers have had to invent a joke name to inure themselves to ignorance so casual and cruel that it rewrites the most crucial relationship between human beings.

Yet, if it were legal, these parents would probably cart their child off to a car-boot sale to swap for one who scores better on maths, who is more popular or more powerful playing sport. A child to be proud of ...

Not this one they've got instead.

The story about DJs syndrome, which could as easily be called Harrods or Sears syndrome, was the most perplexing I came across as I explored the world of the airhead, examining everything from the antics of hotel heiress Paris Hilton to what really happens inside the brain of a management consultant. It's true that the airhead lurks in all of us to some degree. The mother who was capable of saying "I think the whole of year 9 at school are extremely interested in luxury goods in Sydney" may be very level-headed most of the rest of the time. The men and women who run their companies according to the handbooks of *Jargon Incorporated* and *When in Doubt, Downsize* may read Montesquieu and Rousseau in their spare time and work in the local charity shop once a month. A touch of airheadism here and there does not make one a complete airhead, nor someone who exhibits every other trait of airheadism.

Nevertheless, these are times in which, in various ways outlined in this book, we are being encouraged as never before to let our inner airhead bloom. If the airheads are winning, the question has to be asked: what have the rest of us been doing? The answer is, sometimes or even often: being airheads, too. Airheadism pays off, whether it's the politician on the witness stand with memory loss, the business chief pleading the case for even higher CEO salaries, the *Big Brother* contestant wondering aloud if pigs eat through their noses or the newspaper journalist writing seriously about $10,000 watches. If Marilyn Monroe were alive now, her studio bosses would be horrified to think she was seen reading James Joyce. Talk about damaging the brand! Today, the airhead is the ideal twenty-first-century citizen and so airheadism flourishes, sometimes in the most unlikely places.

The job of this book is to show what's behind the triumph of the airheads, and to provide numerous snapshots of what has happened to us as a result. It's about what happens when a society careens off the rails in all sorts of ways, waving cocktail glasses in the air as it goes. It is about an age where vacuity is not just celebrated, it is poured down our throats. The question is: why?

SHELLEY GARE, SYDNEY, 2006

Seven Habits of Highly

The new twenty-first-century politician likes airheads and so do the people who now run our corporations. Here's why:

Airheads are to consuming what Angelina Jolie is to adoption. Their ideal pastime is shopping, and if someone is airheaded enough to pay $28.50 for a jar of imported Piedmontese honey and $4,000 for a handbag that ten of their neighbours have already, this can only be good for the economy. More money for those at the top and more kudos for the politicians (who, these days, very often end up in business and at the top about a lickety-split second after their parliamentary days are over).

Airheads adore numbers. An economic theorist deprived of his statistics is as anxious and irritable as a baby whose blanky has been taken away from him. Statistics about rising living standards matter much more than, say, noticing the beggars on Oxford Street in Sydney or how many Australian children live below the poverty line. When researchers at St Vincent de Paul released stats in 2005 that claimed 4.5 million Australians lived in households with an income of less than $400 a week, a right-wing think-tank rushed out a release proving St Vinnies was wrong and showing that "Australian Bureau of Statistics data indicates the maximum possible figure is no higher than 2.5 million". Oh, no problem then – not a quarter of the population of one of the world's most resource-rich countries living in distress, just a bit over 10 percent.

Airheads don't read much beyond the glossies (business, lifestyle, gossip) and books of self-help or theory, which is why they are so receptive to jargon, slang and management speak. Their ideas and vocabulary cupboards are bare.

Aspirational Airheads

4

Airheads have taken Descartes and *cogito ergo sum* to heart. I think, therefore I am, said Descartes, thus proving his own existence. But, thinks an airhead, does anyone else exist? Where is the proof of that? What if you wasted all that time thinking about other people and then discovered there was, like, no need after all. What if you voted to spend more money on hospitals and schools when you could have had it all for yourself?

5

Airheads are driven only by how the next five minutes may turn out. Like the greedy children in psychologist Daniel Goleman's famous example of emotional intelligence who chose to eat their marshmallow straightaway rather than score two marshmallows if they waited, they cannot put off gratification for a second. The average airhead business plan thus centres on what rewards can be delivered immediately; never mind the calamity waiting around the corner. This is especially so in today's economic climate where news of large-scale sackings always drives up the share price (and thus the value of the share options being shared out at the top).

6

Theory is paramount in the airhead universe, whether it is two airhead teenagers discussing astrological beliefs and boyfriends or a McKinsey & Co management consultant explaining again just why his group once thought mobile phones would never take off and the guys at Enron were so clever. Theory too often gets it wrong, but airheads have the memory of goldfish so it's not as if anyone cares or has to worry in hindsight.

7

Most of all, airheads always do better in packs. One airhead looks mindless, a few airheads are an annoying distraction, but a big bunch of airheads – well, they look exactly like too many of the people who get to run most of the developed world.

CHAPTER 1

Why I Comes Before U

"We're living in a world of perfection and extremes.
Everything is pumped-up and cartoon-like; there are no
nuances. We're becoming these plastic creatures and when
you get that plastic, there's a certain dead quality to it."
TOM FORD, EX-GUCCI GROUP DESIGN HEAD

"Most intelligent f***wit I've ever come across."
MOGUL KERRY PACKER ON ACADEMIC,
EX-MCKINSEY & CO PARTNER AND FORMER FAIRFAX CEO
FRED HILMER, NOW VICE-CHANCELLOR OF
THE UNIVERSITY OF NEW SOUTH WALES

Many years ago, I shared an office with a man who was so vacuous he would have posed a serious problem for any neurosurgeon opening up his head. Naturally enough, in these Teflon-times, he had a stellar reputation in his field. He spoke well, after all, and was fully conversant in the kind of management-think and -speak that later made *Who Moved My Cheese?* a world best-seller among humans, not rats.

Anyone who actually worked with this man, though, knew that if you were to compare the thoughts inside his head with those inside the head of, say, a guppy, there wouldn't have been much difference. In fact, if you'd had to choose who to put in his position, him or the guppy, you might have opted for the fish because then at least everybody else who knew how to do their job would have been able to get on with it.

Such guppy-men – and guppy-women – have been slowly emerging since the mid-twentieth century when Dr Laurence Peter developed the Peter Principle, which rules that people rise to the level of their own incompetence. Now, for all sorts of reasons to which we'll return, they're unstoppable. Scott Adams, creator of the *Dilbert* comic strip, spent almost twenty mind-shorting years in the banking and telephone industries. He once noted helpfully of what he had observed: "First question in the Management quiz: do you believe that anything you don't understand must be easy to do?"

Of course, there have always been airheads. Every office, classroom, lecture theatre, most

Like, whatever

"We couldn't go through the Door of Miracles unless we gave them 10 percent of our money. So we stopped going."
JERRY HALL ON WHY SHE AND MICK JAGGER STOPPED VISITING THE CELEBRITY-HEAVY LONDON KABBALAH CENTRE.

cinema and television screens, and most social groups had one or two. I remember we used to make allowances and even feel sorry for them when they didn't understand a joke or said something in a meeting that showed they were three sentences behind everyone else. That was a big mistake because, somehow, in the hectic rush towards the end of the twentieth century, when there was more economic, business, cultural, social and demographic change in twenty years than in the previous fifty, it was the airheads who soared like hot-air balloons. There was something in the newly postmodern, economic-rationalist[1] atmosphere that gave them lift. I don't think it was irony. Some of the results have been pretty funny.

Plum Sykes, author of chick-lit best-seller *Bergdorf Blondes*, explained the new reality, commenting disdainfully to *Guardian* journalist Hadley Freeman in 2004, "Like, you have to be brighter to write about idiotic politicians than to interview Karl Lagerfeld who's, like, beyond smart?" This new tone, instead of being looked down upon, seems to be the accepted way of talking now. Sensible people might be raising their eyebrows but sensible people aren't being offered $800,000 book deals.

Celebrity singer, wife and mother Posh Beckham claimed she'd never read a book, presumably including her own, an autobiography syndicated for newspaper extract for more than a million pounds. Later, when she scornfully objected – "Of *course* I've read a book!" – the Spanish journalist who had quoted her, squelched the denials, saying she had Posh on tape.

Trends guru, millionaire and founder of *Wallpaper** magazine Tyler Brûlé flew into Sydney and complained loftily that "luxury has dumbed down".[2] He was concerned about something he called "masstige", by which he meant affordable luxury for the masses and the very opposite of prestige. God forbid.

When you saw who was suddenly scrabbling up the poles of television, filmmaking, publishing, education, the arts, politics, management, business and public service, the aphorism "empty vessels make the most sound" had never seemed more apt. The more of them clustered up there, the more they helped other airheads to rise. (How my heart sighs now when I learn that yet another of them has landed a plum job. There goes that neighbourhood, too, I think to myself, as I imagine all the little nongs and nongettes who will soon be recruited by the new kingpin nong.)

There were still plenty of intelligent, hard-working, sensible people around, but they were like a bunch of well-schooled racehorses who had suddenly, for no reason they could understand, been trucked off before their time to lesser races or even the paddocks. From there, they looked back with puzzlement at the gilded ponies now prancing giddily around the racetrack.

If you went into a department store to buy a toaster, for instance, there would be a young idiot manager poncing around and bossing the capable middle-aged ladies in black who would roll their eyes when he disappeared out the back.

Airheads were turning up in all sorts of surprising positions and making the most of their elevation. "The illiteracy level of our children are appalling," President George W. Bush proclaimed to his nation's mayors in Washington early in 2004. Later that same year, he was voted back into the White House. "Bush may not have been born stupid," wrote Jacob Weisberg, editor of online magazine *Slate*, in his deluxe edition of *Bushisms*, "but he has achieved stupidity, and now wears it as a badge of honour."[3] In 2003, Bush invaded Iraq and persuaded the Australian and the British prime ministers along, too, because he swore Iraq had weapons of mass destruction. When it turned out it didn't, they didn't turn back. They just went: oh, whatever.

Then there was the West Australian politician who revealed that he seriously thought the Pope had a wife. State opposition leader Matt Birney, under fire for taking his partner on a taxpayer-funded trip to Greece, was asked on ABC talkback radio if he thought it would be appropriate to take his partner to meet the Pope. His reply: "If it were the sort of function where it was appropriate to have partners there, that is, if the Pope happened to have his partner there, then yes, absolutely."[4]

In quick succession from the late Nineties on, several failed businessmen and women left their jobs at the top of major corporations and were rewarded with millions of dollars for their foolishness. Again and again, a new boss would be brought into an organisation, government department or industry to impose spanking new management ideas. Staff would leave or be sacked, whole departments would be created, disappeared or rearranged and then, in no time at all, the new boss would be gone, too – with a generous pay-off, sometimes more than most of us would earn in a lifetime. It would have been discovered that he/she didn't know what he/she was talking about after all. Bosses with more rat-cunning made sure to get out in time, to another sinecure, promotion or set of board positions, so that when their newly reorganised edifice collapsed behind them, they were out of earshot.

Schools and universities, under the leadership of a bunch of ideologues dosed up on postmodern French philosophers, started turning out students who couldn't spell or construct an essay. They could tell you if you were being gender-specific but not what an adverb was or what it did. The apostrophe in it's went the way of the yeti or rampaged around like a rogue elephant and everybody went: well, so what? Something called a student's "journey" turned out to be much more important. Not that anyone at the top could ever tell you where the journey was supposed to end. It was apparently supposed to be endless and its direction was left to the spelling-flummoxed and apostrophe-challenged youth. No wonder they never found out about adverbs.

Universities, flattened and left gasping by all this wafty, New Age, postmodern thinking, then disappeared under the steamroller of economic rationalism. The modern university has now been so turned over to making money, managerialism and covering it all up with a haze of jargon that a spoof website (www.aiu.name) was created for a supposedly new university. Its slogan is "More better education" and its motto *Rapacitas Bona Est* ("The profit motive is beneficial"). So used are we to what's happened that when I emailed the Web link to a friend, a man who once taught classics at Cambridge, it took him a few minutes to realise he was looking at a joke.

It seems to me now that there are more airheads than reasonable people. Or perhaps they just make more noise than everyone else. There must have been a moment in history when the airheads in ascendancy finally passed critical mass. Now that I look back, I think it was May 1998. That's when I wrote a column about a sudden spate of high-profile forced resignations and retrenchments in the

---

Huh?

Senator Barnaby Joyce:
"So if I shoot a woman in the abdomen and do not kill her, but kill the baby, I have not actually committed a crime."
Roslyn Dundas, for the Women's Electoral Lobby:
"No, you actually have committed a crime by shooting a woman."
SENATE INQUIRY INTO REPEAL OF MINISTERIAL AUTHORITY FOR APPROVAL OF THE ABORTION PILL RU-486, DECEMBER 15, 2005.

business field. "Is no-one good allowed to have a job any more?" I asked plaintively with a columnist's licence.

Good is no longer what it's about. This is what airheads understand: that this is the age of the free market, and the pursuit and acquisition of money at all costs is now considered more important than knowledge, values and commonsense. This is also the post-postmodern age, which means there *are* no such things as objective knowledge or values or truths or commonsense. Postmodernism says they're just figments in someone else's culture or mindset. How lucky is that? It really comes down to you and how you see the world, so you can't lose. It's basically on for young and old. Whatever you can get away with goes, really.

It's amazing how fast a world can change when enough people learn to approach life like this. For centuries, populations have aspired towards greater things, to improving their lot, to making discoveries, to reaching out to the unknown, to celebrating life … Our natural trajectory has always been upwards, out of the primordial slime and towards some wonderful future that involved bright light, radiance and refinement. The work of painters, poets, musicians, writers and playwrights all arc-ed in the same direction, even when, like Samuel Beckett or Sinclair Lewis, they were writing for effect about the very opposite.

Now we favour more tangible, easier-to-reach rewards – designer handbags, a spray-on tan, a berth on the next reality television show or strategic Master of Business Admin programme. Conditions have never been so perfect for the breeding and upkeep of guppies. If the twenty-first century is to keep going the way it is, making its profits, sneakily transferring wealth and power to a select group, it *needs* the ignorant, the thoughtless, the selfish, the vacuous, the narcissistic, the spendthrift and the money-motivated. As long as you're not interfering with airheads' direct interests (see designer handbags and MBAs above) they are malleable, as unthreatening as a soy decaf latte, as unthinking as pod people.

My particular guppy mate's awesome rise had not happened in spite of his being an airhead but *because* he was an airhead. If you peered up the ladder of opportunity, you could see that guppy-man almost certainly worked for another guppy-man or guppy-woman.

Those who can prosper by appealing to the airhead within and without have become a kind of mindless new aristocracy, like Louis XIV's court at Versailles, but with BlackBerrys, a confident bent for self-promotion and a thesaurus worth of self-serving jargon stuffed into their vocabularies. Alongside them, the only people who look as if they have their heads screwed on very tightly indeed are the people in investment banking, and they've been streaming through the cities like the Pied Piper's rats of Hamelin, insinuating themselves into every nook and cranny with a dollar in it. Which doesn't mean they aren't airheads, too. Just airheads of a particularly ruthless kind. You can finally see what people who know the price of everything and the value of nothing look like *en masse*.

Commonsense, meanwhile, has become as rare and as hard to find as the emperor's new clothes. Where is a legion of clear-eyed little boys when you need them?

The successful twenty-first century airhead comes in as many varieties as the Apple iPod. There are political airheads who really believe that you can stop people noticing they've been sold down the river to profit a major corporate (or that you can silence them if they do notice). And there are corporate airheads who can tell such porkies to protect their profiles that you wonder their eyes don't revolve in their heads.

There are rich airheads like hotel heiress Paris Hilton who scream "Ohmigod!" and "Kidnap!" when they forget they've left their pet chihuahua with their grandparents. Social column airheads don't believe anything has happened in their life for real – love, marriage, divorce, shopping, eating, breathing – unless they've been written up and photographed doing it for their favourite gossip columnist. There are celebrity airheads who are now paid the kind of close and flattering attention once bestowed upon, say, Einstein. The celebrity boom has taken off because celebrities sell product and product makes money. Now the few hundred of them have multiplied like a pool of tadpoles and colonised 80 percent of the world's media space.

Serious newspapers paused briefly in consternation at the rise of celebrity journalism but then headed as unflinchingly as George Clooney in *The Perfect Storm* towards the tidal wave of starry stories that normally kept the tabloids and weeklies afloat. Soon, it could be said that no newspaper ever met a celebrity it didn't like or couldn't put on page one on a slow news day. I found myself acquiring knowledge that seemed astonishing: that actors Brad Pitt and Jennifer Aniston had not had sex for the last two years of their marriage, for instance. Even as my brain cells reared back and tut-tutted in polite astonishment at having such intimate access, there was a bit of me that accepted that this was okay, that this was now the way of things. Celebrity is a business transaction and the price of being a millionaire celebrity is that there is no privacy and a billion strangers might be invited to examine the cellulite on your bikini-ed bottom in the celebrity tabloids, magazines and websites if that bottom also appears regularly on big and small screens.

Shopping airheads, meanwhile, are trained to think there's nothing valuable in life that can't be bought. That includes happiness, love and a wrinkle-free face. Politically correct airheads, having got their grip on us in the counter-culture Sixties and Seventies, followed up by the postmodern Eighties, now tell us what we may read, learn, say or think; all of which is profoundly different from what has kept Western civilisation going for the last 2,500 or so years.

The void that opened up, though, provided a space to grow a new strain of empty-heads. More than thirty years of taking the MBA seriously means we now have airheads who can spout the latest management truisms to back up whatever nonsensical cost-cutting scheme they are trying to introduce or defend or promote to big business. These are schemes that, all too often, shore up the airheads' own positions while doling out large salaries, consultancy fees, shares or options to the airheads and their colleagues.

Most powerful of all in today's society are the process airheads who have infiltrated so many of the other layers and types, from management to education to the arts, popular culture and even health and science. These are the people who approach life with a theory and a blueprint – like the executive at one company who decreed that, if employees had ideas, they must fill out an "ideas form". You can always pick a process airhead because if reality collides with the blueprint, that is,

Que?

In Tokyo, a man who took his pet python for a walk in a park, fell asleep on a park bench. When he awoke, Reuters reported, the creature was gone. Japan is seeking to have such dangerous pets micro-chipped, but the python owner told a television network later he was surprised the snake had disappeared because it wasn't that kind of snake.

if a cause ends up having an unwelcome effect – kids can't read because they're not taught how, newspaper circulations go down because editorial staff and resources have been cut, short-changed hospitals run out of beds for patients – they declare it's reality, not the blueprint, that must change. Process airheads live by jargon, theory and statistical measurements, and they are thriving in the new globalised world. Try to remember the last time you had a sensible conversation with someone in Human Resources. They come, they go, only the shape changes.

Basic intelligence has nothing to do with whether someone is or isn't an airhead. According to *Vanity Fair*, ditsy singer Jessica Simpson, who made so much capital out of wondering whether a tuna was a fish or a chicken, has a genius-level IQ of 160. Process airheads can be alarmingly bright, just not very smart. No, what all too often gives away an airhead is motive. Whether it's Paris Hilton or a fiercely ambitious CEO with three university degrees, signs of triumphant airheadism are, one, that "me" always comes first and, two, that they hold on to propositions that promise snappy solutions, profits and outcomes, while overlooking any contrary evidence about how life really works, how humans really behave and how things are panning out in reality and the long term as opposed to in theory and in the short term. Little children behave like this, too, but these people run corporations or countries, or have the power to decide what we get to eat, read, hear and watch.

Airheadism means believing that 2,500 years worth of wise maxims designed to ward off greed, stupidity, selfishness, unhappiness and calamity no longer hold true. It's as if Aesop had never told his fables.

With all these airheads knocking around, rubbing shoulders, congratulating each other and hefting one another up into yet more privileged positions, the rest of us have been left to lurch and crash around like loons on dry land, trying to reconcile what's going on.

There are, of course, more serious examples of airheads in search of a brain. Wall Street investment banks like Goldman Sachs and the management consultancy McKinsey & Co praised American energy giant Enron to the skies for years. When Enron imploded in 2001, it turned out the company, once the seventh largest corporation in the United States, had been kept afloat only on a bubble of fraudulent accounting. Plausible talk and the riveting sight of all the multi-millions being made so dazzled the experts that thousands of Enron employees lost their retirement savings. If other pension funds are included, average Americans lost between

$US25 billion and $50 billion. Various Enron officials have gone to trial, but what of the airheads whose praise egged them and the investors on?

It's not hard to find less public examples, and not only by opening your newspaper every morning. An academic remembers watching, bemused, as her business school rushed helter-skelter into China, eyes fastened on all the fast profits that might be made from all those Chinese students. She asked a couple of wise questions. Would the courses in China be taught in English or Chinese? How profitable would the move actually be? These were brushed aside in the fervour of the moment. "We'll teach it in English!" was the reply. "They don't speak English," our academic responded. "Well, we'll teach in Chinese via interpreters!" "So how will the lecturers mark the essays?" And so on …

Existing university staff went to China to teach the courses, on top of their normal teaching load. They would go to China for a few weeks, then come back exhausted to deal with their "real" students. Naturally, there were problems. One of the difficulties was that not enough provision had been made for being paid upfront. When it came time to pay, one Chinese university announced it didn't have access to foreign exchange. The joke went around that they were hoping they could pay in dim-sum. "They kept getting up more and more crazy ideas," the lecturer says musingly now. "This was probably an extreme example but it's intriguing how so many seemingly sensible, rational people get taken in …"

When the City of Sydney library moved out of its old premises at the Town Hall and into a sumptuous new home at Customs House on Circular Quay in 2005, users were told it would be bigger but it would have fewer books. That was odd, I thought. The answer was that the extra space would be given over to cafes, seating and space. The books that would qualify for transfer would be those that were "the best and most popular". Other books would be sent to other branch libraries, kept in the stacks or "retired". Just half the books in the old library made the cut. Staff librarians, doing a kind of Sophie's Choice of the book world, had to painstakingly and painfully decide which half of the 140,000 came along and which didn't.

The new library is indeed very glamorous, but it feels as if it has been designed by people for whom books are, frankly, a bit of a nuisance. In the main display areas, all the bookshelves are waist-height which, as any keen book reader, browser or buyer will tell you, is hell on the neck and back as you bend over, squinting and squatting to find the title you're after. Some digging gave me the answer, though.

Apart from the designers apparently rather liking the look of low shelves, engineers said the open floors of the historic building simply couldn't take the weight of proper-height shelves filled with books.

Which means that someone in authority decided to move the library to a building that actually can't really hold a library and so the library has had to rid itself of books when books are what a library is all about. But it does have a barista and a coffee bar.

"Do you think the world has gone mad?" I once asked a leadership strategist who advises Fortune 500 CEOs. "Yes, I think it's going that way," she replied – and this from a woman who attends the Davos World Economic Forum every year.

Still, if the world is mad and commonsense has run off with the pool boy, an awful lot of people are doing very well. By 2004, there were 8.3 million people around the world with assets of at least $US1 million.[5] "Being a millionaire ... is becoming commonplace," sighed *The Economist*. By 2005, there were 8.7 million such people. Credit card debt has shot up and so have sales of luxury goods – so much so that queues form to purchase private planes, elite sports cars and beachside shacks that look like mansions. As for the rest of the population, think-tanks on the Right pronounce that we have never lived better, that even the poor are doing well and that these are the rewards of globalisation, the free market and economic rationalism.

Do you believe them? Sometimes it feels as if they're only talking about themselves. When I occasionally suggest to a commentator or economist that maybe he should catch the train to beaten-

---

Really?

"'I don't know why you're talking about Sweden,' Bush said. 'They're the neutral one. They don't have an army.' [Democrat congressman Tom] Lantos paused, a little shocked, and offered a gentlemanly reply: 'Mr President, you may have thought that I said Switzerland. They're the ones that are historically neutral, without an army.' Then Lantos mentioned, in a gracious aside, that the Swiss do have a tough national guard to protect the country in the event of invasion. Bush held to his view. 'No, no, it's Sweden that has no army.' "

THE NEW YORK TIMES MAGAZINE, OCTOBER 17, 2004, PROFILE OF GEORGE W. BUSH BY RON SUSKIND.

down Macquarie Fields or visit a hostel for families in crisis, I don't get any takers. If the economy is so good and the poor have never been richer, why are charities reporting more calls on their stretched funds? What does "richer" actually mean given so many people now claim they feel financially insecure? Sixty percent of Australians aged between thirty-one and forty; one-third of those aged between forty and sixty; 30 percent of those earning more than $100,000.[6] Economics journalist Matt Wade described how, with the advent of the new industrial relations laws, exposure of superannuation to the fluctuating share market, and increased household debt, more and more risk is being transferred from the corporate sector to households.[7] There are indications that what we're really seeing is a growing gap in opportunity between the top and the bottom, and a middle that is being stretched thinner by the year. Some of the middle is migrating up; some of it is going down. Soon there won't be too much middle left.

A television news flash in September 2005 told me there had been a decline in discretionary spending and it was showing up in sudden increased sales for sliced bread: more people were taking a cut lunch to work. Not that there would be many cut lunches at the top, which is increasingly where airheads cluster like party balloons. So if you want to get ahead, here's a tip: be sure to make friends with an airhead, or two or three, so they can take you up with them. Our prosperous, empty-speak, PowerPoint times favour them.

If you're smart, be even smarter: adopt, mentor or even brown-nose a guppy today.

CHAPTER 2

The Unbearable Liteness of Being

*"Well you can study Shakespeare and be quite elite,
And you can charm the critics and have nothing to eat,
Just slip on a banana-peel and the world is at your feet ..."*
"MAKE 'EM LAUGH" FROM *SINGIN' IN THE RAIN*

The year 2003 was shocking for me. First, my father died. Secondly, my cat became the breadwinner of my household. There can't be many people whose pets have turned out to have better career prospects than their owners. Maybe whoever owned Mr Ed, the talking horse. Maybe whoever owned the little rust and white terrier on *Frasier*.

And now, me.

My own job, as editor of a Sunday newspaper's magazine supplement, had vanished when I was made redundant. In a letter to readers, the associate publisher wished me well in "the next exciting chapter of her brilliant career".

So that was me. No job.

It was different for my cat.

She had, under my guidance, taken to writing a short weekly column in the magazine I had been editing. Readers sent in photographs of their cats and, each week, we would choose a picture to publish. Hero-the-Cat would offer her thoughts alongside. Although the column started out as an insider's send-up of columnists, it took off and, after almost two years, Hero was the country's most famous cat columnist. Helped by the fact, of course, that she was the only one. A website labelled her Australia's shallowest columnist.

Editing this magazine was probably the most un-serious job I've ever had, and that's saying a lot in a career that has spanned everything from dreaming up stories on evening gloves for *The Sunday Times* in London to writing about degrees for well-schooled dogs for a family magazine in

Ohmigod

"It took me fifteen years to discover I had no talent for writing but I couldn't give it up because by that time I was too famous."
AUTHOR ROBERT BENCHLEY, WHO WROTE FOR *VANITY FAIR* AND *THE NEW YORKER* DURING THE TWENTIES AND THIRTIES.

Australia. The Sunday supplement was so lite it could have been held down with powder puffs. We happily ran stories on film stars, tips on nail varnish, a cheat's cooking column and a regular on the lowly jobs famous people had once held.

That didn't stop a film publicist complaining to my newspaper editor that the magazine was "too serious". "Phil," I said later, when he dutifully passed on her criticism (for he depended on the publicist for his various Sunday celeb scoops). "How serious can this magazine *be*? It has a column written by a *cat*!"

Just as well for that cat though.

A tortoiseshell Persian-cross, Hero had mostly written about her food, her looks, her fur or herself, and she had acquired both a following and a future. Several weeks after I was let go, it was declared that I owned Hero, along with her copyright, and that she, too, would be leaving the company to pursue her writing career elsewhere.

Not that I should have been taken aback by Hero-the-Cat's fan base. Designer onions, tasting round-ups of latte coffees, Prada handbags, Q&As on modern etiquette, sex and scandal had been taking over newspaper space for several years. A racehorse apparently caught sniffing cocaine made the front page of one broadsheet. Restaurants and chefs had long since become the new pin-ups of page three in the upmarket press and had started to appear as stars in the tabloids, too. A society doctor, a neurosurgeon caught with cocaine at a beach resort, rated not just a matter-of-fact few news pars down the side of a page, but a full-on picture splash story on page three of *The Sydney Morning Herald*. Other newspapers were hardly blameless. *The Courier-Mail* published a milksop poem that a love-struck Bec Cartwright had written for Lleyton Hewitt and read out at their wedding reception. In spite of its political gravitas, *The Australian* showed a frisky penchant, come Paris and Milan collections time, for running photographs of the most revealing frocks on parade.

Of the two of us, naturally enough then, it was my cat that found work first. Hero quickly organised for her column to appear in a rival newspaper, a Sydney tabloid. She was smart enough to share her weekly pay cheque with me, her unemployed owner. For quite some time, Hero continued to earn more than me, especially after she landed herself a second column, this one in a monthly.

About the same time, a chicken scored a rival spot in a weekly magazine. That was mortifying. One night at a birthday party overlooking Bondi Beach, in a room filled with Names – actors, entertainers, media types – I said lightly to a group of people I hardly knew that my cat had a column, but I was hoping she wouldn't find out about the chicken's column because the chicken had more space.

The smooth faces around me remained as buff as if they'd just come out of airbrushing. No-one even snickered. Then a big beefy man said slowly, staring at me fixedly: "So why doesn't your cat write a *dog* column?"

I GREW up in a serious world. All the adults I knew – my parents, my parents' friends, my friends' parents and my teachers – reliably informed me that life was serious. There would be good times to be had but they would be earned by working and studying hard, and if there were too many good times, then I would surely pay for it.

It's true that I can be so serious that sometimes at drinks parties even I want to introduce myself to someone else so I can get away. Still, I'm having trouble trying to put my finger on the precise moment in time when life turned into a sit-com and we all started talking and joking like Joey in *Friends*.

For a brief period there, when I turned on ABC-Radio at 8.45 am to get the overnight news, the new and jolly presenter was instead cheering her morning audience along with stories about burnt custard.

An upmarket girls' school bragged to parents via a bus sign that they should come to the place where learning is fun! "Lighten up" is the cry of the day, around the world, and when President George W. Bush was caught out over missing weapons of mass destruction in Iraq, he was also caught out mugging on a slide show for the Washington press corps, pretending to hunt for the WMDs in his Oval Office.

"Was there a World War II in Germany?"[1] asked a young woman, chosen especially as a housemate in the fifth series of Australia's top-rating television hit *Big Brother* because of her lack of inhibition. A disgruntled former commercial FM breakfast radio host told how executives had seriously proposed a segment that would have as its prize sperm donated by a star. The winning woman would be allowed to use it to impregnate herself.

Paris Hilton, the spoilt young woman who has taken vapidity to such new levels, asks carelessly, "Wal-Mart, what's that? Do they, like, make walls there?" But never mind whether it's a rich girl's joke or genuine ignorance, her notorious celebrity has turned her into both a glamorous icon for tweenie girls and an in-demand businesswoman who earns millions of dollars a year. Remember *Valley Girl*, the

Like, whatever

1982 hit by Frank Zappa and his daughter Moon Unit? It was supposed to be satire, a send-up of young girls and their vacuous conversations and mindless shopping habits. Now, two decades later, we're all shopping and spending like crazy and we're all talking like, like, like, ohmigod, totally, fer sure, y'know … like airhead Valley Girls. The sing-song intonation, the exclamations, the hands-up gestures and slick patter that come from watching

"Launched last Wednesday, the Subservient Chicken site racked up a million hits in the first 24 hours, and between 15 million and 20 million hits so far, according to Crispin Porter & Bogusky, the advertising agency responsible for the site [for Burger King's new chicken sandwich] … The chicken [an actor wearing a chicken suit] tentatively steps out of the kitchenette, wearing a garter belt, a metal anklet and nothing else. A text box invites the viewer to 'Get chicken the way you like it'. The chicken gazes at the camera expectantly… By webcam standards, the chicken is a bit of a prude. It will do jumping jacks, disco dance and watch television. On the slightly edgier end of the spectrum, it will vomit, smoke a cigarette and shake its booty… Originally, the chicken would grant some salacious requests, albeit behind the cover of a censoring black box that popped up to cover the chicken's naughty bits. Now the chicken receives even remotely sexy commands with an insulted look and a finger-wagging scolding.

"But a gallery of still photos on the site seems to document scenes from the chicken's less inhibited days. In one, the chicken reclines on a sofa, legs spread, head propped on a pillow, its beak parted in what one assumes is an expression of avian lust. Another shows the chicken on all fours, hindquarters in the air.

"[Creative director Andrew] Keller, nevertheless, denied that the site contains even a hint of sexual innuendo. What about the garter belts?

" 'The reference was really more like a Victorian-style chicken,' Keller said. 'An elegant old costume was sort of the inspiration.'

"And the gallery of salacious poses? In the photo of the chicken on all fours, he is rooting around for something in the couch, Keller said. In the reclining photo, he is merely relaxing after an exhausting session of break-dancing."

PORNO HEN HAWKS FOR BURGER KING BY CHRIS ULBRICH. *WIRED.COM/NEWS*, POSTED 2 AM, APRIL 14, 2004.

too many television shows; the cadences and phrases that clog our conversation no matter how bright we are. I know four-year-olds who talk like that – and thirty-six-year-old businessmen, too. President Bush talks like that. Even Rupert Murdoch, one of the most powerful and wealthy men on the planet, is susceptible.

Today, everything is a joke or has to look like one. Instead of the equivalent of Edward G. Murrow, the grave and formidable American broadcaster once described as "one of those rare legendary figures who was as good as his myth",[2] we now have comedians and entertainers as our radio, TV and print voices.

As Bebe, the atrociously amoral agent in the sitcom *Frasier*, declares to her psychiatrist client as he frets over a television show offer: "Anyone can heal … You're better than that, you're an entertainer!" In early 2006, the Australian Catholic University decided to bestow an honorary doctorate on four men for their knowledge of early childhood education: they were the Wiggles, millionaire members of an ever-cheerful, boppy children's pop band.

I was as outraged as a tick in mid-2005 when a comedian acquaintance confessed her hope that she might be the next breakfast broadcaster for the ABC's local station in Sydney. I lectured her, as politely as I could bring myself to do, on the importance of having well-trained people, ideally with a journalism background, in such heavy news positions. I said we needed people who could interview politicians and who could act as gatekeepers, working out which guests would be good enough, bright enough, insightful and incisive enough to bless the ears of a waking city's population.

Well, that turned out to be a load of fanciful poncing around on my part. My acquaintance didn't land the gig, but management chose another of her kind: an ex-television comedian and radio broadcaster who liked to joke. And she didn't just treat her listeners to discussions about burnt custard. In the midst of the fury and flurry over the publication of former Australian federal opposition leader Mark Latham's all-too-blunt diaries, I heard her ask earnestly of another political diarist, Rodney Cavalier: "So what *is* the difference between a memoir and a diary?"

She must have thought we were all so scramble-headed we needed enlightening. Fortunately, it also turned out that the comedian hadn't fully understood that doing a breakfast show meant getting up in the dark of the night and, after four weeks that did in her health, she resigned. It was, in retrospect, a brave and sensible thing to do.

Nor was it her fault that an ABC-Radio management obsessed with ratings, jollity, beating the commercial radio stations at their own game and staying middle-of-the-road, had anointed her. In spite of the burnt-custard style, they professed themselves disappointed by her resignation. If she had been able to get up and out of her pyjamas, the job would have remained hers. The people who proved to have more sense than management were the short-lived breakfast broadcaster herself, and the listeners who protested so vehemently to the on-line ABC comments book about her performance that management appointed as her successor Adam Spencer, also known for being funny but with a first-class-honours degree in pure mathematics, a keen interest in science and a reputation as an excellent debater.

When *Age* newspaper staffer Gay Alcorn took incredulous issue with the content on local ABC-Radio in Melbourne, she cited a twenty-minute slot during which, at radio host Richard Stubbs's request, listeners rang to relate stories about "being stuck in strange places".[3] Alcorn quoted an earlier rejoinder made by radio head Sue Howard after criticism of Stubbs's appointment: "People forget that the ABC charter says we have to inform, educate and *entertain*. [People] leave off the entertainment bit."

You might argue that in a world of terrorism, insecurity, violence, natural disasters and threats of plague-like diseases sweeping the planet, we've had to retreat to lightness, levity and occasional inanity for the sake of sanity. But another way of looking at all this might be to wonder if the world would make more sense if, for instance, we weren't being entertained all the time. We might feel the world was turning on its axis with more surety if everything didn't have to end with a punch line. We might even notice what's really going on in the world if we weren't so busy laughing, or being made to laugh, at every opportunity.

Fun!

There's a lot to be said for seriousness.

WHEN, IN February 2005, singer and actor Jennifer Lopez landed the closing show at New York Fashion Week to launch her fashion range, one fashionista critic commented sharply, "We've only ourselves to blame because we've given celebrities these deranged feelings of omnipotence. She'll be doing brain surgery next."[4]

The same year, actor Sharon Stone – who once confessed she was so insulated from reality she didn't know how to use peel-on stamps and kept licking them instead – went to Switzerland to address the hard men of the Davos World Economic Forum. Angelina Jolie, Bono, Richard Gere were there, too, and in 2006 Michael

Douglas turned up. This is not necessarily to criticise the stars, but to question just why some of the world's toughest, richest and most powerful business people couldn't spot a world problem or poverty until a celebrity started speaking to them about it. (How far would you and I get? Not even past the first security gate.) Anyone who wants publicity for a cause or project knows the value of adding a star to get attention from both the media and the public. Celebrities bring glamour and excitement and they look good. If you're lucky or far-sighted, they will also know how to give big smiles and even make people laugh. Celebrities are used to sell sugary breakfast cereals to children, condominiums to millionaires and lavatory paper to everyone. Now that people expect everything to come to them quickly – even knowledge and learning – celebrities are also used as the intellectual equivalent of fast food.

To go with its big 2000/2001 summer show *Buddha: Radiant Awakening*, the Art Gallery of New South Wales hit on the idea of inviting some celebrities to give after-hours talks. The gallery asked five well-known people, including actor Jack Thompson and comedian Paul McDermott, to speak on the influence of Buddhism on the West. *Art After Hours*, as the series of talks was titled, proved so popular that the venue had to be moved from the original small room to the 320-seater Domain Theatre and, even then, people were turned away.

This is heady stuff. Unexpected success has a giddying effect. It makes us shiny-eyed and ambitious. Now the celebrity talks are well established at the gallery and feature a number of

Totally

When the serious British news analysis programme *Newsnight* popularised its format yet again so that a weather report ended the show, rather than the previous management-inspired innovation, a sharemarket update, host Jeremy Paxman did it in his own style: "So finally and controversially, tomorrow's weather forecast. It's a veritable smorgasbord. Sun. Rain. Thunder. Hail. Snow. Cold. Wind. Not worth going to work really." After ten days of this, an audience poll brought the return of the market update. Not that Paxman liked either option much, noting sarcastically, "So farewell then, weather forecasts. *Newsnight*'s brief flirtation is over. From Monday, it's back to the dreary old markets." He also pointed out that just 0.37 percent of the BBC programme's audience had bothered to vote on what segment they wanted.

people who are also known for being, if not exactly comedians, then certainly quick with the apt light and sharply honed comment. They put work into their talks; they're entertaining. Columnist Emma Tom has given lectures on sixteenth-century Italian artist Caravaggio, nineteenth-century impressionist Camille Pissarro and Pablo Picasso. Comedian and radio host Libbi Gorr has also shown off her knowledge of Caravaggio. Comedian and ABC-TV host Peter Berner has lectured on Picasso, and Sydney radio host, author and journalist Richard Glover has taken on both Pissarro and Picasso. (The dramatic Caravaggio obviously spoke to the hidden side of many celebrities: other lecturers scheduled were film director Bruce Beresford, barrister Clive Evatt, comedian and interview host Andrew Denton and theatre director Jim Sharman.)

The pairing of celebrity with renowned painter lends the guest speaker an intriguing intellectual patina, a hint of hidden depths, but not so deep that it's difficult for the audience. You also have to admire the levels of chutzpah, roughly what I might need if I were to agree to appear as the surprise factor in a show called "Let's Talk Quantum Physics". The twenty-first century is clearly not for scaredy-cats, nor for anyone who has forgotten the mantra, particularly apt for our times: nothing ventured, nothing gained.

When the gallery defended the programme, two of its staff put it like this in a paper: "The engagement of celebrities to draw people to museums is considered by some to pander to populism. And yes, the program is unapologetically popular but with serious intent and substantial content. The mix of speakers that *Art After Hours* has engaged since its inception, and the tremendous insight each individual brings to their topic, continually confronts and dismisses the charge of 'dumbing down'."[5]

When Peter Berner spoke on Picasso as a cartoonist, he helpfully pointed out to his audience that the artist's "graphic work would not be out of place in newspapers today. If you go downstairs [to the exhibition] there are several etchings in the genre of 'bearded man in lusty embrace with young woman, with someone voyeuristically peering from under the bed at them', and if you play the game as I do, you can subtitle that '[politicians and former lovers] Cheryl Kernot and Gareth Evans with [journalist and squealer] Laurie Oakes looking on' ... you'll realise how incredibly relevant they are today ..."[6]

It's lively stuff and people who have taken part talk warmly of a large audience that is both smart and relaxed. Still, I wonder if it eats away ever so subtly at the idea that serious lectures can be riveting, too. Has a laugh with everything really become as rooted in our culture as chips with everything? An academic friend is enraged because a museum of ancient artefacts at his university has suddenly acquired a range of "funny" headings on its commentaries: a mummy is having a bad hair day, for instance. When the gallery audience goes away from a celebrity talk, who and what do they talk about? Picasso's drawings – or Peter Berner? Or maybe some of the patina rubs off on the audience members, too. We've been to listen to a talk on Picasso, they might say to friends and neighbours. It was very funny.

IN 1953, American author Ray Bradbury wrote the classic *Fahrenheit 451*. The title refers to the heat required to burn books and Bradbury wrote of a barren and empty-headed society in which books were forbidden. A lead character says in defence of the burning: "You must understand that our civilisation is so vast that we can't have our minorities upset and stirred ... People want to be happy, isn't that right? Haven't you heard it all your life? I want to be happy, people say. Well, aren't they? Don't we keep them moving, don't we give them fun? That's all we live for, isn't it? For pleasure, for titillation? And you must admit our culture provides plenty of these."

Nobody wants to be a party-pooper. If everyone is having fun, and seeming to do well out of it besides, who wants to be Old Sourpuss pointing out that joshing might be all very well in its place but, please, those are frivolities to be kept for frivolous occasions, and life generally is serious.

No, indeed, and the message I keep getting is that life isn't serious – or rather, it shouldn't *look* serious. No-one wants to be a snob either, or an elitist, which is what those with a questioning look on their faces are often called. That's the extra burden on those who still think an IQ is something to be cherished. They have become the "intelligentsia", a word that sounds flattering but isn't. They are also referred to as "the chattering classes". Or even, "an elite".

My sister, a nurse-practitioner, writes to me from Perth: "I'm sick of being referred to as the 'middle class intelligentsia' as if we are a minority whose views don't count."

It's an odd thing to contemplate: a society so devoted to the pursuit of airheadedness and so derisive of careful intelligence and learning that it invents pejorative labels, names and phrases for abilities that used to be thought essential for the maintenance of a civilised society.

Writer Nick Place, best-known for his sports reporting, muses to me on the sneer that often goes with the description of someone being "left-wing" or part of the "intellectual middle class" or, if they're concerned about the environment, a "tree-hugger". "Why should I apologise because I'm concerned about these things?" he asks.

An insider on Australian *Big Brother* tells me the audiences don't like contestants who are considered to be older or more clever. When one bright housemate started training in preparation for the 2005 series, he practised with a mirror and friends for weeks to stop himself rolling his eyes when people said stupid things. He knew that would lose him votes.

In an afterword to *Fahrenheit 451*, Bradbury wrote simply, echoing one of the book's characters: "… you don't have to burn books, do you, if the world starts to fill up with non-readers, non-learners, non-knowers? … If the primary grades suffer meltdown and vanish through the cracks and ventilators of the school room, who, after a while, will know or care?"[7]

After the Australian federal election in October 2004, I met a thirty-something designer friend for lunch. It was only the Friday following the Saturday, so I started talking about the result. He responded with some astonishment to my seriousness: "You know, you're the first person I've heard all week even *mention* the election."

MY PARENTS were serious people. It was expected of their generation. There was a lot of laughter, but it was accepted that that was the reward you got in your off-time — at the beach, over

---

Huh?

eBay auctioned a fine but small –300g – piece of extra-strong Somerset cheddar cheese, called TNT, for £152. Associated Press reported that the successful buyer intended to feed it to his cheese-loving cat, Huggy.

a Swan Lager, in front of *Monty Python*, with friends – for taking life and responsibilities seriously the rest of the time. My mother married my father, she once confessed in a letter, because he owned so many books. It was just before World War II and my father had a room in a guesthouse on Adelaide Terrace, the wide tree-lined boulevard just outside Perth's CBD, flanked with grand houses which had come down in the world and been turned into lodgings.

My mother had a room in another mansion along the terrace. My father was twenty and had come out of Albany High School in the far forested south of Western Australia. He had done very well at school but gone straight into the Postmaster-General's Department, while taking units at night school so he could eventually get a cadetship to study engineering full-time. His parents had spent the Depression moving from farm to farm as managers. My grandfather had had to walk off his own farm. Their life in the bush meant my father, who had won an inspector's scholarship, boarded in Albany from the age of thirteen so he could go to high school.

My mother had grown up in a large family in Adelaide. Her father, my grandfather, had belonged to an established family who had reacted in horror when he married my grandmother, who came from somewhere well below the salt. That was that. He made his life as a harness-maker and bet on the horses every Saturday. My grandparents had seven children and took in an eighth. Theirs was another family with not much money and my mother left school at thirteen to work in a smart frock-shop where she happily pressed crepe de Chine gowns and parcelled up straw hats before training for office work.

An uncle had offered to put my mother into art school but my grandfather looked to his pride and wouldn't have a bar of it. It took my mother three decades of reading and writing and studying on her own, fitting in life classes and such, before she had her first book published, and started painting seriously.

She died suddenly, in 1994, and I had not had a chance to say what any daughter wants to say to a mother. I was not going to let that happen with my father and so I often spoke to him about my gratitude for the upbringing I had had. Even now, three years after his death, when I'm wrestling with a sentence, trying to remember which famous writer delivered such and such a quip or observation, or what really happened during an historic battle, I reach for the phone on my desk to ring him. When, some mornings I hear the radio news telling me what the weather is like in my hometown, Perth, I forget again and automatically think about what kind of day

Dad will be having.

When he was twenty-six, and a few months before the end of the war in Europe but eight months before Hiroshima, he wrote to the academic and essayist Walter Murdoch offering his services to a new cause. Murdoch had written a piece for the newspapers urging the formation of an idealistic new political party to be called either The Common Sense League or the Silent Australia party. My father listed his age, occupation, education, ability ("reasoning powers fair, I think") and his enthusiasm: "In this instance, enormous."

A few months before he died, when we were discussing something very similar to the ideas in this book, I told him how lucky I thought we three kids had been to have been brought up knowing that education and learning were important and understanding things like duty and obligation and caring about other people, even if we did, of course, slip.

In a drawer, I once found a note written by my mother. It said that the rich should help the poor and the strong should help the weak. She had also written, "It isn't as hard as people say it is to work out what is the right thing to do".

IN APRIL 2003, in Sydney, Justice Owen handed down his report from the Royal Commission into the 2001 collapse of the insurance giant HIH with losses of $5.3 billion. It was an account of rich and powerful people out of control; of people with no concept of corporate governance or thought of what might happen to thousands of ordinary people as a result of their management shenanigans and sheer fecklessness. The HIH collapse happened because there was not enough money to keep the company going in the first place, especially after it took over another company, FAI Insurance, which turned out to be a basket case. It simply did not have the funds set aside to pay claims. HIH lasted as long as it did because executives used aggressive accounting to cover up the holes. Those same executives and colleagues were known and embraced around Sydney for their award-winning, fun-filled Christmas parties, millionaire lifestyles and widely publicised donations to high-society charities.

Neville Owen was, at the time of his appointment to the commission, a Supreme Court Justice in WA. He had presided over many complex commercial cases, was a father of five and a keen bush-walker. In exasperation and with a kind of exhausted incomprehension, Justice Owen in his report asked rhetorically of the HIH executives and office bearers: "Did anyone stand back and ask themselves the simple question, 'Is this right?'" We need people and organisations in our society to ask questions like that, to make rightness an everyday affair, a habit. But in the last thirty years, almost every body with the prime purpose of promoting rightness has been subtly undermined and weakened. The family, the Church, newspapers, television and radio news, universities and the public service have all been diminished, mostly through being starved of respect and money or time, or all three. HIH itself was badly policed because, in 1998, after the Howard government had run a review of the various regulatory authorities aimed at minimising regulation, the Australian Prudential Regulatory Authority had replaced the Insurance and Superannuation Commission. The authority was understaffed and repeatedly ignored warnings about HIH.

Public servants, often now dependent on their contracts being renewed, don't so much give independent advice as to the "rightness" of a state or federal government policy as advise on how the policy can be spun to look as if it is right. In big business, ethics has been turned into a consulting industry, as companies write mission, vision or value statements which draw heavily on the thesaurus for different ways to say "ethical" and "profitable" at the same time, and investment banks employ "integrity officers" (but still – surprise – get into trouble). None of it, on the evidence that comes to light every day in the media, seems to mean much more than that ethics is now a highly saleable and good-looking badge for a company or manager,

Liberal Senator Mitch Fifield: "I mean, Clerk, it comes to my mind that if you don't like the laws passed by the Parliament, you know, 'stiff cheese' is a phrase that comes to mind." Harry Evans [Clerk of the Senate]: "That is an extremely silly statement, Mr Chairman, if I can say so very respectfully. What do you keep an adviser for? You keep an adviser to give you frank advice ... Now, if you only keep advisers to say that everything you've done is totally correct and perfect, then it's not much good keeping them at all."
EXCHANGE IN A SENATE COMMITTEE INQUIRY INTO FEDERAL GOVERNMENT SPENDING ON TAXPAYER-FUNDED ADVERTISING, AUGUST 19, 2005.

along with, say, those other something-nothing phrases: forward planning, a commitment to excellence, fair dealing, spiritual intelligence …

Actually *doing* the right thing is quite another thing.

After all, during the last fifteen years, did Justice Owen or anyone else really imagine that gatherings of bank chief executives fretfully asked each other if closing down all those branches and downsizing thousands of their people was right? Did he or anyone else really imagine that when heads of industry got together, they discussed the growing inequalities between rich and poor and what should be done about the rising numbers of families queuing up for help from the Salvos and Anglicare? Did he or anyone else really think that they fretted about not having enough staff who might question what they were doing?

More tellingly, I thought at the time, what did Justice Owen think happened when a gung-ho super-boss announced, in some inane bit of neo-liberal econo-speak, how he was going to increase profits and cut costs while maintaining quality? Did he believe that some gentle soul who didn't mind losing his or her job was going to pipe up: "Sir, do you think this is right? Or possible?"

These days, such a line of questioning is called a "career-limiting move".

DO YOU know what is a career-enhancing move now? Going to business school. It's much easier today, too, and lots more fun. Once upon a time, Master of Business Administration (MBA) students toiled for two years full-time or three or four years part-time to get through the slog of a degree that had originally been created in the newly industrialised United States for young college graduates who were going into management and needed to fast-track their organisational knowledge. Now you can choose an MBA or another kind of business-oriented degree that "suits your lifestyle". It can be done on-line. You can do an eighteen-month MBA or a one-year MBA or, most popular of all, a part-time MBA. The MBA has been split up and finessed, massaged and re-created to attract and net as many customers as possible. There are also single-subject courses, short courses customised for a company, certificates and diplomas. In the last few years, other courses have crowded in, with mid-career executives deciding on a masters in commerce or a masters in finance. At some of the best management schools in Australia, you can even learn "elevator talk", which is how you use the 1.5 minutes in a lift to shine and impress anyone senior standing beside you.

The overall message from all this promotional activity? C'mon, it's not that hard. It's fun. At the Krannert School of Management at Purdue University in Indiana, MBA students can take a golf elective so that, later on, they can network on the green without making fools of themselves.[8] One student told *BusinessWeek* she had chosen to "study" golf so she'd make a good impression on her boss some day. There's a waiting list of students, and now fifty or so other universities are copying Purdue.

The Purdue course is titled "Golf: For Business and Life" and includes successful business people coming into the lecture room to "share stories about how golf has influenced their professional achievements". The Professional Golfers' Association of America has kept up the pressure with programmes aimed at tournament winners using their money to set up golf courses at their alma maters. More than $US5 million has gone into these so far. "Golf is an honourable game that teaches ethical behaviour," one Purdue spokesperson pronounced firmly.[9]

And it's certainly fun. It may not teach you to question things or to analyse or to reflect, but it helps you entertain your clients and bosses. It helps you hum along.

There is one saving grace: at least golf is still a non-credit course at Purdue. So far.

CHAPTER 3

Power, Money and Isaac Newton

"It's good to be the king!"
MEL BROOKS AS LOUIS XVI IN
HISTORY OF THE WORLD, PART I

"One of the first things you have to do is attract your audience and then work out how best to monetise them."
ALAN REVELL, GROUP EXECUTIVE, JOHN FAIRFAX
HOLDINGS, ON THE INTERNET IN *THE SYDNEY MORNING
HERALD*, SEPTEMBER 27, 2005

In 1936, American *Vogue* sent a reporter to Berchtesgaden in Germany to write an "at-home" on Adolf Hitler's country retreat there. In the August issue – the same month as the Berlin Olympics – *Vogue*'s writer enthused blithely of Hitler's taste in design: "German, jumbled, and *gemütlich* [genial] ... On the side of a mountain, the chalet has a suburban neatness, with a sun porch and canaries, and its rooms a cosy podge of clocks, dwarfs and swastika cushions."[1]

Proximity to power overwhelms the brain cells. *Vogue* wasn't the only one to embarrass itself. Randolph Hearst's newspapers offered Hitler a regular column in the Thirties. He lost it only because he kept missing his deadlines.

For a kind of amoral airheadism to thrive, all it takes is for people to be distracted by money or power, or both.

In early 2000, Dior's John Galliano sent his models prancing down the catwalk wearing couture inspired, he said, by the rags worn by Paris's homeless living under the bridges of the Seine. God knows what the millionaires' wives in the front rows made of the clothes, which came with holes, pulled threads, used tea-bags, whisky bottles and bottle caps. Protesters with more sensitivity pelted Dior's windows with rotten eggs.

"I saw just the romantic side of it," said the designer of the tasteless frocks that cost well up into five figures. "The poetic side of it. The criticism was that I was taking the piss out of homeless people, but the point was that they are creating beauty out of necessity. I loved that collection."[2]

Ohmigod

"The two James Hardie executives found responsible for depriving future asbestos disease victims of up to $2 billion yesterday walked away with a $10 million golden handshake between them."
PAGE ONE LEAD STORY,
THE WEEKEND AUSTRALIAN,
OCTOBER 23-24, 2004.

A few fashion seasons ago, I was transfixed to read that Marie Antoinette, the dizzy but beautiful French queen guillotined in 1793 for the sins of lavishness and heedlessness, was about to become the new last word in style-setting for the twenty-first century. Whether it was to be with or without her head was unspecified by the troupe of giddy retailers and creative types who were busy pushing their wares and declaring her to be the icon of our day.

"It's all about sparkle and embellishment ..." a spokesman for the glossily upmarket London store Harvey Nichols declared to *The Financial Times*, egging on customers to buy just one fabulously expensive, over-the-top item so they, too, could have their Marie Antoinette moment. Dior, Chanel and, perhaps more understandably, filmmaker Sofia Coppola were also smitten and busily either designing clothes inspired by the empty-headed queen or working on her sumptuous but tragic life story for the movies.

As the fashion and film crowd were falling for Marie Antoinette, a woman once described by an historian as a "warm-hearted but indolent girl who hated the sight of books",[3] a Parisian perfumier was re-creating the doomed queen's scent, a blend of rose petal, vanilla, jasmine and ambergris. It was so costly that it was not, at first, intended for general release. It was simply a public relations gesture to accompany a new book and a fund-raiser for the preservation of Marie Antoinette's furniture. But the makers were flooded with requests from rich women, sniffing out rarity snob value, and so the scent went on sale in early 2005 for £1,050 a small bottle.[4] It was unveiled at the palace of Versailles, that shimmering edifice outside Paris masterminded by Louis XIV, great-great-great grandfather to the young queen's husband, Louis XVI, and the man who set off the events that led to the French Revolution by almost bankrupting the nation, over-taxing the peasants and cosseting the nobility with riches, luxury, beauty and spectacle in order to keep them preoccupied and under control.

It's impossible to think of this era without remembering Madame de Pompadour, the mistress of the Louis-in-between, Louis XV. She it was who remarked, while enjoying the same privileged opulence: "*Après nous, le déluge.*"

In other words, this can't go on. Actions have consequences.

Mme de Pompadour thus recognised Isaac Newton's third law of motion: for every action there is an equal and opposite reaction. That is more than the airheads running the world and our lives today can understand. It is also a prime defining characteristic of the modern airhead: the increasing inability to recognise that chickens don't just get hired to write columns; they also come home to roost. Airheads, instead, operate according to the same principle that purportedly guides goldfish: what's in front of them, at that moment, is all that matters and all they can remember. This is probably unfair to goldfish although spot-on for airheads.

One of the key developmental stages in childhood is the one that occurs around two years old when a child learns that the world includes other people and if he or she does A, then B will happen. The history of the world is told through that equation. Airheadism, though, is essentially a failure or refusal, for whatever reason to understand that A will equal B. From Enron's founder and former chief executive Ken Lay to HIH's tricky goose Rodney Adler, befuddled as they were by greed, vanity and flattering headlines, airheadism at its most arrogant is a belief that the laws of physics, history, empirical evidence and grammar can be subverted. That cause will not have an effect.

How wonderfully simple and easy that belief makes life. It's why airheads, at their most extreme, can worry only about themselves and the rest of the world can go to buggery. Airheadism thrives on concerning itself with the next five seconds because, with any luck, the next five minutes, days, months, years may, like, you know, never happen … or at least, if something does happen and it's bad, it won't happen to you.

The best place to see all this in action is not in a Krispy Kreme doughnut store, or watching a twenty-something flashing a credit card on a Friday night over a $300 meal. It's in the business pages of our newspapers, and on page one.

Short-term thinking is the scourge of our times, its disastrous effects showing up in everything from our passion for distracting frivolity and luxury to our dysfunctional cities, creaking for lack of infrastructure, to the constant reorganising of companies (combined with massive retrenchments and re-training) that happens every 4.9 years as one chief executive goes and another takes his or her place. Governments do not worry about the twenty-year effect of their policies. They worry about what will keep them in power or get them back into power. People who do think long-term are an embarrassment. They are squeezed out of organisations, they don't get elected to boards and their dissenting, querulous voices are drowned out as much as possible by the other eager voices going yes-yes-yes to whatever scheme is being promoted which, while clearly troublesome or even calamitous in the long term, will bring huge benefits to its promoters in the short term. Twenty years on, of course, they will have long flown.

With previous generational change, it was simply about the old versus the young, each with their own habits and tastes and neither having much liking or respect for the other's. But this is a much more fundamental change, from accepting, even if reluctantly, that one plus one must equal two, to the joyous notion that one plus one can equal anything we choose it to equal if it benefits us or our particular game plan.

Plenty of people made millions out of Enron, the massive energy company which was once America's seventh largest corporation with, at one time, a valuation of $US68 billion. It crashed with debts of $31.8 billion and five thousand people immediately lost their jobs. Worse, about $1.2 billion in employee pensions went. But in 2001, Enron paid out $800 million to 152 executives. Apart from the insiders who together had made hundreds of millions of dollars during Enron's glory days, there had been rewards for others. One small investor went into a venture masterminded by Enron's chief financial officer, Andrew Fastow, in 2000 and put in $5,800. She ended up with a million dollars in her bank account a month later.[5]

Alex Gibney, director of the film about Enron, *The Smartest Guys in the Room*, said this of big business in his production notes: "The world of investment banking and big business is a world unto itself in which a few powerful people wheel and deal out of the public eye and, particularly in the case of vital markets like energy, exert 'market power' that has nothing to do with competition among equals, or open relationships between

---

Totally

"Ultimately it was Enron's tragedy to be filled with people smart enough to know how to manoeuvre around the rules, but not wise enough to understand why the rules had been written in the first place."
FROM *CONSPIRACY OF FOOLS* BY KURT EICHENWALD, BROADWAY BOOKS, 2005.

consumers and producers ... Enron is important because it takes the predatory nature of 'business as usual' to its logical extension ... Enron is not an exception to the rule; it's an exaggeration of the way things too often work."

Gibney also wrote of people's willingness to be accomplices: "I was amazed by the degree to which virtually everyone – journalists, stock analysts, business school professors, even [former head of the Federal Reserve board] Alan Greenspan – believed the Enron story. Perhaps one of the reasons they were so convinced was that [Enron heads Jeff] Skilling and [Ken] Lay wrapped their mission in an ideology that everyone in the American business community wanted to believe: if there are no rules and regulations, everything will work out fine. It was like being guided by the keynote slogans of Gordon Gekko ('Greed is good') and Alfred E. Neuman ('What, me worry?')."

It's argued that globalisation, the liberalisation of trade, the booming stock market and the new market-driven economy have raised living standards everywhere and that argument will go back and forth for decades. What can't be disputed is that a lot of the new money suddenly washing around the globe has still gone disproportionately to a small and powerful few positioned to take advantage. In 2006, a group of 85,400 people around the world were identified as ultra-wealthy, with fortunes of at least $US30 million.[6] If in India, a graduate has gone from earning a starting salary of 9,000 rupees a month ($A270) to 30,000 rupees ($900) now, it doesn't make it any easier to stomach the $US60 million wedding of Vanisha Mittal, daughter of steel magnate Lakshmi Mittal. In Russia, the number of billionaires increased by a quarter – from thirty-nine to fifty – in one year, reportedly the result of an oil-driven consumer boom, and the number of rouble billionaires went up by 50 percent.

The unfettered market forces of the last quarter-century mean American CEOs now earn 386 times the pay of the average American worker. In 1980, a CEO earned forty-two times the average.

In Australia, the figures are just as telling as big bosses scramble to ape what is happening overseas. Between 1990 and 2005, one study[7] showed that the average annual cash pay (not including the equity component) of chief executives from fifty-one of the largest Australian listed public companies rose by 564 percent, from $514,000 to $3.4 million, a notional weekly average of $65,700. In the first year of the study, the Australian CEOs of these top organisations earned eighteen times the average salary. Only fifteen years later, by 2005, the multiple was 63 times.

Another study[8] claimed even higher figures: that CEOs' salaries were now ninety-eight times the average worker's salary, while American researchers dug around productivity gains and discovered that half of the gains made since 1966 had gone to the top 10 percent of earners.

IN LATE August 2005, BHP Billiton announced Australia's largest company profit in history – $8.6 billion for the financial year ended June 30, 2005, almost double the previous year's figure. The profit was due to a surge in global resource prices. Matt Wade and Jamie Freed wrote in the front-page splash of *The Sydney Morning Herald*: "Strong world growth ... has triggered an unprecedented rise in prices for mineral exports. This has led to a huge transfer of wealth to Australia from the rest of the world. The Access Economics director Chris Richardson estimates the world economy has pumped $40 billion into the Australian economy in the past two years ..."[9]

The very next morning, though, on ABC-Radio 702, I heard that a Sydney city school was forced to advertise McDonald's hamburgers in school grounds to raise money for reading materials. Some Australian schools have to pay teachers out of the proceeds of fund-raisers and, in New South Wales, there are hospitals relying on community groups to buy pillows and linen.

A year later, in August 2006, BHP Billiton had broken its historic record, announcing a profit this time of $13.7 billion. The situation for schools and hospitals was still the same. Of that massive profit, $3.3 billion was paid in company tax to the Australian government and hundreds of millions of dollars went to the states in mining royalties.[10]

These days, stuff happens. Inexplicable, unconscionable, unimaginable stuff happens. Wilfully careless stuff happens, too. And the response to it all from those with the power and privilege to do it all better? Whatever. Shrug.

Take, for instance, the situation that confronted the President of the United States in September 2005. When Hurricane Katrina deluged the Louisiana, Mississippi and Alabama coastline and sank New Orleans, George W. Bush waited until day three after the floods had hit his people before popping out of his holiday burrow to grin like a chipmunk and promise aid.

He seemed not to understand how shocking it was for the rest of the world to watch citizens of the richest nation on earth wandering dazedly like nuclear victims over their highways, scrabbling for food and water and trying to protect themselves from whoever was taking advantage of the cataclysm that had destroyed their lives and homes. Could any pictures have sent a clearer message to terrorist groups that the United States had lost the plot?

Five days after the hurricane, police issued a "shoot to kill" directive to try and keep order as the rumours of murder, rape and looting got out of control. Louisiana is one of the poorest states in America, its population overwhelmingly black, and the murder rate in the capital nearly ten times the national average.

An editorial[11] in *The New York Times* seethed: "Publications from the local newspaper to *National Geographic* have fulminated about the bad state of flood protection in this beloved city, which is below sea level. Why were developers permitted to destroy wetlands and barrier islands that could have held back the hurricane's surge? Why was Congress, before it wandered off to vacation, engaged in slashing the budget for correcting some of the gaping holes in the area's flood protection? It would be some comfort to think that, as Mr Bush cheerily announced, America 'will be a stronger place' for enduring this crisis. Complacency will no longer suffice, especially if experts are right in warning that global warming may increase the intensity of future hurricanes. But since this administration won't acknowledge that global warming exists, the chances of leadership seem minimal."

There was one heartbreaking sentence in an early press report[12] from an Australian correspondent: "Poverty has exacerbated the problem, with many people staying [behind in New Orleans] because

Really?

"We do not really know what causes economic growth," admits Francois Bourguignon, chief economist at the World Bank. "We do have a good sense of what are the main obstacles to growth and what are the conditions without which an economy can't grow. But we are far less sure about what are the other ingredients needed to create and sustain growth."
FOREIGN POLICY,
MARCH-APRIL 2006.

they could not afford to leave – particularly as the storm came just days before the next welfare payment." While the better-off citizens were able to evacuate, there was little local or state government effort to help either the poor who had no cars – or, if they did, no petrol – or the sick to get out before the hurricane and flooding. As one website commented, "Everyone was expected to devise their own way out of the disaster area by private means, just as the free market dictates ..."[13]

What became more appallingly, disgustingly obvious over the ramshackle days after the storm breached the city's dykes or levees was that the residents still had no-one rooting for them. People were dying in full view for lack of water or medical aid. Bodies lay in the streets. Where were the community organisations? Where were the aid agencies? What were the emergency services doing, for heaven's sakes? Instead, the government finally started shipping in National Guard to try and control the lawlessness that threatened to become outright anarchy.

In Australia, the story also took time to grow. It coincided with the death of a thousand pilgrims in Baghdad, and newspapers here, in what seemed to be a fit of political correctness, concentrated on that. It was only on the Friday, five full days after the hurricane hit, flooding New Orleans, Biloxi and Mobile and leaving hundreds of thousands of people homeless, and corpses, sewage, toxic chemicals and rubbish floating through the submerged communities along the Gulf of Mexico, that people started to realise something was horrifically wrong.

Even then, days after local newspaper editors must have read reports on the Web and seen television footage, *The Sydney Morning Herald*'s page one Louisiana coverage that Friday came from a syndicated reporter. The *Herald*'s US correspondent had filed for the sports pages out of New York, covering glamour-boy Lleyton Hewitt's tennis match at the US Open. Did the paper's news editors think the celebrity tennis player might sell more papers? That the Hewitt news story was more important? Or was it simply that the reporter and news desk, brainwashed by years of enforced cost-cutting, had instinctively held back in case a trip south proved an unnecessary expense? The blur of time turns out to have blurred memory about the reasons.

That same Friday, when I called various aid agencies to donate money, I could find no-one who had set up an appeal. Not Care Australia ("we do Third World undeveloped countries"), not World Vision ("we had a meeting today and decided not to start an appeal"), not the Salvation Army and, in the end, not even the Red

Cross, which was the one fund supposedly collecting on behalf of the American Red Cross. Their website announced they were yet to get the donor hotline organised.

When the tsunami hit Asia on Boxing Day, 2004, donor lines opened very quickly. But for these people who live on the nightmare underside of the American dream of luxury and promise, there seemed to be no immediate charity, understanding or compassion. The Asian crisis reminded people around the world of the paradise holidays they had taken there and of the exotic people they had enjoyed meeting, and millions of dollars flowed in. Louisiana, along with the devastated areas of Mississippi and Alabama, didn't have the same resonance.

Those affected were mostly the under-educated and poorly paid, often in ill-health, living on welfare or eking out a living picking up after rich folk. They had no exotic appeal. They were Westerners, but not Westerners other Westerners seemed able to identify with, or even recognise. There was even a common and prejudiced attitude among those who leaned to the Left in Australia, in spite of the evidence in front of their eyes: the United States was rich, they said; they could look after themselves.

But hang on. These were also the people whose ancestors had grabbed our imagination for decades through the harrowing tales of slavery followed by racial discrimination in the deep south, the blockbuster book and TV series *Roots*, the civil rights movement. Weren't these the people who we all knew had had a rotten deal most of their lives at the hands of their countrymen?

Instead of rushing food and water and health help to them, the United States government seemed more intent on policing them. Troops poured into the state as the violence grew. Exhausted workers at New Orleans' Charity Hospital were furious. "I'm beginning to wonder if the government is more concerned about the looting than they are about the people who are dying in these hospitals," one told David Mark, the Australian ABC's reporter there.[14]

Hurricane Katrina had dealt the region only a glancing blow. What caused the destruction of New Orleans, which is located in a kind of bowl two metres below sea level, was the breaching of the levees that held back the water on all sides, from the Gulf of Mexico, Lake Pontchartrain and the Mississippi River. The levees were old, the accompanying pump system dating back to the early years of last century, and local officials had been pushing for years to have them rebuilt and strengthened. Two state universities had created computer models showing exactly how the levee system might fail under a surge of high water. Instead, federal funding had diminished. In 2004, instead of receiving the requested $US100 million or so for flood control and hurricane-protection projects, the city received $42 million.

Meanwhile, $200 million went towards building a single bridge between Anchorage in Alaska and a virtually uninhabited point of land. The difference was that Alaska was lucky enough to have influential politicians, including a senior senator who had been chairman of the Senate Appropriations Committee from 1997 to 2004. These poor southern states didn't and their politicians were preoccupied with looking after special-interest groups, often corporate.[15] Funds and National Guard manpower that could have come to the aid of the stricken were instead tied up in Iraq. One in three of the area's guardsmen was in the Middle East.

The police force fell apart. Two officers committed suicide and about 250 others, or 15 percent of the force, went AWOL. A few may have been trapped themselves; maybe many others went to look after their own families and flooded homes rather than those they had pledged to serve. That would have been unthinkable a generation ago when people felt there was more quid pro quo between the ordinary person and the bodies above them, and when the habit of following duty and obligation was ingrained, broken only if the breaker wanted to invite shame and castigation.

If all that wasn't enough to turn the disaster into a catastrophe, bureaucracy got in the way. Relief

---

Huh?

United States officials in states from Texas to Minnesota announced in late 2003 they planned to cut the costs of running jails by cutting prisoners' food allowances, sometimes by 1,200 kilojoules a day. Prisoners had not complained, they said, although the Civil Liberties Union said it had received hundreds of letters.

was turned aside; lines of empty buses waited kilometres away from crowds desperate for evacuation.

None of it made sense, most of it could have been prevented and, in that, it was a perfect example of the triumph of the airheads.

BY THE time Katrina struck, my brain and my house were stuffed with examples of airheadism at work and at play, in business, government, society and in schools, leading from one to the other and back again like wisps of smoke. I could see what was going on, I could sense it, I could list numerous examples of idiocy, of commonsense thrown out the window, of buffoonery in high places, of decisions that defied all logic, but it was still tantalisingly hard to pin down – in neat statistics and proven statements – the trail from one to the other; how one outbreak of airheadism propped up the other, how one caused another, how the thinking that produced chaos here was the same kind of thinking that led to lost chances elsewhere …

And then Katrina came along, like the Commendatore at the end of Mozart's *Don Giovanni*, a massive and unstoppable force rising from the earth. It showed just how shockingly, and how shockingly fast, a phalanx of decisions made by airheads, or made by people under the influence of airheadism, can pile up into catastrophe.

New Orleans turned into such a disaster because the federal government was thinking short-term and gambling that the levees would never be threatened. That was in spite of a pattern of regular hurricanes. The crisis was about not shoring up essential infrastructure in spite of repeated warnings. (Which did not stop President Bush blustering – preposterously, airheadedly – in the first days of the crisis that no-one "anticipated the breach of the levees".[16])

It was about saving money, looking after better-fed and better-represented interest groups and lobbies, spending the money there instead, and being prepared to play with the lives and happiness of the most vulnerable. It was about being prepared to risk an entire city. It was about local officials taking risks, too, while being worn down by lack of money, and lack of understanding from the presidency. Again and again, it was the US Congress which insisted at budget time that the President's funding for Louisiana's levees be raised (although never back to the levels requested by the US Army Corps of Engineers in charge of the Hurricane Protection Project).

And when the hurricane struck and the levees flooded, it was about lack of communication and lack of organisation. It was about a mobile hospital with a hundred surgeons, a full pharmacy and the latest equipment never getting the orders to move. When National Guardsmen in New Mexico offered their services, Pentagon bureaucracy muddled the offer; firemen who volunteered were sent to Atlanta for community relations training first.[17] It was about dunder-headed cronies of the President in sinecures, running the crucial agencies and getting in the way.

It was about no-one seeming to understand what Mme de Pompadour had expressed so memorably: the basic laws of nature. That decisions have results. That actions have consequences.

Through all of this in the days immediately after the hurricane, George Bush seemed to think the horror was happening on another planet. I guess, given the world in which he lives, it was. It's a strange world, his, a universe of privilege, ignorance and nonsense masquerading as know-how and leadership, a slippery universe of subterfuge and obfuscation, where nothingness puts on a bland face and pretends to be something. It's a place where the airhead keeps coming out on top. A barrister who practised criminal law told me once that the hardest person to shake on a witness stand was someone not very bright, a little empty-headed. He said, "Witnesses who are intelligent can see where your questions are leading and so their answers start reflecting that or they start explaining themselves. They answer in too much detail, leaving themselves open to more cross-examination."

Dumb-clucks, though, stick doggedly to their version of events no matter how outrageous this may seem in the light of evidence or questioning, no matter how seemingly untrue. So it is with the airheads of today. They see what they want or where they want to get to, and, like collie dogs on the scent, they are impossible to deflect with appeals to commonsense or truth or logic.

That's what happened in Louisiana, what led to the fiasco and what came afterwards.

Within days of the disaster in which 1,300 people died and a million were displaced, including 400,000 children, and which caused so much damage that it will take billions to fix, the White House went into spin mode. It claimed any number of reasons why Louisiana's devastation was not its fault, mostly, it claimed, because of federal versus state issues. Louisiana's governor, Kathleen Babineaux Blanco, was put on the back foot. She declared, and you could hear the frustrated puzzlement in her statement, that it was true that when she implored the President for help on the Monday night at the very first sign of the rising waters, she hadn't actually specified what *type* of soldiers she wanted. "Nobody told me that I had to request that," Ms Blanco was quoted in *The New York Times*. "I thought that I had requested everything they had. We were living in a war zone by then."[18]

In this case, anyhow, Blanco's President was in San Diego next day to give a speech to naval personnel on the war in Iraq, and later that week, the Secretary of State went shoe-shopping at Ferragamo in Manhattan after enjoying a Broadway comedy the night before. The man responsible for emergency relief, Bush's friend, Mike Brown, was otherwise engaged, too. It was later discovered that, even as the waters were rising, and the President had declared a state of emergency, Brown was joking with his staff about his wardrobe and calling himself a "fashion god". Six months later, a news agency unearthed videotapes proving that top officials, including the President, were either aware of or had been briefed on the hurricane's potential to wreak devastation even before it hit.[19]

But guess who immediately rushed to appoint himself head of an investigation into the catastrophic disaster relief immediately in the wake of the hurricane? "I'm going to find out what went right and what went wrong," President Bush announced stoutly to his Cabinet. He also insisted to news outlets that he was not going to "play the blame game".

That'd be right.

AIRHEADS believe no-one else has any more memory cells than they do. Airheadism takes away the efficacy of public hospitals, roads, railways, schools and telephone systems – by insisting on

Que?

"What I'm hearing, which is sort of scary, is they all want to stay in Texas. Everyone is so overwhelmed by the hospitality. And so many of the people in the arena here, you know, were underprivileged anyway, so this, [chuckles slightly] this is working very well for them."
BARBARA BUSH, WIFE OF THE FORMER US PRESIDENT, ON THE LUCK OF HURRICANE KATRINA REFUGEES TO FIND THEMSELVES LIVING IN THE HOUSTON ASTRODOME, SEPTEMBER 5, 2005.

savage cost cuts because of blow-outs elsewhere or by selling others off willy-nilly to private enterprise – and then tells you that you are mistaken: those services weren't any better in the past. *Now* it is better. On August 19, 2005, Prime Minister John Howard, speaking of Telstra, told ABC-Radio that "when we owned Telstra, the services weren't as good as they are now ... When it was totally owned [by government], does anyone seriously believe our telecommunications were better?"

I do, given that the last time my phone was out of action I was told it might take five days to be repaired. It ended up taking three. I remember a time, maybe five years ago, when my out-of-order phone was fixed the same day and I didn't need to sit down in amazement when I got my phone bill every quarter.

In Sydney in 2003, because of a long drought, water restrictions were introduced and people were told to cut down on household water use. So people did. The water restrictions got tougher. People cut down on water usage again. It was then announced that water prices would have to go up. The spin people and bureaucrats got to work. When a price rise of 9 percent, rising further over the next few years, was put in place, Sydney was told sternly it was for its own good; it would now *force* us to use less water. As it turns out, Sydney Water officials had been warned in 1979 that the city would run out of water by 2000 if urgent action weren't taken. Some attempts were made but, in the end, as a former manager told *The Australian*'s John Lehmann, there was more interest in keeping costs down than planning for the future.[20]

The new airheadism is good at fudging. That's how you get around the law of consequence. But it's also why if you are bright, questioning and independent-minded, you are no longer considered an asset to society, to faction or to employer. If you think there are more important things to life than consuming, getting ahead and doing deals that make you and your boss bucketloads, your drive and commitment and right to a comfortable place in society become suspect. (Unless, of course, you are a workplace consultant, in which case companies will pay you hundreds of thousands of dollars each year to give life-work balance seminars to employees on subjects such as how to deep-breathe, how to stand correctly in the office – true! – or how to turn off your email at home.)

Airheadism signifies thought that never goes below the surface but, instead, glissades over problems like a skier navigating gingerly over a tricky slope, trying not to dislodge and set off whatever lies underneath. It uses euphemism, jargon and oxymoron instead of simple language because, that way, it's easier to cover up what is really going on. People are as confused by long words and phrases as they are by a recital of numbers.

When the Australian government changes the industrial relations laws so that workers negotiate with their employers separately rather than as a collective with some muscle power, it uses a positive word, "flexibility", to describe the promise in the new scenario. This is no accident: consultants with psychology and linguistic qualifications coach politicians and officials on how to word their announcements to score direct hits on our psyches. There is a blow-up when it is revealed the government has pulped half a million copies of a booklet setting out the new industrial relations rules because only the words "simple" and "national" appeared in the title. The government wanted to include the word "fairer" – even though it was manifestly obvious that the new rules would not be fairer, given that single employees would have to negotiate with employers who, by their very title, are in the catbird seats. The Council of Catholic School Parents, sensibly, started campaigning to have older schoolchildren taught how to negotiate and fend for themselves in the new "fairer" work regime.

The Sydney Morning Herald's Matt Wade writes that company profits have been rising steadily as a proportion of the economy, equal now to 27 percent of gross domestic product and up from 16 percent in 1975.[21] More wonderful numbers, but as he then writes, wages have meanwhile declined from more than a 60 percent share of the economy in 1975 to about 53 percent. He quotes economists who say that the fall in wages share shows that the gains in our expanding economy are going towards capital and away from the workers.

New markets for capital keep on opening up. In an American documentary screened on PBS, *Merchants of Cool*, about marketing to today's teenagers, a media observer says: "They look at the teen market as part of this massive empire that they're colonising. Teens are like Africa."[22]

There are now more than 32 million teenagers in the United States, the largest generation of teenagers ever. This also means there's a growing bulge in the twenty-something age group. Products from films to technological toys to alcoholic drinks and snack foods are pitched at that combined massive young market. It can have bizarre consequences. Marketers worry whether a young audience will "get" something. Adults don't shape our new world; increasingly, the tastes and foibles (and limited knowledge) of the youth market do because they are the ones who, researchers have decided, will spend the most.

Then there is the Asian sub-continent with its growing, newly acquisitive middle classes. *The Times* ran a piece in London about India's young middle class. Headed "No-one saves for a rainy day now",[23] the article dwelt on the unprecedented levels of disposable income and the explosion in consumer spending. Goods once unavailable in India – Revlon lipsticks, Johnny Walker Black Label – are now everywhere. The young eat out, take out loans for Poggenpohl kitchens and buy Korean and Japanese cars. "With money to burn and no time for the Gandhian asceticism of the earlier generation, the young are fuelling the retail boom … Amit possesses hardly any savings, nor does Reddy. Both live for the day. Their parents spent their entire lives squirrelling away the little that was left after running the house. Among their friends, no-one saves much. 'I'll tell you why my friends are not saving for a rainy day, it's because they don't see a rainy day coming,' Reddy says. 'If they lose a job, they'll get another one. They're optimistic about the future so there isn't the same fear.'"

One interviewee tells the *Times* reporter that he spends on two restaurant meals what his mother once used to run the house for a month. In that, it sounds very much like the consumer boom that hit Western society as young baby boomers came into their first pay packets in the Seventies. (Ask a baby boomer today what they wished they'd done with at least part of those earnings.) On a subsequent web-log about the 2004 *Times* article, reader Rajiv

---

Ohmigod

In 2005, to raise money to send her son to a private school, 30-year-old American Karolyne Smith sold advertising space on her forehead by auctioning herself on eBay, attracting 27,000 hits, according to newsagency *Agence France-Presse*. Lucky winner here was gaming company GoldenPalace.com, known for its outrageous advertising stunts, which paid $US10,000 to tattoo its name on Smith's forehead. "It's a small sacrifice to build a better future for my son," said Smith.

had this to add: "It mentions that there are 19 million mobile phone users. In February 2005, just a year later, the number has gone up to 50 million …"

Inspired by the enormous wealth to be made from such new free-spending, non-saving, non-thinking customers, from deregulation and from globalisation, the money market has stuck its enormous piggy snout into the communal trough and snorted up every dollar it can, oinking all the while that what the market demands is always right. In which case, how do the free marketers explain, for instance, that about 17.5 percent of alcohol sales in the United States are to under-age drinkers, making that market worth $US22.5 billion in 2001?[24] Market growth has been helped by the industry's development of sweet, often milky, concoctions that mask the taste of alcohol and are hugely popular with new and young drinkers. Am I supposed to believe that the liquor industry would lift its skirts in horror if it thought all this was going on? An Australian report reveals that a large proportion of young adolescents felt such drinks as Bacardi Breezer were packaged to appeal to them.[25]

Enough is now never quite enough. When Apple Computer delivered its fiscal 2005 results, it showed a 384 percent rise in net profit and revenue growth of 68 percent, year on year, the best results in the company's history. Within half an hour, the shares fell 11 percent. The market felt it had been promised more: "… results did not soar like an eagle, as analysts predicted, but simply set all-time records".[26]

Where is all this concentrated wealth taking us?

Andrew Leigh, an economist at the Australian National University and co-author of a paper about the distribution of top incomes in Australia, speculated to me, choosing his words carefully: "There's always a risk that the rich will have a disproportionate influence on election outcomes. It could skew election results with such things as campaign donations. There's also the potential for people to buy their way into politics. There are certainly examples of that in the United States and the potential is here to do that."

The more that large amounts of money go to a small group of people – and that is one clear effect of our market-driven economies – the more power these people have. When you accumulate that much power, the consequences of your actions aren't something you often have to think about.

CHAPTER 4

Salute the Rich

"... if you didn't get richer this year then you weren't really trying."

JOURNALIST NARELLE HOOPER ON THE VAST SUMS
WASHING AROUND THE FINANCIAL MARKETS, *THE
AUSTRALIAN FINANCIAL REVIEW*, DECEMBER 23-27, 2005

The trouble with the rich and powerful is the way they bring out the Uriah Heep in so many of us. And there are now such a lot of rich and powerful people. Australia has 146,000 of them,[1] each with at least $US1 million in liquid assets – their average booty is $US3 million and their numbers are increasing at one of the fastest rates in the world. Until or unless these millionaires are dragged huffing, puffing and protesting into a courtroom for wrongdoing, they seem unable to do any wrong. Unctuousness instead is on display.

When the Nokia phone company spent $88,000 on 88 guests at a lavish dinner at the Museum of Contemporary Art in July 2005 to launch an expensive new mobile phone, and inveigled the likes of designer Collette Dinnigan, Grandiflora's Saskia Havekes, architect Tina Engelen, publisher Deke Miskin and Louis Vuitton boss Philip Corne to join in, decorate the tables and invite eight guests each, nobody blinked in print. Instead, the social and gossip scribes of Sydney turned up to report on the spectacle and to note enviously that guests also went home with a free mobile worth $1,599. One even went so far as to write: "Nokia's lavish bash was the party on everyone's lips."[2]

As the rest of us know to our cost, you have to be rich to get things for free. You have to be stinking rich to be fed on caviar and Champagne every night of your life because someone somewhere either wants you at their party or the imprimatur of your presence at a product launch. (And these days, everything from perfume to new

"In some ways, although we don't expect to get a thanks, they should be at least saying, 'Gee, for an industry that's in so much turmoil, we've still got decent jobs.'"
QANTAS CEO GEOFF DIXON ANNOUNCING PLANS TO CUT JOBS AND SHIFT THOUSANDS OF OTHER POSITIONS OVERSEAS. THE SAME REPORT, IN *THE SYDNEY MORNING HERALD*, REVEALED DIXON STOOD TO EARN $2 MILLION PLUS A POSSIBLE $1.2 MILLION IN BONUSES IN 2005 AND THAT QANTAS HAD JUST REPORTED A RECORD PROFIT OF $763.6 MILLION.

bed linen gets its product launch.) You also have to be very rich and powerful to become used to the idea that you should get things for free, whether it's someone picking up your airline tickets for your next holiday or providing you with a free car when you fly overseas. You have to be especially rich to enter that exclusive club where wealth begets wealth, where insiders are invited in early on stock offerings and deals and board positions so that more and more money comes in buckets as if delivered by a chain of sorcerer's apprentices. In Australia, the wealthiest – in assets rather than income – pay about 25 percent in tax, easily avoiding the top personal rate. The very rich simply get most of their income from business investments and shares and claim tax breaks not available to most regular workers. They then declare earnings down in the five figures after deductions.[3]

At this heady stage, it becomes easy to believe that you are so rich you deserve to be richer. This is called the "rich airhead" syndrome.

Six months after the splashy Nokia party in Australia, news broke that in 2004, the Finnish company's CEO-to-be had been picked up slipping $18,000 worth of goods through the duty-free line at Helsinki airport.[4] Although he had made sure to claim every bit of his tax refund of about $1,000 as he left Switzerland where he had bought the clothes and antiques, Olli-Pekka Kallasvuo said it simply hadn't occurred to him that duty and taxes might be payable at the other end. This is how a rich airhead's mind can work, given that, first, Kallasvuo is a lawyer and, second, in the year of his offence he had taken home pay and bonuses of $1.7 million. He was fined $50,000.

Just before Christmas 2005, as retailers braced for a slump in spending because the average consumer was concerned for his or her future, economics writer Ross Gittins put it like this: "Truly, we live in an age where the more powerful you are, the more you believe the less powerful owe you a living. The less well-off must pay because the well-off have convinced themselves they're the ones doing it tough. You see this in the company executives laying off staff and holding down wages so as to fatten their own million-dollar bonuses, having convinced themselves there's nothing morally questionable about doing so. You see it in the way politicians of all stripes have lost the will to improve working conditions in any way that would add even a little to business costs. Increase business costs by imposing paid maternity leave? Unthinkable."[5]

It seems quaint now to think that for a brief period at the end of the Eighties and the beginning of the Nineties, we really did think we had learned our lesson and survived the greedy decade made forever famous by the film *Wall Street* and Gordon Gekko's catchphrase "greed is good". Just as *Vanity Fair* editor Graydon Carter got it seriously wrong when he said after the cataclysm of September 11 that the age of irony had ended, so were the bulk of us ordinary citizens gulled by the imprisonment of Eighties high-fliers like Michael Milken, Martin Siegel, Dennis Levine and Ivan Boesky.

While we were poncing on about karma, life and work balance and the new simplicity, corporate life was undergoing the biggest transformation of all – the arrival of globalisation and, with it, the realisation among the canny and clued-in that if globalisation was handled carefully, there would be riches galore, munificent abundance, rivers of gold ... available to a select few. In the United States, the top 1 percent owned 57.5 percent of corporate wealth by 2003; back in 1991, their share was 38.7 percent. For every group below the top 1 percent, shares of corporate wealth have declined since 1991.[6]

Economist Andrew Leigh's new study[7] of top income distribution, mentioned earlier, states: "At the start of the twenty-first century, the income share of the richest 1 percent of Australians was higher than it had been at any point since 1951 while the share of the richest 10 percent was higher than it had been since 1949. The rapid rise in Australian CEO salaries during the 1990s suggests that much of this recent increase may have been caused by higher executive pay, possibly driven by the internationalisation of the market for CEOs."

In twenty years, salaries at the top levels of management have soared out of control, so much so that, according to the McKinsey business consultancy, even 50 percent of Australian board directors think they're too high.[8] If you look at CEO salaries in Australia's largest 300 listed companies, the average remuneration for 2004-5 was $1.9 million. (The average Australian annual wage at the time was supposed to be about $50,000.) Those figures look like a parson's pay-out, though, compared with the $3.4 million average for CEOs in our biggest 51 listed companies,[9] to say nothing of the massive multi-million-dollar salaries at the top of the United States tree. At the same time, no doubt to make it easier for the average salary-earner to swallow, the pursuit of money has been glorified. The grubbiness we associated with the Gordon Gekkos has been all but obliterated from community memory. The wealthy are honoured simply for being wealthy, not for how they might have made their wealth. There is no such thing as respecting a man who made his fortune through innovation and diligence while disrespecting another because he made his in a series of bodgy property deals courtesy of his friends and contacts. No, in the new twenty-first-century world, only the zeros count. Nobody cares from where they come.

For the truth of this statement, watch a glossy and sleekly maintained art gallery owner at an opening, pulling up attentively alongside a rich client, a businessman just this side of crookedness. You will know straightaway the meaning of the phrase: money makes fools of all of us. Or just examine the guest lists of some of the major social events in your town or city.

In September 2003, convicted fraudster Alan Bond, who went to prison after his business dealings crashed in a $5 billion heap and he was found guilty of embezzling $1.2 billion, was the toast of the town, as columnist Miranda Devine described.[10] It was the twentieth anniversary of Bond's America's Cup win and he was invited along to a commemoration at the flashy Cruising Yacht Club in Rushcutters Bay, Sydney. Later that week, he would do a lap of the Melbourne Cricket Ground in a "parade of champions" for the football grand final. Devine quoted one exchange:

"'Can you be a corporate criminal and a national hero?' the ABC's Mick O'Donnell asked Bond this week.

"'It seems to be so, doesn't it?' replied the shameless one."

And indeed, as Devine went on, nobody else seemed bothered: "Last week Bond was honoured at a slew of balls and parties in Perth, where he and

---

Ohmigod

"Late in 2005, MLC Investments coined a phrase destined to pass into the investment vernacular: 'barbecue risk'. It neatly sums up the pressure we feel when we hear that someone else's investments have done better than ours."
THE AGE, JANUARY 14, 2006.

second wife Diana Bliss are rebuilding a beachfront dwelling in the swish suburb of Cottesloe. He even unveiled a likeness of himself in Perth's maritime museum. Tonight he is scheduled to appear on the grand final edition of *The Footy Show Late* alongside Russell Crowe."

Devine was incredulous. "There is still another punishment left: old-fashioned ostracism," she challenged, especially given one newspaper had published a poll that showed 75 percent of readers – that is, average people – disapproved of the Melbourne invitation.

Fat chance of ostracism at the top though while you have enough fat zeros next to the figures on your bank statements. You have to be fallen businessman John Elliott, and bankrupt to boot, before the upper echelons turn. (As nineteenth-century American writer Henry Wheeler Shaw pointed out, "It ain't often that a man's reputation outlasts his money.")

Not surprisingly, this magical power of the zero has affected the way young people plan their careers and jobs. A friend of mine, a middle-aged Jewish mother, commented on how many of the local community's children were choosing careers in the CBD. She said wonderingly, "Twenty years ago, Jewish kids were going to university to become doctors and lawyers. That's just the way it was. Now, they want to go into the city. Even my daughter. They see that's where the money is being made and that's what they want."

So keen – or obsessed – are people about joining prestige investment banks and the like that one vice-chairman at Goldman Sachs in New York underwent 150 interviews before she was hired away from a law firm. *The Economist*, reporting this, noted dryly that if this wasn't a record, it should be.

Sometimes the only way to see how far a society has drifted in one direction is to go back to newspapers and magazines from decades ago. In 1987, the same year the film *Wall Street* was released, and a few months before the October stock-market crash, American journalist Ron Rosenbaum wrote a satirical piece for the magazine *Manhattan, inc*. It was for a special issue about "New York's greediest cases".[11] While the rest of the issue picked apart various scandals and examples of corporate greed, Rosenbaum's opener pretended to be a primer for young upwardly mobile types who wanted to purge themselves of their venal ambitions and lifestyles. His last pointer was titled: "The difference between crack-dealing and investment banking as professions." Both, he wrote, involved destructive addictions and both involved choosing addictive substances over any human values or ideals. "Come to think of it, there's not much of a philosophical difference between crack dealers and investment bankers at all," he concluded. "Except that these days most decent people would rather admit they're crack dealers than investment bankers."

How times change, and to think that was at the height of the "greed is good" decade. Economic progress is such that now every kid on the block wants to be an investment banker, and single women hang out in bars hoping to snag one of them.

At the 2005 annual general meeting of Berkshire Hathaway, billionaire investor extraordinaire Warren Buffett's sidekick, Charlie Munger, told the audience of 20,000 shareholder millionaires that too much of the intellectual capital in the United States was now tied up in the management of money.[12] One transcript has this quote from the vice-chairman: "The present era has no comparable referent in the past history of capitalism. We have a higher percentage of the intelligentsia engaged in buying and selling pieces of paper and promoting trading activity than in any past era. A lot of what I see now reminds me of Sodom and Gomorrah. You get activity feeding on itself, envy and imitation. It has happened in the past that there came bad consequences."[13]

In a 1999 piece for *The New Yorker*, writer Nicholas Lemann, now dean of Columbia University's Graduate School of Journalism, wrote about the "McKinsey Kids", the top-notch graduates cherry-picked by the giant management-consulting firm which advises the world's top corporates and which basically sends in teams to advise companies on how best to organise themselves and whether to make an acquisition or move into new territory. "The rise of consulting as a first career move has been dramatic," Lemann commented. "The essence of the phenomenon isn't so much the number of graduates who actually become consultants as the size of the psychic space that consulting occupies at Ivy League schools. The general feeling is that in all the big wide world there are only two default fields of endeavour, as far as postgraduate employment is concerned: investment banking (ever so slightly fading) and management consulting (on the rise) …"[14]

Senior-year students, who weren't interested in either consulting or investment banking, found themselves wondering if there was something wrong with them, he observed. Like Munger, Lemann was bothered by the idea of so many bright young Americans being recruited from the elite universities to the service of money, remembering a time when universities, if not producing pure scholars, were about training statesmen, ministers, doctors and lawyers, the last being "business at a remove, business as scholarship, not business itself. It is remarkable how rapidly the ancient prejudice of educated elites against business has disappeared, not just in the United States but all over the world." The Ivy Leaguers Lemann met talked about business as "cool" and, even if they were idealistic about using McKinsey training to "change" things, the idea of working in public life to "make a difference" didn't seem to have crossed their minds.

Looking ahead, Lemann hypothesised that if the trend he was observing continued and strengthened, three things would have occurred: "The United States will have decided, in effect, to devote its top academic talent to the project of streamlining the operations of big business. This is a new development in the history of Western culture." The second was: "We will have created a direct hiring track from elite colleges into a particular sector of the economy. This will only intensify the already considerable hysteria over college admissions, by giving it a hard rational basis for the first time: if you don't get into the right college, you still have another shot at graduate school, but you'll never be a business analyst."

Third, he concluded, "McKinsey and the other management consultants will have got a great deal. They stand at the end of a huge system that sends tens of millions of people to American public schools every year ... and processes more than a hundred thousand applicants to the Ivy League colleges – all of this done either directly by government or by non-profit organisations

Really?

"Two Melbourne brothers suffering muscular dystrophy have settled with Westfield after they were left to crawl to their car when forced to abandon wheelchairs [owned by the] Fountain Gate shopping complex. Tony and Ross Costa have accepted Westfield's offer to pay $50,000 to the Muscular Dystrophy Association."
AAP REPORT IN
THE AUSTRALIAN,
JANUARY 31, 2006.

subsidised by government – and then they pluck its ripest fruit."

When I wrote to Lemann asking what he thought of this hypothesis now, his guess was that these conditions hadn't changed much. In a 2006 survey[15] of American MBA graduates, McKinsey still came out on top as the most desirable place to get a job, with two other consultancies, Bain and Co and Boston Consulting, rating fourth and fifth. Investment bank Goldman Sachs came in third. Interestingly, though, Internet search engine Google ranked second. Something similar can be seen in Australia, where the number of students studying for business degrees doubled between 1990 and 2000.[16] Our universities encouraged the trend because, while training engineers and doctors and scientists is expensive because of the equipment needed, all that is needed to turn out economists, lawyers and commerce graduates is a classroom, a library and a couple of lecturers.

They are not only cheap to produce, they are also in demand. In 2006, accountancy positions made up almost a quarter of all graduate jobs, while graduates going into investment banking, law or into mining as engineers earned the highest salaries. Banking and legal areas are expanding because of the economy and the boom in shares as well as increasing complexity in the financial markets, hence the need. Similarly in a resources boom, mining engineers are needed, except there's a real shortage there and that has driven up the starting salaries.

The Institution of Engineers, worried by this shortage, made a submission[17] to the Department of Education, Science and Training in 2002, describing what was happening with enrolments. While student numbers for engineering and surveying went up 26 percent between 1991 and 2000, numbers for the arts, humanities and social sciences rose 40 percent and numbers in business administration and economics leapt 60 percent. A 2006 overview by Engineers Australia showed shortages of graduate engineers from 1999 on were becoming more acute.

University of Melbourne maths professor J. Hyam Rubinstein pointed out in a 2002 submission to the department that Monash University had recently appointed six new professors to business studies. Meanwhile, the university's maths and statistics department didn't have the resources to hire one professor of statistics and one professor of pure mathematics at the same time.[18]

The Singapore government, worried that too many of its bright students were going into business rather than science or engineering, prepared a review of fee policy in 1997. It found that students who had studied science successfully at high school and should have continued to study it at university, were going into business courses because tuition fees were cheap and – importantly – the private returns were higher.[19] In Australia, engineering, accounting, economics, commerce and administration all fall into the same fee band. But, as one careers adviser pointed out, if you go into the business areas there's pretty much a guaranteed outcome. "And," she added, "these days, kids don't want to go into the outback of Queensland to be an engineer." Or take up a career that might put them in Brazil for five years.

A Macquarie University study found school-leavers turning away from the hard sciences because their parents were pushing them towards more prestigious and potentially more lucrative areas of study. One professor said that where bright maths-science students might once have gone into science at university, now they go into economics, financial studies and accounting. "They can use their maths, not so much their science, and make considerably more money than they would if they went into straight science," he said.[20]

In hard, cold, real terms, it's difficult to blame young business-minded students in the current climate. The riches in store for those who have gone for the civilised CBD option put you in mind of Marco Polo arriving at the court of Kublai Khan. Early in 2006, Manhattan saw a real estate spending spree because $US17 billion had just arrived as bonuses in the pockets of the bankers, brokers and traders on Wall Street. One 33-year-old had earned a bonus of $20 million, a real estate broker said. She sold him a Southampton property for $28 million. She talked also of seeing the property-buying trend trickling down even to those on "smaller bonuses" of $3 million.[21] Another realtor described three hedge fund players competing for a $6 million "celebrity-style loft" called the Glass Farmhouse. "All these guys are in their thirties," he said.

Tom Wolfe in *Bonfire of the Vanities* described how bond traders made their money out of percentages and fees. His protagonist's wife explains to their child that he didn't actually create anything useful like hospitals or roads; what he did at work all day was a bit like handing around slices of cake and, every time he did that, he was allowed to take a crumb from the cake slice so that eventually, if enough slices were handed around, he would have enough crumbs to make a gigantic cake for himself. Columnist Mike Seccombe noted, "It's not just bond traders who scavenge these crumbs [now], of course. Also merchant bankers, management consultants, business advisers … Like magpies, these crumb-gatherers flock to anyone who might feed them."[22]

Huh?

In the Sixties, University of California Berkeley students had a reputation for political and social activism, but in 1986, senior students at the university's business school asked Ivan Boesky, then worth $US130 million but later convicted of insider trading, to address their commencement ceremony to mark graduation. During his address, Boesky provided these lines, later shortened for the movie *Wall Street*: "Greed is alright, by the way. I want you to know that. I think that greed is healthy. You can be greedy and still feel good about yourself."
The applause was enthusiastic.

In his book *American Theocracy*, Kevin Phillips, an American political commentator and former strategist for the Republican Party (which he now accuses of unbridled greed, fiscal irresponsibility and ideological extremism), calls this the "financialisation" of an economy. Thus, such an economy is based on nothing more than moving and managing money.[23] People make money simply because of the money deals they are doing — in finance, in real estate, in insurance. It is not about manufacturing any more; when these people go from a business meeting, they leave nothing concrete behind except for the deal they have created which then creates money for them.

At a conference for graduate recruiters and university careers staffers in Sydney in November 2005, Elizabeth O'Leary, head of human resources for Macquarie Bank, the private investment banking house known as the millionaires' factory because of the wealth it has created for its founders and employees, gave the opening address. She was charming, warm and forceful with her reminders of how far the bank's "tentacles" reached and how large the bank had grown: it now has 8,600 highly paid staff in 24 countries and its total operating income for the financial year to March 2006 was $4,393 million, a rise of 17 percent on the year before, which in turn had featured a rise of 52 percent on the year before that. By the end of her PowerPoint presentation, you could forget about anyone in the audience thinking about the future prospects of graduates; 99 percent of the recruiters and HR personnel in the packed-out room would have put up their hands to join Macquarie. In the year to March 2005, the bank's top nine executives shared almost $100 million in remuneration. After the 2005 results came out, federal treasurer Peter Costello remarked he couldn't understand how one person could be worth $18 million in pay. A fair call, except that when Macquarie's next results were released in early 2006, the 18 Million Dollar Man, managing director Allan Moss, had turned into 21 Million Dollar Man.

The investment bank, which started out in 1969 as a Sydney merchant bank called Hill Samuel with just three staff, became trading bank Macquarie in 1985 and listed in 1996 at $6.50. It now commands a share price of between $60 and $70, and expands every year like a latter-day Roman empire. In ten years it has gone from net profits after tax of just under $100 million to $916 million in 2006, growing ever more successful as it inserts itself into the middle of deals between governments and the public. It specialises in buying into projects such as tollways, airports, tunnels, facilities which governments have to provide and the public must use; a deal strategy that also allows it to reap millions in fees. Wealth, as we know, creates wealth: net profits at Macquarie in 2004 were $494 million, so profits increased by almost 85 percent in two years. Staff numbers went up 25 percent in the year to March 2006, and 2005 was up 15 percent on the year before. (To get those precious new staff, O'Leary said just over 75,000 applications were processed in the financial year ending March 2006 and about 5,000 of those applicants got to the psychometric assessment stage. The student hirees among them didn't just come from accounting and finance either; the net spread across faculties from engineering to science and law and even to history.)

The bank has its fingers in everything from Chicago's Skyway toll road to New York's biggest parking-lot operators. It has stakes, to name but a few, in a Japanese turnpike, a Chinese port and Rome's airport. More than 2,500 of its staff work outside Australia, and *The Wall Street Journal*, surprised but intrigued by the bank's innovative move into big-ticket infrastructure projects, profiled its new and different methods on page one.[24] In a column for *The Australian Financial Review*, Deirdre Macken, with bemused fascination, likened the bank to a leech: "[It] is both ubiquitous and nowhere … It's all fees and no shopfront … its forte is as a siphon …"[25] Macken declared this leech the icon of the new privatised world. What Madison Avenue was to early consumerism, and McKinsey to modern management, this unnerving Australian bank is to our times. "They can make a bid for anything, or at least find a way to suck a fee out of it." The bank does not have to worry about voters or the media or pernickety boards. "In Macquarie, if it makes enough money, you get the go-ahead."

On the day I listened, in the converted ballroom of a conference hotel, the pert O'Leary described hearing people talk about the long, long tollway from South Korea's Seoul airport into the capital. "And I think, 'Yep, and it's ours!' " she finished triumphantly. "And we also own Sydney airport, Rome airport, Brussels airport."

It comes at a price, of course. Not to Macquarie Bank though.

In December 2005, the Australian Competition Tribunal decided the landing fees charged by Sydney airport might have to be regulated because the airport had "misused its monopoly power". By January, one international airline was complaining that the airport was "the worst in the world for punctuality".[26] Checked bags that might take ten minutes to reach an aircraft in other airports were taking more than an hour, sometimes two. "It's completely unacceptable," another insider expert said. A spokesperson for the Australian Consumers Association was quoted saying of the airport, "They have got us over a barrel. There's no competition because they own and run everything."

Before Macquarie Bank took a majority stake in mid-2002, the airport was generating revenues of $106.5 million a quarter. In the April to June 2006 quarter, under Macquarie, revenue was up to $160.2 million a quarter. The average profit per passenger has risen by 35 percent, from $13.25 to $18 in 2006, courtesy of increased parking and retail revenue.

At the graduate careers conference, O'Leary described with relish the way Macquarie's tentacles (her words again, not mine) extended all over the globe. The last time I looked, Macquarie had taken over the world's largest luggage trolley company, had been fined $20,000 by the Sydney Futures Exchange because a London-based trader had created a sham futures contract and lied to the exchange about it,[27] was well into aged care facilities, had ingenuously offered to take over the parking meters in Sydney suburbs, and had just failed in its attempt, as a hostile suitor, to take over the London Stock Exchange. Macquarie exists only to make money. The board of the LSE was less than impressed. "A blatant attempt to acquire the exchange on the cheap," it said of the bank's second bid attempt. Nor were analysts reassured by the level of debt the bank envisaged using to fund the acquisition and what that might do to the way the bank ran the exchange.

IN HER history of the Middle Ages, *A Distant Mirror*, American historian Barbara Tuchman describes the period in recent times when the world at large discovered avarice: "There never was a time when more attention was given to money and possessions than in the fourteenth century …"[28]

By 1509, the Dutch humanist Desiderius Erasmus was writing, in *The Praise of Folly*: "The most foolish and the meanest profession of all is that of merchants, since they seek the meanest goal by the meanest methods; even though they tell all manner of lies, perjure themselves, steal, cheat, deceive, still they think they outshine everyone else just because they wear gold rings on their fingers. Naturally, there is no lack of flattering friars who stand in awe of them and openly call them 'venerable' – clearly for no other reason than to get a little share of their ill-gotten gain."[29]

Money can make us do mad and bad things. But most of all it makes us forget.

It seems like only yesterday that I thought an annual income of just under a million might mean a life of ease, comfort, security and contentment. But of course, it doesn't signify that at all by today's standards.

In my collection of daily clippings from newspapers and magazines, I have an item from a July 2005 *Australian Financial Review*. The then 40-year-old chief executive of upmarket store David Jones was being dilatory about re-signing with the group after his initial contract. The item includes a picture of the young man, Mark McInnes, looking smug as he climbs a set of marble stairs inside the store. He had improved DJs' bottom line with cost efficiencies and tight inventory management. I had read elsewhere that revenues from the store's high-interest credit card were continuing to grow strongly, later accounting for almost a third of the store's total earnings, which tends to be how the financially canny, debt-happy twenty-first century works. There were rumours McInnes wanted a lot more money. The clipping quotes a retail analyst commenting understandingly: "He didn't come in on a very big package … He was a young man at the time and unproven … so presumably those negotiations reflect all those things."[30]

McInnes's base salary for the year 2004 was reported to be $856,096, with incentives, options and superannuation puffing that out to $1.8 million. Well over a million. Almost two million. And that was without factoring in long-term incentive share schemes. But not big enough apparently.

A direct rival was on a salary of $2.5 million (and a package worth $18 million over three-and-a-half years, it was later disclosed); a chain store head was on

$2.2 million. McInnes wanted that kind of money, and more, too. By August, he had done his deal, signing for another three years at a base salary of $1.45 million but with the possibility, if he met targets, of reaping a yearly bonus of between 100 and 150 percent of his salary. This made him one of our highest-paid retail executives.

A later news cutting had him already "trousering" a total package of $5.5 million in 2005, including long-term incentives, options and so on.

Comparisons are invidious. The problem with a million dollars is that it only looks good if everyone else is earning half a million. These days, our newspapers are full of stories of Wall Street executives exiting with stupendous sums, like the $US113 million for the former CEO of Morgan Stanley, Philip Purcell, who was forced to retire. Average movie stars command $20 million a picture and Harry Potter creator J. K. Rowling has passed the billion-dollar mark. I remember reading about a famous Harvard study in which research subjects, given a choice between earning $50,000 when everyone else is earning $25,000, or $100,000 when everyone is earning $250,000, plumped for the $50,000 option.

A note of panic arises when people are told again and again, via the media and anecdotal gossip, how much money other people are making and how quickly. *New York* magazine has always had a nose for sniffing the mood in the air. In the Seventies, it picked up on Tom Wolfe's "Me Decade" for an epic cover story. It also squirrelled the notion of the "couch potato", a phrase that first appeared in 1979 in *The Los Angeles Times*. By the turn of the century, the magazine was running cover stories such as "Envy" with its subtitle "Manhattan is becoming an island of megamillionaires. So where does that leave the rest of us?" and another called "Washed up at 35?" The former opened with this question: "If you are standing still while others are getting richer, are you, in fact, getting poorer?" The latter was a feature about successful young people feeling less than successful because of all the under-35s heading up new ventures and making their fortunes.

Clouds of anxiety started bunching around the spires of Gotham and the international CBDs beyond so that, after a while, anyone not earning a base million started feeling like the fat kid at school who always comes last in the running race. A friend who hobnobs with the rich and powerful of London tells me no-one is considered truly wealthy there unless he/she can live comfortably off the interest off the interest.

When former New South Wales premier Bob Carr announced, within weeks of his resignation in mid-2005, that he would be signing on with investment bank Macquarie, there were rumours his new salary would be a handsome $500,000. Not bad for part-time and if you're also entitled to a lifetime pension of $130,000 a year. But insiders were contemptuous. They thought the figure was an insult to a lobbyist of his talents.

When the public broadcaster signed Julie McCrossin to do the breakfast slot for Sydney ABC local radio for a little more than $150,000, one newspaper deemed it a "relatively modest salary".

But possibly the most egregious example of a man not understanding just what planet he lives on was Fred Hilmer, the former CEO of John Fairfax, the newspaper company which produces *The Age*, *The Sydney Morning Herald* and *The Australian Financial Review*. Having pocketed almost $20 million over his seven years at Fairfax, including the surprise (well, to the journalists anyway) $4.5 million payout on leaving, it was announced that he would become the next vice-chancellor of the University of New South Wales. David Gonski, a former board member of Fairfax and a fellow member, with Hilmer, on the board of Westfield, is the university's chancellor.

The V-C's salary is $750,000. Three-quarters of a million dollars. Sounds good to me. The cat and I could live very nicely on that and holiday at the Cipriani in Venice every year, too. But, said Hilmer grandly, rather as if he were explaining why he had decided to go to India to work barefoot among the poor for a pint of gruel, "I actually don't work for money. If I worked for money, I would never have moved out of corporate life ..."[31]

Like, whatever

Millionaire celebrity chef Jamie Oliver was mortified when the marketing people at Heinz let the cat out of the bag and revealed that he had been persuaded to put baked beans on the menu of his London restaurant in return for £15,000. He told one British newspaper, "The next thing I know we've got giant baked beans running across the restaurant and paparazzi outside shouting 'Oliver's a wanker'."

Not that he seems to have considered handing back Fairfax's $4.5 million farewell handshake, in spite of a hundred editorial staffers turning up at the company's annual general meeting to protest such a payment. Incoming CEO David Kirk had just announced a 7.5 percent redundancy measure in their ranks because of falling profits. Circulations had also dropped during Hilmer's time and on-line opportunities, which might have bolstered Fairfax's classifieds revenue, had been missed. Maybe that's why Kirk himself received more than a million for simply signing on.

About this time, Pepsi-Max was screening a particularly objectionable television ad. A hunk of a young man with hair like a bear's pelt leaps out of a moving helicopter, its propeller blades causing such sandy havoc on a beach that sunbathers scatter in all directions. "You can do anything when you're heaps rich," the hunk chortles to the camera.

American sociologist Richard Sennett, author of *The Corrosion of Character*, has produced a book, *Respect in a World of Inequality*, [32] which questions the automatic respect given to the upwardly mobile while the less fortunate or less ambitious can be treated as then being less than human. Sennett, who grew up in a Chicago housing project, writes, "The unusual person who makes full use of his or her abilities can serve as a social icon, justifying inadequate provision of resources or regard for people who are not developing as fully; the celebration of self-sufficiency and fear of parasitism can serve as a way of denying the facts of social need; the compassion which lies behind the desire to give back can be deformed by social conditions into pity for the weak, pity which the receiver experiences as contempt."

Melbourne historian Mark Peel, author of *The Lowest Rung: Voices of Australian Poverty*,[33] once told me, "What hurts people in poverty most is the disrespect they've learned to expect from others."

On the television show *CSI: Miami*, another young rich thug, the scion of a powerful family, says contemptuously to the lead detective: "Money is the best defence." Naturally enough, our detective, Lieutenant Horatio Caine, responds: "No, honesty is the best defence."

But that's TV. In real life, the message is clear. These days, this is what we're all up against: the irresistible lure and clout of money when it has been decided that money is all that matters and that $750,000 is small beer.

CHAPTER 5

The New F-Word

"I would make them shine and give them — what's that thing called? A makeover."

TIFFANY MINERVINI, 21-YEAR-OLD BOSTONIAN,
AUDITIONING TO BE ONE OF THE BEAUTIES ON
AMERICAN REALITY TV SHOW *BEAUTY AND THE GEEK*.
THE BOSTON GLOBE, AUGUST 28, 2005

Fatuousness is the cruise control of our fairhead society. Australian *Harper's Bazaar* had no qualms about putting out a one-off special in 2005, The Big Red Book, based on the seven deadly sins. The book, a huge A2 format in hardback, was a "style bible" of fashion, photography, stories and essays that dived headfirst into the sins of sloth, gluttony, greed, envy, anger, lust and vanity, treating them much the way you might use a spray of ostrich feathers as an amusing backdrop.

Cristal Champagne and caviar were served at the launch party, which was covered approvingly by the gossip columns, and editor Alison Veness-McGourty was quoted, calling her new product a "bookazine". Now there's a word that's perfect for a twenty-first-century dictionary for airheads. "It comes in a hard case, it is fabulous and luxurious," she said. "I think it will become a collector's item."[1]

God save us, I hope not, but it probably will. The first "bookazine" for *Bazaar*, The Big Black Book published the year before, had a print-run of 30,000 and reportedly sold so well that distributors Random House asked for a 40,000 print-run for this one. Next up, The Goddess Book. With a white cover and a $4.95 price rise from $25.

Fatuousness works.

So God save those of us, too, who have felt obliged to become fatuous to further our careers.

For years I admired the American journalist Maureen Dowd for the acuity and wit of her knife-edged columns for *The New York Times* that get syndicated around the world. I admired her, that is,

Totally

"We call it celebrity news, but it's really gossip … Thirteen years ago, the tsunami would have been on the cover on its own, but, you say: do you want to take a bath at the newsstand? For us, it's clear that celebrity gossip and photos are the big sales drive." ONE WEEKLY MAGAZINE EDITOR, JANE NICHOLLS, OF *WHO*, IS DECENT ENOUGH TO TELL THE TRUTH ABOUT READER PREFERENCES TO *THE SUN-HERALD* IN AUGUST 2005.

until she did her publicity for her latest book, *Are Men Necessary?*[2] At which stage I wondered instead just what the hell was going on.

"You know," she drawled in one public interview session in Australia. "This is a good book to take to a restaurant or on the subway and meet someone." In the same performance, she volunteers that she's interested in hearing from men, that she's staying at the Sydney Hilton and her room number sounds like 26-something-or-other, although that bit is drowned out by a gulp from her on-stage interviewer.

Dowd, who has spent several years complaining that men are intimidated by her (and presumably, by her reputation for critical commentary and wit), started off her round of media interviews in the United States with a publicity shot that made her look as if she were auditioning to be a hat-check girl at a Bunny Club. She wears her flaming red hair *à la* Veronica Lake, has a penchant for very high-heeled shoes and told author Ariel Levy in one interview that she subscribed to the philosophy of Thirties glamour actor Carole Lombard. That is, as she expressed it: "'I live by a man's code, designed to fit a man's world, yet at the same time I never forget that a woman's first job is to choose the right shade of lipstick.'"

Really? *Really?*

Was she joking? Sending herself up?

I'd like to think so. Is it possible that this Pulitzer-prize-winning journalist, a columnist with *The New York Times* for ten years whose skilful writing on politics and society puts you in mind of a sashimi chef going about his filleting, is the kind of disorganised, faff-headed woman who, as she coquettishly let slip to Levy, can also leave a laptop in a taxi three times, lose her mobile continuously, wear a watch that doesn't tell the right time and be seemingly unable to keep her diary straight?

It is preposterous to think that Maureen Dowd might be an airhead for real. Please, not that. Could she be in the same game as singer Jessica Simpson who claimed in a *Vanity Fair* interview that she loved playing the ditz in spite of her IQ of 160? "That's how I charmed people," Simpson said.[3]

Dowd, from her columns, is anything but clueless, yet on stage in Sydney, she played the ingénue, confessing to the audience that she'd never imagined that her book about whether men were necessary would be seen as reflecting her personal life. She joked with her friend, Sydney journalist Julia Baird, who was conducting the interview, about how within days of first meeting, the two of them were gambling in Las Vegas, and then how Baird and Dowd's sister bought matching bikinis and then ... oh, you know, girly, giggly, madcap things. The interchanges sounded like what might have happened if you'd slipped Nan and Flossie from the Bobbsey twins some Ecstasy in their morning cereal. So cute, so whacky. If the Stepford Wives concept had gone as far as including women journalists, this is what they might have looked and sounded like. When a man asked later why someone as critical of President Bush as Dowd wasn't at the barricades the way he himself had been over Vietnam, Dowd and Baird looked at each other gawp-eyed. They seemed not to have the slightest clue what the man meant.

Watching Dowd in bemused fascination, I fantasised that maybe she had done a kind of Faustian deal with her agent and publisher to produce a sexy, playful bestseller – and now was starting to rue it, especially in view of the often quizzical reviews her book had received. Her own newspaper published a sniping review by novelist Kathryn Harrison that implied Dowd was manipulative and a namedropper, and worse, that her smart, staccato style, so successful in her 800-word columns, was unable to sustain a full-length book.

If I am right and Dowd, alone at midnight and with the doors barred, rants to the moon about the foolishness of ever taking on this book deal, whose fault would it really be? Would the publishers at Putnam have embraced as enthusiastically a serious book by Dowd about, say, women in world politics? I doubt it. In any case, this book has certainly worked for Dowd as far as making the world aware of the Dowd brand.

Baird herself had caused some consternation when, in 2005, in *Good Weekend* magazine, she launched a column which featured a sexy full-length photo byline. It's true that editors, rather than columnists, come up with such ideas, but it's still up to a columnist to have the wit to say ... mmm, let's maybe not do that. As for the columns, Baird told me later they were pretty much a reflection of what she and her friends were talking about at the time. Certainly, they read as if rather more IQ had gone into finessing her figure-hugging outfits for her photo-shoot. The dinkus kept changing each week: this week stomach-baring hipster jeans, next week stomach-baring hipster jeans but a different top, etc, etc. The fatuousness quotient of the copy remained about the same, whether she was confessing to kind of liking Arnie Schwarzenegger (even after telling us that he enjoyed the idea of burying a woman's face in a toilet bowl), thrilling to Angelina Jolie's desire to walk around topless, tattooed and in leather pants, or sounding off about the responsibility of men surprised by fatherhood (always safe). And this from a woman with a PhD in history whose doctoral thesis on how the press treats female politicians had become a book, *Media Tarts*,[4] later short-listed for the NSW Premier's literary awards.

But however much fatuousness can be seen in these public performances, and however clear it is that both Dowd and Baird have gone with publicity photos designed to titillate, the pair have certainly captured the zeitgeist, as did Veness-McGourty. They are re-creating themselves or their work as highly desirable, highly marketable brands that appeal specifically to the non-cerebral part of the cortex.

After all, as one thirty-something Sydney magazine executive exclaimed to me about Baird's ever-changing dinkus shots: "But I *love* looking at what she's wearing. It's like the cream on the cake; it really enhances the column!"

That's why, if the twenty-first-century has one message for survival, appeal and getting to the top, it is this: don't be too smart. In fact, be really smart; act sweet and just a tad confused. Sexiness, the showgirl kind, is in. Vacuousness is in. Who needs books when you can have a bookazine?

FATUOUSNESS is everywhere; a kind of languid vacancy, assumed or real, that makes other people laugh. A friend tells me about a rich grandmother who counsels her daughter-in-law, a new mother, on the raising of children, by saying lightly: "Just do whatever you think is right and then if he still grows up with any problems, you can get in a counsellor."

Biographer Helen O'Neill, whose most recent book was on adventuress and wallpaper designer Florence Broadhurst, has another persona, Popsi

---

Que?

"Few women would begrudge their lover a night with Angelina Jolie."

THIS FAR-FETCHED CLAIM IN A SYNDICATED PIECE MAKES ITS WAY THROUGH THE EDITING RANKS OF VARIOUS NEWSPAPERS FROM *THE NEW YORK OBSERVER* TO *THE AUSTRALIAN FINANCIAL REVIEW*.

Bubblehead. What she has discovered is that Popsi is much more popular than she is. The nickname came out of some banter she had when she was researching a science documentary for the Discovery Channel. Then her partner, who was food reviewing for *The Sydney Morning Herald*, decided Popsi would make a good dining companion for him in his pieces. Popsi took off. (Bit like my cat really.) A dinner with Popsi and her reviewing partner was auctioned off at a charity fundraiser for cancer. A PR from David Jones meticulously invited Popsi to a food party and even made out a name tag for her. If her partner started talking to a chef or owner, quite often they would ignore him and turn to Helen and exclaim, "So YOU must be Popsi Bubblehead." Sometimes they were a little disappointed. They'd go: "I thought you'd be a blonde."

Today's most famous blonde, Paris Hilton, well knows the worth of fatuousness. Having left the world gobsmacked after her appearances in her television show *The Simple Life*, and on the social, glitz club, freebie and sex-tape circuits, she wrote her memoirs, *Confessions of an Heiress*, which came out in 2004. It was mostly pictures of Paris proving that millions of dollars still can't help a girl with naturally bad taste. Then she complacently watched her book whiz into the best-seller charts where it stayed for many months. The memoirs have now been joined by *Your Heiress Diary: Confess It All To Me*. ("Let Paris guide you as you write down the details of your own fabulous life.") The rewards have been excellent. Between June 2004 and June 2005, demands for Ms Hilton's appearances, her books and services on television earned her $US6.5 million, up from $2 million the year before.[5] In the year to June 2006, she earned $7 million. "She is the Donald Trump of the younger generation," the chairman of a marketing consultancy in Georgia told *The New York Times* admiringly.

Nonsense presented as something worthwhile and smart is very much in. Take the way British *Vogue* covered the 2004 Hay-on-Wye literary festival. It sent along a fashion writer. As you do. So on one warm Friday in late May 2004, Lisa Armstrong tells her readers she popped on a tweed jacket, jeans and a pair of Donna Karan boots and disappeared up the train line from London to Hereford on her literary assignment. It was a stretch, as she later wrote in a feature piece resplendent with artfully staged photographs of major literary figures. "Being an intellectual is quite hard sometimes," she observed in her second paragraph.

Indeed, and so readers got to find out about the famous festival – featuring on this occasion American novelist John Updike, playwright Arnold Wesker, authors Tony Parsons, Zadie Smith, Hari Kunzru and Jonathan Coe, and filmmaker Ken Loach – through the eyes of a seeming nincompoop.

Admittedly Armstrong, who writes for *The Times* and is a successful chick-lit novelist, sent herself up a little by playing to the role. On the other hand, British *Vogue*, whose managing director is Nicholas Coleridge, a fine journalist and author, let the archly empty-headed piece run for about 4,000 words and over thirteen pages.

The piece was termed "intellectual chic", which shows just how far we've come in the fatuousness stakes. What next? Vacuous chic?

A friend of mine recently fell out of a car after having travelled for several hours in the company of a clutch of former beauty editors. She swore, "If I hear the shriek "ohmigod!" once more, or if anyone says anything about shoes, handbags or lip gloss in the next 24 hours, I'll shoot myself."

More fool her. She should bone up on the lingo. My friend doesn't get it, although the beauty writers certainly do. Over the years, they have amassed vital contacts throughout the international beauty product conglomerates which spend billions in advertising each year around the world. The beauty editors have sat at numerous lunches, dinners and presentations, watching highly paid executives giving long lectures on why a new mascara wand is the year's most significant invention. They have been flown first-class thousands of miles to attend the launch of an eye cream in Tokyo. They have written reams of copy about nail polish, moisturisers, what to look for in a facial and how to use a luminiser.

It takes a certain mindset and depth of brain-pan to be able to do this for more than three months without wanting to either stare into space for a very long time or volunteer to work in a starving African village as atonement. The women – and now some males are getting in on the act, too – who stick it out thus prove themselves, rather like young Maasai undergoing gruelling initiation rites without whimpering. And just as the African elders do with their adolescent charges, so does the beauty industry embrace those beauty editors who last the distance. If you could see the twinkly-eyed, rat-a-tat-paced, intense conversations that go on between executives, who are basically skin-care salesmen, and beauty writers, you'd think you were getting an up-close seat at a debate between Simone de Beauvoir and Jean-Paul Sartre.

What all that sparkle and flirting and back-and-forth really means though is that the conglomerates will advertise in the magazines where the beauty editors work, and the beauty editors will write copy and organise pages that make it worth their while. Consequently, these beauty editors have passed another initiation test. They have proven their fitness for editor duty in women's magazine-land where nurturing advertisers is rather more important than providing copy that a reader over the age of fifteen might actually find interesting and enlightening.

We need to find the moment when this kind of ditsy fatuousness became sexy, appealing and what the market wanted. After all, for years, women who were smart and talented were presumed to be the ones who were desired, desirable and useful. Men who yearned after dumb blondes were considered to be either dumb themselves or a little off. Max Bialystock in *The Producers* was the caricature: a sweating, overweight, sleazy, no-hoper sexist who longed for the blonde, big-breasted receptionist whose dumbness was a caricature, too. We were expected to look down our noses and snigger at such choices.

Hollywood and show business instead made icons of women of the calibre of Myrna Loy, who, in the Thirties, played the tough, smart half of married amateur sleuth duo Nick and Nora Charles in *The Thin Man* series of films. In 1957, a delicious Rita Hayworth sang "Zip!" in the film version of the Broadway musical *Pal Joey*. Hayworth plays a successful and wealthy socialite exposed as a former stripper. In a wonderful up-yours melody, with lyrics by Lorenz Hart, she announces to her audience:

"*But before I unzip one zipper, I want you to know I was quite the artist, the intellectual kind …*

Really?

"'The [former] award-winning editor of UK *marie-claire* Glenda Bailey said to me, "You should be the editor of *marie-claire* in Australia,"' Jackie Frank says. 'And I said, "But I can't write," and she said, "Neither can I!" And we both roared with laughter.'"
MEDIA SECTION,
THE AUSTRALIAN, AUGUST 11, 2005. FRANK MADE THE MAGAZINE AUSTRALIA'S NUMBER ONE FASHION TITLE.

"What was I thinking while I worked you might ask,
While I worked, these thoughts were crossing my mind ...
"ZIP! Walter Lippman wasn't brilliant today,
"ZIP! Will the Giants ever make it a day?
"ZIP! I was reading Schopenhauer last night,
"ZIP! And I think that Schopenhauer was right!"
And so on.

Poor doomed Marilyn Monroe, forever the curvaceous, wide-eyed blonde, also knew it was good for the box-office to be perceived as a closet intellectual. She married Pulitzer-prize-winning playwright Arthur Miller and was seen reading James Joyce's *Ulysses* on set between takes (albeit upside-down, as one catty Hollywood gossip writer had it).

These actresses knew that seeming to be smart would pay off with audiences. They stood for a cavalcade of bright, intelligent women from the Twenties to the Sixties who were in the public spotlight and who could argue anyone under the table: Dorothy Parker, Helen Lawrenson, Lee Miller, Nancy Mitford, Clare Booth Luce and on.

All gone now and where are their like today? We should be grateful, I suppose, that pin-up queen Angelina Jolie has turned her attention and fortune to helping the world's less fortunate for, apart from her and a few other notables (George Clooney, Sandra Bullock, Susan Sarandon and Tim Robbins, Bob Geldof, Richard Gere), the celebrity landscape is pretty barren of any star with more on their minds than themselves. Efforts by others to pose for pix associated with the Green movement or famine are, for me, a tad too, too much what happens when good causes become the latest fashion accessory; kind of like babies a few seasons ago, except requiring longer faces.

Empty-headedness is the look of the moment, something to be pursued wholeheartedly by the market. Much has been made of British author Helen Fielding's love affair with Jane Austen and how she based her best-selling novel *Bridget Jones's Diary* on Austen's most famous story-line. "Actually, I just stole the plot from *Pride and Prejudice*," she told *Entertainment Weekly* for a 1998 special on that year's top twelve entertainers. "I thought it had been very well market-researched over a number of centuries."

Artfully, the hero is called Mark Darcy and there are umpteen twists through the first book and its sequel that play upon the name Darcy and the actor Colin Firth who played Darcy in the 1995 BBC version of *Pride and Prejudice*. All very sexy and compelling, but what happened to the woman who awakes Darcy's passion, Elizabeth Bennet, Austen's most memorable heroine? For, if Fielding based her novel on *Pride and Prejudice*, she forgot to actually read or re-read the original, or she had a particularly spectacular airhead spin-out as she reworked it for a modern audience. Or worse, maybe she took account of the current ideal of mindless womanhood and edited away furiously. Then the film company got to work.

Dunderbritches Bridget bears no relation to Austen's sharp, elegant, sassy and witty Elizabeth Bennet, first made famous in film by Greer Garson in 1940 and then by Jennifer Ehle for the BBC and, finally, with a little less sangfroid, by Keira Knightley in the latest 2005 movie. In Bridget, the cool intelligence, the wit, the sexy warmth, the commonsense are all erased. Instead, the closest our heroine for modern times comes to one of the Bennet girls is Lydia, the squawking, over-sexed teenager who almost ruins the romances of her two elder sisters.

So in 1813, it was apparently acceptable to have a heroine who was both bright and acute as well as having fine eyes, but at the dawn of the twenty-first, we must have someone who, in one hilarious episode in the Fielding book, turns out not to be able to find Germany on a map. (Life imitates fiction: in the 2005 season of *Big Brother*, one of the inmates asked: "Where's the Berlin Wall?")

Now of course Bridget Jones is having a second life, having been resurrected by Fielding and *The Independent* newspaper in the UK. The first column of the new series revealed that Bridget had learned nothing from her adventures, and indeed, may even have slipped back in the IQ stakes owing to too much fat consumption, too much fast food and too much alcohol. Whatever ditsy, funny charm she had when I first met her, in the opening paragraphs of *Bridget Jones's Diary*, had virtually disappeared. Can we deduce that someone somewhere in marketing, publishing and film-land has said to Fielding: "Look, they laugh at the funny bits; don't make her as sharp this time."

What are we to make of the fact that the people we are encouraged to admire now are not bright so much as rich, not great thinkers so much as great performers, not intelligent so much as street-smart? And if someone *is* bright and an acute writer, like Maureen Dowd, then she must caper and giggle and give every appearance that her intelligence is not nearly as important as, say, her ability to wear pencil heels. In a

Totally

"Creating a cultural icon out of someone who goes, 'I'm stupid, isn't it cute?' makes me want to throw daggers. I want to say to them, 'My Grandma did not fight for what she fought for just so you can start telling women it's fun to be stupid.'"
ACTOR REESE WITHERSPOON, WHO LATER OBJECTED TO REPORTS THAT SHE HAD BEEN TAKING AIM AT A PARTICULAR CELEBRITY. ON THE RECORD, SHE ADDED: "I BELIEVE THERE'S A MOVEMENT AMONG YOUNG WOMEN TO PLAY DUMB, AND I DON'T THINK THAT'S A GOOD MESSAGE TO PROMOTE IF YOU'RE A PUBLIC FIGURE."

December 2005 *Vanity Fair* questionnaire, Dowd teasingly listed her greatest achievement as "covering six presidential campaigns in heels" and declared "gravitas" the most overrated virtue.

Remind yourself again: who are the women whose faces sell magazines today and who get radio play and television hours? (A magazine executive semi-seriously confides that she has sleepless nights because of the airheads she chooses to put on her covers. "But," she says, "I don't own these magazines. Someone else does and it's my job to make him money.")

To discover the moment when vacancy became sexy and ravishing, we don't have to go back very far – only to the beginning of the Eighties to find the Princess of Wales, the first person to receive worldwide adulation while clearly being thick. At first, we were mildly charmed by Diana's naivety and the romantic situation in which she found herself – a young, pretty and unpretentious woman marrying a prince and heir to the throne of Britain. Then something else kicked in. Diana got a makeover from the ladies at *Vogue*. Some of the world's best photographers took her portrait. She lost weight. Before our eyes, she turned into a gorgeous, sapphire-eyed pin-up wearing hugely expensive clothes and living a luxurious life she hadn't earned. If magazines put her on their cover, sales soared. Little girls dreamed of being her and big girls envied her. Books were written about her and sold in their millions. Drama, scandal and sex entered her life, which meant the virginal fiancée had now metamorphosed into a seemingly sexually available vamp. We couldn't get enough, even when it was revealed she had once tried to kill herself by slashing her wrists with a lemon zester. In short order, Diana had exactly what we were all beginning to be fascinated by: looks, privilege, wealth, sex appeal. Never mind the silliness and the airheadedness; these were passed off as quite charming, really.

Through it all, as Diana proved a money-maker extraordinaire for everyone from newspaper proprietors to paparazzi photographers to publishers, she remained as thick as we'd always known she was and as thick as she had always admitted. Diana was the original adored airhead of the new age. However much admirable charity work she did, however much people pondered whether she was a superb manipulator or a wounded dove, no-one ever thought that, in her, we had anything other than a blonde with not much upstairs.

The line from Diana to Paris Hilton (roping in the likes of Maureen Dowd along the way) is as direct as the Central line from Holland Park to Holborn on the London Underground map.

Vapidity, so long as it is linked to money, looks and fame, has officially become the new thing. It is enormously appealing and completely unthreatening.

"I'd like to be a queen of people's hearts, in people's hearts, but I don't see myself being queen of this country," Diana remarked perspicaciously in her infamous BBC interview in 1995 in which she dished the dirt on Charles and Camilla and owned up to some of her own. Some 15 million people watched the interview, one of the corporation's highest-ever audience figures.

IT IS a couple of centuries since small children in upper-middle- and upper-class England could routinely speak Latin and ancient Greek, recite large chunks of Virgil and do complicated calculations without using pen and paper. "No-one in this world … has ever lost money by underestimating the intelligence of the great masses of the plain people," wrote cranky H. L. Mencken in 1926. Now, almost a hundred years after, with far too much of the business world making its fortune from following his aphorism, few of our teenagers even know how to speak and write English, let alone how to read a book like *Crime and Punishment* or *Madame Bovary*. Instead, it's the Harry Potter mysteries being devoured not just by nine-year-olds but also by nineteen-year-olds, and everyone applauds because, thank God, at least they're reading.

An empty head is not necessarily the same as an airhead but in society's pursuit of the ideal twenty-first-century citizen – that is, an airhead who consumes but neither questions nor thinks too deeply about consequences – the promotion of empty-headedness is a twenty-four-hour occupation for far too many people who should know better.

Our appetite for the easy and entertaining has emptied our heads and in doing so has actually made it harder for us all to have common intellectual ground. In the Forties, Lorenz Hart could write those lyrics for "Zip!" and take it for granted that the audience knew Schopenhauer was a German philosopher. Cole Porter could write a jokey song for the musical *Kiss Me Kate* called "Brush Up Your Shakespeare" with wordplay on *Troilus and Cressida*, *Coriolanus* and *As You Like It*, and know that the audience would laugh. But that frame of reference has all but disappeared.

Biographer and editor Jacquie Kent, in a paper on the future of research libraries and biography, referred to this with a story about tabloids in the mid-twentieth century: "…one example was an article in the Sydney *Daily Telegraph* in which the [Australian] poet Hugh McCrae was compared to the fifteenth-century French poet Francois Villon. Presumably the readers understood the reference … a tiny detail that says so much about the popular press of fifty years ago."[6]

Ross Campbell, who used to write funny columns about his family of four children for *The Australian Women's Weekly* and *The Sunday Telegraph*, was also a classics scholar. In one delightful line in a short piece about children's reading habits, he described Baby Pip getting her first "libry" book. It was *The Story of Horace*. "(The bear, not the poet)," wrote Campbell in wry parentheses, knowing his mass audience would get the joke and its reference to the Roman poet. It's doubtful if the same joke would even make it to the printed page today, being deleted by an editor or sub-editor on the grounds that not enough readers would understand it. Especially if the editor or sub-editor didn't get it either.

In just fifty years, our tastes and our methods of education and dumbing down have removed frames of references that previous generations had possessed for centuries. We can't even keep up with our recent history. A few years ago, I made a reference to the Algonquin Round Table to a couple of thirty-something senior journalists. They had no idea what I was talking about. One of them had a Masters in English literature.

In 1965, Helen Gurley Brown created the mass circulation women's magazine phenomenon *Cosmopolitan* from a pre-existing title. At last count, there were fifty-six editions around the world and it was the world's top-selling magazine for young women. The original United States edition traditionally carried long pieces with pages and pages of text, often written by well-credentialled therapists and respected writers. That has changed drastically in the last few years, and now the US edition, more and more like its overseas sisters, looks like a children's book, a sea of big type, coloured headings, breakouts and dot points and, above all, pictures.

"Pictures are the new *words*!" an American *Cosmo* exec enthused to the dubious Gurley Brown.

A friend in magazine publishing notes sardonically that what the reader really wants now, or is presumed to want, is the in-depth picture caption. Noted biographer Deirdre Bair blew the whistle on book publishers who have decided that readers no longer have the attention span to read an entire life story. Instead, they ask authors to write a "dip-in". That means, Bair explained, that it might just be the most exciting part of someone's life or, better still, an event at which several important people were gathered together. She quoted one editor saying to an author proposing a biographical subject: "Just give me a weekend when something terrific happened."[7] These shorter biographical books are also far cheaper to produce. Natch.

No wonder that sometimes when we listen to people, it really does feel as if there's a big cartoon bubble coming out of their mouths. Fantastic rubbish is prattled and we are supposed to go along with it as if our brains have turned to cheese. As of course, all too often, they appear to have.

Vanity Fair, the same magazine whose editorials have been bollocking George W. Bush over the

Que?

"Anybody who knows anything of history also knows that great social changes are impossible without the female ferment. Social progress can be measured exactly by the social status of the beautiful sex (the ugly ones included)."
KARL MARX IN A LETTER TO A FRIEND, DECEMBER 1868.

invasion of Iraq since the war started, put Paris Hilton, bare-topped in white jodhpurs, on its October 2005 cover. Hilton's interviewer declared in that issue's contributor notes: "She's a fantastic train wreck of a bimbo, but ask her a serious question and suddenly you find an articulate young woman."

Really?

This of a woman who, two months later, revealed in a legal statement for a pending court case that she didn't know London was in the United Kingdom and that she knew so many people she didn't know the names of some of her friends. Given it's hard to credit that even a self-obsessed heiress could be that ignorant, it's highly likely that what we're witnessing here is mouth before brain. As in, the mouth is engaged but the brain is not. What comes out of the mouth doesn't even get a dusting of brain cells on the way out and nor does the owner of the mouth seem to believe that's necessary.

In the piece itself, a business partner of Hilton's claims: "She makes a lot of money, and the system doesn't pay out that kind of money to airheads. You don't make millions as an idiot." The man concerned is the CEO of a cosmetics company which hired Hilton to be its spokesperson for a lip-treatment product that, at $US29.99, promises to increase lip size by 40 percent. Just who exactly is the airhead in cases like these is the question of the day but, certainly, whenever the whiff of snake oil is in the air, you have to acknowledge that someone is hoping someone somewhere is going to be an idiot.

Meanwhile, my doubts about Ms Hilton, even after reading *VF*'s positively glowing piece on her, were not assuaged by subsequent events. Hilton, who, in the article, was supposedly madly in love with her fiance, shipping heir Paris (another Paris) Latsis, broke off the engagement the same month the magazine came out. She then engaged in a round of public flirtations and propositions.

It was feminist and author Naomi Wolf who supplied the *VF* writer with the most apposite quote about Hilton, picking up on her constant smile, her pigeon-toed girlishness and that sense of sexual availability: "It's almost like white noise in an over-stimulated environment. Paris Hilton is like a palate cleanser. She's like, as semiotics would say, an empty signifier, so you can project absolutely anything on to her, which is the perfect situation for branding." And there, of course, is the real reason *Vanity Fair* put Hilton on the cover.

By sheer determination to win fame, Hilton has put a ring through all our noses.

Now we take Paris more seriously than she takes herself, and magazines and newspapers flog her and her image relentlessly.

Mia Freedman, former editor-in-chief of Australian *Cosmopolitan, Dolly* and *Cleo,* now Nine Network creative director, explains the appeal to young women of Hilton "and all her talentless, unemployed It Girl mates": "They see these young women with huge wealth having men and discarding them as they please, and they see that as meaning those young women are in control.

"And that's what they want, too."

Really. *Really?*

CHAPTER 6

The World is My Oyster Shell

*"Porsche's new baby.
An excellent reason to delay yours."*
ADVERTISEMENT FOR THE PORSCHE CAYMAN S IN
THE AUSTRALIAN FINANCIAL REVIEW

*"Ask not what you can do for your country.
Ask what's for lunch."*
ACTOR ORSON WELLES

Back in the Eighties, the newsroom of *The Sydney Morning Herald* was big, broad, low-ceilinged and often dark because of faulty fluorescents. I can't imagine that management ever spent much more than tuppence on its decor, although upstairs, where the executives and the Fairfaxes had their offices, swelled with polished antiques and Australian masters. The newsroom below swarmed with a bunch of eager twenty- and thirty-something journalists bright with the new idea that newspapers didn't just have to report on local and foreign news as they had done for decades. Goodness, no. Instead of the world being our oyster, and the farthest reaches accessible, we were more interested in the oysters on our plates, on the minutiae of what we could find in our own living rooms, kitchens, bathrooms, on the dishes in front of us at restaurants, and what we were doing with our leisure time. Decks and courtyards became big news. So did summer berries and chefs.

The Washington Post, home of Watergate investigative journalists Woodward and Bernstein, had started its *Style* section in 1969. It was to be a place that examined popular culture and social trends for men and women, with no relation to old-style women's pages. (Ironically, given what has happened to lifestyle sections since, and their now relentless focus on product with a frothy topping, the original *Post* section was staffed by highly experienced men and women who later became editors, managing editors and publishers of various illustrious United States newspapers, magazines

Ohmigod

"She employs a PA as a 'human ashtray' to follow her around everywhere so she can chain smoke red-pack Marlboros. (Donatella is full-strength in all her tastes.) She speaks in a treacle-thick drawl and gesticulates wildly as she cheerfully massacres the English language. She moisturises her toes with £100-a-pot Crème De La Mer. And she never leaves home without wearing [at least] £100,000 worth of jewellery, including a giant yellow diamond ring Gianni gave her." A FLATTERING PROFILE OF FASHION DESIGNER DONATELLA VERSACE IN *THE OBSERVER*, OCTOBER 13, 2002, THAT ENDS WITH THE SALUTATION "BRAVA, DONATELLA".

and news services.) The idea behind the *Post*'s section was not that you took social events and lifestyle per se seriously, but that you discerned social currents through them. One of the early writers on the section, Jane Amsterdam, told me it was "tea-leaf reading through social events". The *Post*'s then editor, Ben Bradlee, also refused to give the section its most obvious name because, as he wrote, "I thought 'Lifestyle' was a bogus word, suggesting the worst of Madison Avenue."[1] Bradlee probably would never have believed at the time what a long line of dominoes his baby section would set tumbling.

By the mid-Seventies, *The New York Times* had begun its own softer sections. If that bulwark of serious journalism could start incorporating lifestyle, taking ratatouille, Parisian designers, cabernet and cushions seriously, so certainly could *The Sydney Morning Herald*. If the room around us was full of dreary desks, bulky computers and walls plastered with peeling maps, lists of politicians, conversion charts and deadline times, our young heads brimmed with tales of chefs' specialties, fashion shoots with models perched trickily on high ledges, the cutting edge in furniture design, film festivals, late-night happenings and what was hot in gourmet takeaway and sofa design. We were fascinated, liberated by the idea that such everyday objects, such familiar things, could generate pages of copy and win admiration and readers. Who needed to furtively read up on the issues of the day before going out to dinner? Why, half the time taken to eat the first course could be filled with a discussion of the best olive oil to buy.

One day, the newspaper's young editor, Eric Beecher, approved a picture story for the news pages about beachgoers on a weekday. Supine bodies in a news photograph were circled and their owners queried as to why they were able to sun themselves when everybody else was at work.

After that, there was no stopping us and our inventiveness. Our aim was to chronicle how people were living their everyday lives – in a surprising way, of course. One boiling summer's day, a bright-eyed news editor is supposed to have instructed a reporter to take an ice-cream cone into the sun and time how long it took to melt. Bradlee's original idea, the notion that you can tell a lot about society by the food it eats, the clothes it wears, the friends it keeps, was transmogrifying into something else. Lifestyle, for lifestyle's sake.

So mindless did we become that I can remember telling Beecher importantly that one of the sections I edited, Thursday's *Style*, was about to do a "hard" story on kitchens. Heaven knows what I had in mind. An investigation of pine cupboards? The truth about dishwasher installation? (If I had stuck with kitchen stories, I would have been only twenty years ahead of my time. There are now journalists on excellent six-figure salaries who do nothing *but* chart the changes in kitchen surfaces, layouts and whether to have white or brushed-steel appliances.)

Another news editor was Richard Glover, now a successful author and Sydney ABC-Radio host who still writes a Saturday column for the newspaper. He remembers being inspired when the British porcelain manufacturer Royal Doulton balanced a Rolls-Royce on four upturned Royal Doulton teacups at The Royal Easter Show to demonstrate the superiority of British produce. Glover got a mate's Holden Ute and balanced it on four Vegemite jars and the picture ran on page three next day.

Glover also remembers how much mail he received after writing a cover story on the death of wallpaper. "I'd written about uranium policy and Aborigines, but I'd never received so much hate mail as when I wrote that piece for a section called *Life and Home*. How they'd spent their life-savings on their wallpaper and I'd ruined their lives. At that point I realised the passion that was in lifestyle."

Lifestyle gave new life to the newspaper ad sales departments and turned into a demanding monster that paid the rent. Many of us are aghast, all these years later, at what our unchecked enthusiasm has wrought. Glover, a fierce defender of the notion that newspapers should cover both the ordinary realities of everyday life as well as war zones, economic policy and what's up in Washington, still remarks: "Sometimes today's newspapers can remind me of a weary old man dragging along a huge cloak of sections and lifestyle paraphernalia. The little old man is what remains of the traditional newspaper – news, analysis, foreign news."

Beecher arrived at *The Sydney Morning Herald* in 1981 from *The Age* where he had been running the Saturday feature pages. "The paper was dying," he remembers now of the *SMH*. "It was just a two-section paper, with one feature page a day, and it was very staid and traditional. The aim was to try and reinvent it in a way that would appeal to younger readers and to women. We used to look at the obituaries in the newspaper and it was like recording our dwindling readers. They literally were dying off."

David Jones, the upmarket department store that had serviced the well-heeled in the city and the pastoral aristocracy since 1838, had always been a major advertiser in the paper, taking ten to twenty pages a week. But by the time Beecher arrived, the store's advertising had shrunk so much that he remembers one week the only ad was a half-page for men's hats. "That was the only thing they thought the *SMH* could sell for them."

It was Beecher's job to introduce lifestyle sections such as *Good Living*, devoted to food and fashion, *The Guide* for TV and radio, and *Style*. All were modelled on the sections that had been launched in *The New York Times*. *Good Living* kicked off in June 1982, six weeks after *The Guide*. David Jones looked at the broadsheet dummies and instantly booked three pages. By the mid-to-late-Eighties, as Beecher moved to *The Herald* in Melbourne (where he also introduced daily lifestyle sections which he hired me to start and run) and John Alexander moved into the *SMH* editor's job, circulation had turned around at the latter and was starting to rise.

But better still for revenue, lifestyle advertisers such as furniture stores, wine shops and kitchen designers had been given platforms to reach all those quality newspaper readers. The more advertising the lifestyle sections brought in, the more necessary they became to the commercial viability of host papers. Sections such as foreign news and even books started looking like wallflowers. No advertisers wanted to dance with the former, and few with the latter.

Meanwhile, the pages allocated to lifestyle grew lustily and continue to do so. Lifestyle, after all, is what burns a hole in your wallet. The term hardly existed until British businessman Terence Conran invented the Habitat homewares store concept in London in 1964. Since then, it has become as effective as any social anaesthetising drug dreamed

Really?

"'We did not give that 10 seconds' worth of thought,' [Burger King chairman and CEO Greg Brenneman] says. 'I'm not bothered by the food Nazis.'"
THE CHAIN'S NEW CEO RESPONDS TO CRITICS OF HIS NEW ENORMOUS OMELET SANDWICH IN *USA TODAY*, MAY 23, 2005. THE SANDWICH, WHICH CONTAINS 46G OF FAT, BOOSTED THE CHAIN'S BREAKFAST SALES BY 20 PERCENT AND SAVED ITS BACON.

up by Huxley or Orwell, creating a vast, suffocating blanket of neediness for everything from Asian-inspired crockery to plasma televisions to gas barbecues as big and threatening as mortuary tables to Internet butlers who'll find your special socks for you and auction sites that will deliver couturier knock-offs.

Lifestyle is what you can concentrate on when you're not too sure where life itself is taking you. The new airheadedness is what happens after that, when a society stops dreaming about the far horizons of human endeavour and concentrates on its navel instead: what it might be wanting for dinner, for instance, and how it wants to decorate its kitchen.

Lifestyle is how we now define ourselves and express our all-important individuality. Self-realisation for the generations before us extended to work, community and having a family; that was how people established who they were and how they found out about themselves. That was how they got their identity. Now we know who we are because of the stuff in our lives that we've bought; the names on our shoe leather, sunglasses and suntan bottles, the wine label we choose, the T-shirt we buy in bulk, our mobile phone, car, the vitamin and mineral supplements we take, where we get our hair cut, where we buy our wardrobe and where we go on holiday.

Like most phenomena to do with airheadism, lifestyle crept slowly, slowly into our lives, making itself look at first like an innocuous convenience. Of course, we all needed a proper salad bowl back in the Sixties because unless we used our china mixing bowls, we didn't have anywhere to put this fashionable new green salad addition to our daily menu. Have you clocked up how many salad bowls the average household has today? People have serious conversations about their choice of salad bowls. (And what this choice says about you.) That's how lifestyle takes over your life and your mind. We are wooed to think it and its latest manifestation are indispensable. Build a better mousetrap and the world will beat a path to your door, the old adage went. Now we are encouraged to want "mousetraps" that have no earthly use except to clutter up our lives and daily schedules and use up our money.

A male friend muses that all the spam email he gets either promises penis enlargement or luxury watches at bargain prices. "So obviously the ideal man these days is one with a huge penis and many watches," he concludes.

As for today's woman, you can gauge what she values or is supposed to value by the news that, as *The Economist* reported close to Christmas 2005 in a story about the democratisation of status symbols, it is now possible for aspirational, but financially challenged American women to rent designer handbags on the Web. I clicked on a Louis Vuitton Ellipse bag on the "From Bags to Riches" site and discovered that, yes indeed, I could "borrow this great bag for as little as $US72.90 a week!"

In December, anyone over forty who isn't an airhead pleads with friends not to give them any more "stuff". What they mean is no more of anything that can be loosely categorised under the name "lifestyle". The rest of the developed world, though, rearranges its cupboards, wardrobes, shelves and flat surfaces as it loads in truckfuls more of the things, all in newer, shinier, smarter versions.

Once upon a time, a high street or main street would be lined with shops that sold the necessities of everyday living: the butcher, the baker, the greengrocer, the smallgoods store, the dry-cleaner, the hardware and so on. A bank and a post office were obligatory. Now, a main street can be one unending line of outdoor cafes, bars, restaurants, health-food stores, gyms, dress shops and clever little stores that sell either postmodern lamps, ornaments, fake-fur throws, scented candles and platters or, if they're in the food line, exotic breads, coffees, oils and salads with what looks like yesterday's leftover antipasto plate dumped in them.

Looking after the necessaries now virtually involves getting out the dromedary, compass and road map so that you can at least come home with half of what you actually need as opposed to sackfuls of things from the chichi shops down the road that no-one in their right mind needs.

The big high streets and shopping malls now look all the same as they've been taken over by the big chains. After Terence Conran showed the market how willing customers were to buy in stores that were well designed and laid out, shopping in general got an art-directed makeover. The first shops to be redone felt exciting and unique. Now they are no such thing, as even chemists and supermarkets have been given the low-light, high decor, carefully co-ordinated treatment. It becomes a quaint delight to find a higgledy-piggledy, old-fashioned corner grocer reeking of spices and Italian sausage, or a hardware store with rods, nails and paint-tins stacked every which way.

Cafes are ubiquitous, displacing hardware stores, butchers, dry-cleaners and greengrocers. Our consumption of cafe lattes doubled in four years, from $112 million's worth in 2001 to $225 million in 2005. Don't bother to eavesdrop at a cafe either: Sartre and Camus discussing an indifferent universe it is not. Instead, you may hear where to get a rare tile for your new bathroom, the great shoes that were a steal in a sale for $500, or whether it's worth chucking out all your cookware to install an induction stove top (which will require new pans).

A lifestyle story in a newspaper prattles on about the move towards cocktail bars combining with restaurants so they become a hybrid called a bar-restaurant or a restaurant lounge. A cocktail-maker muses to the reporter, showing thinking the depth of a scallop shell, that, "People go out for an evening and want their tastebuds satisfied by both their food and their beverage ... drinking just wine or lager is now very old-hat."

No, it's not. It's just that even with the 100 percent-plus mark-up on wines at most upmarket restaurants, an establishment will make a whopping lot more out of pushing $20 cocktails down your throat. An insider reminds us that there are better margins on cocktails and they require less time and fewer staff than food.

The cocktail-maker reminds me of the builders and tradespeople I kept nudging into my home at one stage because I wanted some work done on my kitchen. There was a hitch though. Unlike all the people portrayed by the booming home magazines and weekly newspaper supplements, I was not panting for a "full renovation". I did not want the kind of surgical kitchen with appliances designed by French stylist Philippe Starck that takes up so much modern editorial space (to say nothing of conversation between adults). I did not want to spend the next year of my life deciding on taps and tiles and drawer-dividers.

Que?

"We're delighted to be stocking AUSTRALIAN winter truffles from Manjimup about 300 kilometres south of Perth. Just the second season for Manjimup Truffle Company – the truffles are on par with the black winter truffles we usually import from Périgord, France during our summer ... "The current price for the first choice truffles is $2,500 per kilo. To serve finely shaved on a pasta or risotto, we recommend using a minimum of 10 grams per person. Thus a decadent truffle main course for two could cost you as little as $50. "We look forward to seeing you in store soon!"
EMAIL NEWSLETTER FOR SYDNEY-BASED SIMON JOHNSON PROVIDORES, JULY 2006.

I just wanted a bit of general tarting-up, some new appliances, maybe a central bench and re-painting. The builders looked at me as if I were asking them to re-configure the ceiling of the Sistine Chapel. Nothing seemed to be more impossible than my puny requests. "It'd be much easier if you just pulled all this out and put in a new kitchen," they'd say at last after they'd looked around without enthusiasm. Easier and about five times the cost, and twenty times the pain.

Their quotes for total kitchen fit-outs always meant pulling out the solid oak cupboards that had lasted twenty years and looked as if they would go another twenty. These would be replaced with oak veneer.

"It's very *good* veneer these days," they'd say before sloping out my front door.

WE LIVE in prosperous times – or at least the privileged billion of the world's total of six billion do. But instead of sharing the wealth around the globe, we spend and spend and spend on ourselves or on the people closest to us, and so our economies continue to grow, thriving on our appetite for more *things*. And more services. It's what keeps us prosperous. It's also what keeps us in hock and preoccupied.

We earn, we spend, we accumulate debt, we earn more, we spend more, we accumulate more debt, and so it goes. And because we're so busy working and have so little time or energy, we pay for services to do everything from walking our dogs to manicuring our nails. A pampered, stylish colleague, rushing to a beauty appointment, asked me recently who did my eyebrows. She might as well have asked me who cut up my toast for me in the morning. Shopping for stuff or services is not just the new sex; it's the new everything. Is there life *without* shopping? In one episode of the hit TV series *Desperate Housewives*, Carlos, who has found the light while in prison, explains to his beautiful, hard-edged, spendaholic wife that shopping doesn't bring happiness. Eva Longoria's character, Gabrielle, retorts: "Sure it does. That's just what we tell poor people to stop them rioting."

There is now a branch of shopping science called neuromarketing which claims to use the latest advances in brain scanning, with functional MRI (magnetic resonance imaging), to show just which bits of the brain are activated when we see something we want to buy or a colour that sets off our spending instincts. This, said the neuroscientist who told me about it, Professor Tomás Paus, of the University of Nottingham's Brain and Body Centre, whose research is into how our brains grow and develop, is "bad science". Others, though, refer to it as one of the hottest new retail tools and commission their own MRI studies. Daimler-Chrysler, for instance, was delighted to find that its sportier models stimulate the brain's reward centres.[2]

In Australia, the fastest-growing consumer title by the end of 2005 was *Shop Til You Drop*, a bible for shopaholic airheads which, as its publisher explains, is successful precisely because "it's simply all about shopping – there are no articles on sex or politics".[3] Now a second title has been launched: *Shop Til You Drop 4 Kids*. Thankfully, it isn't aimed at kids but at mothers-to-be and anyone who has a connection to a kid and wants to buy it yet more stuff. That's despite most kids these days already having wardrobes the size of an adult's and half the contents of Toys R Us dumped in their bedrooms. As the child-free also know to their amazement, no baby or toddler can come visiting unless its parents are hefting enough regalia to keep Queen Elizabeth content.

Australia, of course, like the rest of the world, is in the midst of a debt crisis fuelled by the explosion in credit cards and an ignorance of Charles Dickens, who noted in *David Copperfield*: "Annual income twenty pounds, annual expenditure nineteen nineteen six, result happiness. Annual income twenty pounds, annual expenditure twenty pounds ought and six, result misery."

Economists around the world are rumbling worriedly about the huge debt the Western world is carrying and the way the world seems complacent about it. The United States alone, through health and social security obligations, national debt, corporate debt, state and international debt and consumer debt driven by credit card spending and home mortgages, faces a bill for present and future debt that some, like *The New York Times*, estimate to be as high as $US70 trillion. In the preface to his book, *American Theocracy*, former Republican and political analyst Kevin Phillips talks of the "rapid ballooning of government, corporate, financial and personal debt over the last four decades". "Excessive debt ..." he writes of America's predicament, "is on its way to becoming the global Fifth Horseman ..."[4]

Lifestyle, meanwhile, which we mostly pay for with our personal debt, flourishes because of our insistence that spending and buying are how we express our individuality. But individuality, the very thing that shopping promises to deliver to us, disappears as we fall into line to buy versions of the current looks bought by the celebrities we are encouraged to admire and ape. We know exactly what they buy because we see them parading their houses, wardrobes and even their choices in beauty products in weekly and monthly magazines and lifestyle sections. Celebrities

Ohmigod

"In the old days people said you needed to wear a power suit to make an impact in business. Now you need a power face."
UNNAMED PLASTIC SURGEON ON STUDIES THAT SHOW MEN THINK LOOKING YOUTHFUL IS A CAREER ADVANTAGE.
THE WEEKEND AUSTRALIAN, JULY 30-31, 2005.

are seized upon to sell us skincare, sunglasses, clothes, fur coats.

Everything is product; everything is a selling opportunity. Even non-celebrities get their day in the sun if they can be dressed up appropriately by marketing. I live in a narrow street just off Sydney's Hyde Park. The street dates back to the early 1800s and is lined with little cottages and terraces. A few years back, a massive office building that had been forced on the street was turned into a luxury apartment block. When it came time to sell the apartments, which had been given the ultra-hip treatment, the developers produced a glossy, thick-papered, big-format magazine. There were no pictures of the new apartments though. No close-ups of taps and window treatments. No floor plans. Instead, our street was bemused to discover that *we*, along with the area's bars, restaurants, public swimming pools and nightclubs, were being offered as attractions alongside edgy pictures of young couples wearing not many clothes. *We* were examples of the great, cool, quirky life that anyone who bought into the apartment block would be able to buy for themselves by just taking out a mortgage. I supposed we were there to supply authentic colour, given anyone actually moving into the block would find themselves living in sparklingly austere interiors that allowed for few possessions.

This is another of the paradoxes of lifestyle. Our decade-long love affair with acquisitions, with *stuff*, means we now also pine for order. With all these possessions in our life, we yearn for the clean lines and clutter-free serenity that greet us when we check into a luxury hotel. As the promo for the

British television series *Hotel Babylon* stated, a hotel is the place where everything works, everything is clean. There is no mess to make you feel you should be doing something else. Interior designers started planning private homes that felt as blank-faced as hotel rooms and then the real hotels got in on the act, offering their beds, sheets, towels and accoutrements for sale. Product, product, product. We'll buy anything if it promises a different, better life.

Stuff to house our stuff has become a sales opportunity. The more we buy and acquire, the more we want our houses and lives to look simple and serene, and so we buy boxes in all sizes from Bo-Peep tiny to Fee-Fi-Fo-Fum giant size, in all colours and materials from rattan to aluminium to shiny pink card. We install shelving systems and cabinets with shelves that revolve. We get special cupboards and racks made for our shoes and bring in wardrobe and storage experts to tell us how to store our knits and T-shirts. In the United States, people now pay serious money to "garage organisers" who come in and sort through all the accumulation of acquisition and give you a designer garage in return for upwards of $US12,000. *The New York Times* reported: "Suburban homeowners are so full of angst, guilt, despair and frustration over their bulging garages that they spent $800 million on garage organising products last year [2005], double the amount spent in 2000, according to the market research firm Packaged Facts. Alleviating that garage guilt could easily cost $12,000 per job."[5]

So synonymous is modern lifestyle with order, cleanliness and art direction that the practice of anal bleaching has started to worm its way into mass-market women's magazines. How neat can we get? Who seriously thought they even needed teeth-bleaching five years ago? Now whole shelves in supermarkets and chemists are given over to expensive teeth-brightening pastes, gels and treatments. Anal bleaching is just the newest whitening product on the block.

Give it five years and, unless commonsense and the medical profession stamp out the practice, it too will have become a must-have. God forbid that with all this stuff in our lives, there should be any mess, anything that reminds us we are human with mammalian needs, habits and imperfections. Instead, we'd rather pay to defuzz and bleach our bottoms. It figures.

IT GOES without saying that lifestyle is something that comes with upwardly mobile status. People who live in caravan parks are not considered to have pretensions towards "lifestyle" and you will not see the insides of their vans depicted in *Interiors*. Having a "lifestyle" means you have handed over good money to someone to get it and it is very likely that you would like people to know that. When Wal-Mart in the United States decides it wants to go upmarket and advertise in *Vogue* magazine, it isn't because it wants to show all those rich people how they can save money on home and fashion products and live more cheaply. It's because it wants to upscale its image and attract shoppers with that kind of money and those free-spending habits. When companies fight tooth and claw to be among the chosen few stuffing iPod covers or diamond-studded lingerie into the goodies baskets doled out to Oscars hosts and nominees, this is not about celebrity fanaticism and proximity to the stars. This is about "positioning" your "lifestyle" product and hoping desperately that Jennifer Aniston will be seen using it, thus encouraging the rest of us to follow suit.

Lifestyle is inevitably about envy, too. Once a luxury becomes affordable, and therefore available to more than the elites (which is what design maven Tyler Brûlé means with his disdainful term "masstige", a parody of prestige), then other luxuries must be discovered and developed. We have seen extra bathrooms, built-in wardrobes, granite-topped kitchen benches, gas barbecues and plasma TVs become commonplace. That's okay. There are people whose business it is to discover the new luxury. As we strain greedily and lustfully upwards, fitting out our houses and our bodies with gewgaws once reserved for the rich, so do the rich move onwards beyond us. A little while ago, interior designers and architects focused their attention on what was once the second smallest room in the house, the bathroom. They declared – and were eagerly backed up by the home magazines and lifestyle sections – that the bathroom was in fact the new living room, a place where people could go to pamper themselves, relax, conduct salons … or so we were almost led to believe. Of course, one cannot have a wet living room in something that is two metres by three, or where your guest has to perch on the loo while you occupy the bath. A wet living room requires a lot of space. It has to have the dimensions of the old standard living room. It has to be big. Big enough for maybe a freestanding tub for two and a sofa or built-in marble recliner. Big enough so that part of the floor can be covered with a Turkish rug and the rug will never get wet. Who has bathrooms that big? Not you and me. Rich people have bathrooms like that.

Lifestyle is what divides the population into them and us. Or you and us, depending on what your bank account looks like.

A FEW YEARS after my adventures in lifestyle journalism with kitchens and oysters, I made a disastrous career decision.

It was bothering me that I could commission a story about evening gloves or upmarket garden designers but was uneasy if I was editing a profile of a politician or leader out of Canberra or the Middle East. I had a brain and an honours degree and I felt I needed to use both. If I'd only thought to look up at the broader media landscape first, I might have realised that I was clearly barking up the wrong tree. While I started to sweat over the harder bits of the newspaper, making myself understand the cut and thrust of politics so I could commission serious, analytical stories out of Washington, London and Canberra, a major chunk of the rest of journalism rushed into those very areas I had turned from in embarrassment.

Plump middle-aged men were making serious money writing about the surfaces of griddle-pans, milk-fed veal or discoveries in New Zealand white wines. A tribe of fusspots took up restaurant reviewing and wine reviewing, and curtains, cushions, sofas and sheets with a thread count of 400 became weighty subjects. In the United States, Anna Wintour, now editor of American *Vogue*, took over a home magazine, *House & Garden*, and packed it so full of celebrities and their homes and furniture that it was nicknamed *Vanity Chair*.

At the same time, a contingent of tough women journalists started turning away from the standard features and news rounds to investigate inner peace, aerobics, wholefoods, organic living and enlightenment. This was the wholesome version of

Totally

"It is a lie that anti-ageing creams will get rid of wrinkles. They won't. You'd be better off spending the money on a good bottle of pinot noir ... Tomatoes make you happy. Have you ever met a miserable Italian? They are irritating but never miserable."
BODY SHOP FOUNDER ANITA RODDICK DISPENSING ADVICE AT A LAUNCH FOR HER BOOK, *BUSINESS AS UNUSUAL*, AT THE CHELTENHAM LITERATURE FESTIVAL, 2000.

lifestyle, which meant that even people into recycling, astrology and mung beans could become lifestyle addicts. A serenely beautiful woman who always wore white, and who had migrated from America to England to work on one of the high-powered, upmarket glossies, wrote about giving birth late in life to a last child – after which she and the rest of her family sat down around the dinner table and ate the placenta. So rich in nutrients, she told her devoted readers.

As the lifestyle boom continued – there is no lifestyle without product and where there is product, there are advertisers and profits and thus more attention paid to lifestyle everywhere – other journalists started boning up on sports cars, luxury travel, handbags like the Hermès Birkin, which costs between $8,600 and $56,000, so they could write stories for lifestyle magazines and sections pitched at the seriously wealthy or delusional. Watches continue to be perfect fodder even now that no-one needs a watch any more because of mobile phones and constant flashing digital displays on electronic equipment. But still, any newspaper or journal with large numbers of highly paid readers will run page after page devoted to luxury watches selling at between $2,000 and blue sky, as modelled by Brad Pitt and the like.

You can, for instance, pay $US460,000 and get yourself the Tourbograph "Pour le Mérite" watch, produced by Germany's Lange & Söhne. From the pictures, I can tell you it looks nice. Not too fiddly. Indeed, when luxury watches couldn't get any bigger or heavier or shinier, it was suddenly put about by the stylemeisters that chunky was way too reminiscent of bling and the millionaire rapper stars who were buying the watches formerly worn only by film stars, sports stars and financiers. The new watch to own was the exact opposite – slim, discreet, albeit set with diamonds. And it cost even more.

The watch peddlers are without shame. An Italian Condé Nast website devoted to watches and jewellery, *Vogue Gioiello*, tries very hard to achieve the impossible, writing: "Watches no longer show the time of stress but follow the rhythm of idleness. The passing of the hours becomes an elogy [sic] to slowness, an invitation to indolence, a hymn to *dolce far niente*." This is a bit like saying you don't have a fancy new stove to cook food, but because it reminds you of how very much you love to diet and eat nothing at all.

A PR trying to place an author with some upmarket magazines lamented to me that his author's name wasn't the name of a new $10,000 watch from Patek Philippe. "Then they'd be interested and we'd get the editorial space we want," he grizzled, accurately capturing our new interest in lifestyle objects as opposed to living people.

The growth in the power of advertisers whose main aim is to get us to buy their products has led to another odd phenomenon of the narcissistic age – the magazine that looks like an onanist's fantasy. These are magazines that range from the *How To Spend It* supplement in *The Financial Times* in Britain to News Limited's *Wish* to Fairfax's *Sydney Magazine* and *Melbourne Magazine*. There are other plush examples in niche slots at the newsagency but mostly these new-style magazines are supplements produced by newspaper groups wanting to capitalise on their captive quality audiences.

They're odd these publications because when you first pick them up, they almost look like a normal magazine. There are features and regulars and pictures and service sections. Invariably, they are printed on thick, shiny paper with fabulous colour reproduction so the experience is luscious. But you notice something rather strange when you put them down. It's as if you've been locked up in a room with the greediest, most acquisitive and exhibitionist bits of yourself for the last thirty or so minutes. You haven't been taken to new horizons, new frontiers. The magazine has not opened doors on the world out there unless it's to inspire you to spend $20,000 on a luxury yak-trek in Tibet so you can brand yourself as someone with an adventurous lifestyle.

Instead, it has pulled off a kind of funfair reflecting-mirror effect. No matter how much you read of these new lifestyle magazines for the airhead age, you cannot escape yourself. What vitamins are you taking? Do you know how to buy a yacht? Here's how to spend $100,000 on a souped-up kitchen. What winter wardrobe do you need? How much money should you be saving? What are the best investments for you? Here's how to know if you've got class. Here are the best 20 seafood restaurants in your city. Can you mix a perfect martini? What 100 books do you need to read before you're dead? On and on and on and on …

It's like having a spendaholic, egotistical chatterbox shut up inside your brain. And there's no end to it as a chunk of society grows richer than was ever envisaged even ten years ago, and the rest of us pant to keep up or at least copy. There are new phrases and words to describe our lifestyle affliction. One is "hedonic treadmill", the idea that the more we earn, spend and acquire, the more we become compelled to do so, convinced it is the only path to happiness. (It isn't, as countless other studies have found.) There is another new word, "hyperconsumption", invented by a French philosopher, Gilles Lipovetsky,[6] to describe the way we shop now. It's what happens when consumption invades all spheres and people are encouraged to consume simply for the sheer pleasure of doing so. Alongside these phrases, the term "recreational shopping", which came into being at the very beginning of the over-spending Eighties, looks like playtime in a romper suit.

We're not completely stupid or completely greedy. We dive into lifestyle as an escape and for pleasure and reinforcement, but lifestyle has been able to get its fingers around our throats because it promises something else. Reinvention. The bleached-bottomed, Hermès Birkin-carrying, designer-suit-wearing shopper is probably congratulating herself secretly on the fact that, just ten years ago when she entered the job market, she was a nobody with a nobody's wardrobe (and a normal bottom, it can probably be said). Renovate your house, install umpteen new storage spaces and import your bathtub from Italy and you will feel – for the moment – that you have life where you want it. The lure of the new home, the new kitchen, the new outfit, the new computer program, the new oven, the new set of saucepans is that somehow they will make you a more efficient, more pleasing, more desirable, more successful-seeming person. For the moment, you will feel just that little bit more secure in a very insecure world. It will be simpler to be on top of your impossible workload if you have a BlackBerry. It will be easier to prepare a meal for eight – which of course you must if you are to impress – if you have a new kitchen. It will be easier to feel at your best and

Que?

"When you cast away last season's favourite, you create a vacuum, a fleeting weightlessness and a sense of expectation that is often more compelling than anything you could imagine in its place. People who understand this principle sooner or later find their way to Condé Nast. One of the most colourful editors-in-chief, *Self* magazine's Alexandra Penney, used to give away her entire wardrobe once a year – showing a rare gutsy spirit and manifesting ahead of time that she was suited for the top position."
A FORMER CONDÉ NAST INSIDER INTERPRETS THE CORPORATE ETHOS IN AN ARTICLE TITLED "MAKE IT RIGHT THEN TOSS IT AWAY", COLUMBIA JOURNALISM REVIEW, JULY-AUGUST, 1991.

most confident in the precarious, political workplace if you have that pair of $550 pumps. Advertisements, whether they are for hotels or travel or clothes or electronic equipment, look as if they have been styled by feng-shui consultants. The glossy pages beckon us towards smooth brows, lightness of heart and confidence ... which of course is not how any normal human being gets through an average day, least of all a day in this crazy, strung-out twenty-first century. That's why, within a week or two, we will be yearning for something else to add to our new purchase to *really* make it work.

It is part of the natural human trajectory to *endeavour*. Like sharks, if we don't go forwards we die, at least a little bit inside, and it's worse if we go backwards. But this trajectory has been turned vertical by the new economic, social and political pressures on all of us. Lack of job security and tenure means we feel as if we are hanging onto a slide by our fingernails. I remarked on my own insecurity – one earning cat, one half-working human – to a man who has been at the top of his profession for decades, owns properties in a few states and has a large and lavish house in one of the city's velvet suburbs. "Yes," he answered, "I feel financially insecure, too."

NO WONDER. Not only do we spend money on things we don't need, we also use money to try and acquire things that either can't be bought with money at all, or certainly can't only be bought. Happiness. Health. Fitness. Slimness. Freedom from stress and anxiety. Peace of mind. Longevity. Goodness, we seem to be thinking to ourselves, if we can buy a smooth forehead by paying the cosmetic surgeon $500 for Botox injections, surely we can also buy something soothing for inside the head. If we can buy a lifestyle, can't we buy a life?

A billion-dollar group of industries will tell you yes. But the simple, commonsense rules that can make good skin, a good figure and physical and mental health available to almost everyone who doesn't have a serious disorder get rather less coverage than products and regimens and services which cost money.

Walk around gardens and parks in the early morning and the greenery teems with people toiling away at their jogging and sprinting. Sometimes they are in groups, and are being lectured and bullied by an instructor who has them doing knee-jumps and sit-ups and squats. Whenever I walk past them, their eyes seem to roll agonisedly towards me, like those of cattle being herded with an electric prod. These are men and women who, ninety minutes later, will be decked out in high-priced suiting and sitting in massive offices dealing in grave matters to do with money. They could achieve similar results for their health, mind and body by going for a gentle walk, but a walk takes longer, maybe three or four times as long, and they don't have that kind of time. Instead they must go for the painful, sweaty, joint-crunching, bosom-stretching, knee-crushing supervised jogging, exercising and running because they have been told it's the fast way, the best way, to stay fit. Hang the expense!

Eventually, if they have any sense, they will do as one of my friends did. When the trainer knocked on her door at 6 am, she leant out the window, tossed him down his $80, bid him goodbye for good and went back to bed. Her joints were grateful.

Our spending is egged on by a gazillion pages and websites. Swallow a vitamin B complex supplement and you will have more energy and be calmer. Follow a strict food plan (low carbs, all raw, bought-in calorie-controlled meals, whatever) and you will lose weight. Sign up with a gym – or even a cosmetic surgeon – and a new body will be yours. If you have ever had a one-to-one with a New Age healer you will know what I'm talking about. Not for them the basics (good eating of a variety of foods, enough sleep, enough exercise and don't forget the water). Instead you are advised, at a cost, to undergo numerous tests so that everything from your aura to the mineral content of your body can be assessed. Are you tired, they ask eventually. Yes, yes, I'm tired, I'm tired, you reply, delighted that they have spotted the problem. (*Everyone* is tired.) Then you are plied with complicated eating plans, rules about what times you can eat, a list of supplements to buy and a fortnight's worth of even more complicated detoxing to start.

Staying slim, as the thin know, depends on a simple if rigorous formula: eat less, exercise more. Energy in (food) must equal energy out (exercise). If you want to lose weight, what goes in should be less than what goes out. Nobody ever got fat or stayed fat using such simple maths. Meanwhile, too much of Australia lumbers about, trying to get into its trousers or walk to the shops without sweating. Too much energy in, not enough energy out. We are now one of the two fattest nations on earth and, pro rata, fast overtaking the other, the United States. Twenty percent of small children in South Australia in 2003 turn out to be porkers in the making. Twenty-five percent of Australian children are either overweight or obese (in 1960, the figure was 5 percent). About 2.4 million Australian adults are obese and almost five million are overweight. It's like watching a giant flock of geese force-feeding themselves so they can turn into foie gras.

One study of children in North and South America projected, to the researchers' astonished horror, that by 2010, almost half of the kids could be overweight and 15 percent of them obese.[7] Ten percent of European children would be obese. Meanwhile, it's predicted that almost two million Australians will have diabetes, mostly type two, a disease associated with diet and lifestyle, by 2010. The number of children with the disease is growing by 5-10 percent each year. A visiting American endocrinologist described our environment as "obesogenic", by which she meant that we are so surrounded by bad food choices – courtesy of those good old market forces – that it becomes difficult to find the right food.

Not that it feels as if too many of us are trying. Have you listened to what people order from takeaways and sandwich bars at lunchtime? It's as if they've been programmed in their sleep by the big bad food fairy. A news story on a typical kid's lunchbox recites a menu – muesli bar, fruit wrap, fruit juice, dip and crackers ... What are parents thinking? A newspaper story about junk-food-eating parents haunts me: a plump little boy would go without food all day while at school because he was so embarrassed to be seen eating.

The airhead way – that nothing should take too much effort, and no action has consequences – is seen in sharp relief in these growing weight, health and lifestyle problems. The average Australian woman is now size 16, and shapes are changing, too, so that waists are gradually disappearing. The apple-shaped body is associated with increased risk of heart disease. And instead of tackling it, people

Ohmigod

"'Laurie touched different areas of my body and asked every organ what it needed,' she says. Now ... she checks in with her organs on a daily basis to ask them what they need."
BODY + SOUL SUPPLEMENT,
THE SUNDAY TELEGRAPH,
FEBRUARY 20, 2005.

attack newspapers and magazines for running pictures of fashion models. One market researcher reported that mothers, far from worrying about their children's unhealthy obesity, fretted that their child might develop an eating disorder if put under pressure. "So what if he's carrying a couple of extra kilos as long as he's happy?" was how the researcher characterised the typical response.[8] Somehow the idea has got around that no-one is a "real" woman unless her cheeks shudder when she laughs. Real women apparently start at size 14. The same researcher later told me that when adult women did happen to notice their own extra kilos, they talked not only of diets and exercise, but also of the quick fix of liposuction.

The other night a friend said to me: do you remember when you were at school and there was always one fat kid in the class? I did remember. She said it isn't like that any more. Her niece is tiny and spends her life complaining that she's the littlest in the class and everyone else is fat. The other day someone sat on her to teach her a lesson.

I know it's supposed to be great to let it all hang out, but there's a bit of me that feels the way *The Newcastle Herald* columnist Jeff Corbett felt in October 2002, when he complained vigorously and with many adjectives about all the fat tummies and hips he was seeing bulging out of hipster trousers and low-slung jeans. He wrote, with tongue in cheek, "Belly blubber and horribly deep navels are taking over as the new anti-fashion … That it is girls flaunting their pudding bellies makes it even more repugnant … The midriff look is for young women with flat stomachs, which is why it is so delightful on Ms Spears and co. It might be pleasantly decorous on a girl with the slightest hint of a roll, one whose diet has gone off the rails just recently.

"But when it's blubber it is abhorrent, the visual version of scraping a fingernail on the blackboard.

"The shock has three elements.

"The first is the vision itself.

"The second is the very number of overweight young women.

"Whoever would have dreamed there were so many? This is much more rife than, for example, the aberration that is a fat woman in Lycra bike shorts.

"The third shock is that they would want to expose their grotesqueness."[9]

As soon as his column was published, a lot of feminist students invaded his office and tried to sit on him, too.

This must be the first assertive, self-satisfied generation that has been too full of self-esteem to ask: does my bottom look big in this? For all that I keep hearing about eating disorders and the media coercion of us to be skeletal, the majority of people I see seem to have no trouble resisting any pressure to eat less.

As well as being genuinely surprised that too much of the wrong food and not enough exercise makes people overweight and unhealthy, we also seem to have forgotten that sound health can't be bought over a pharmacy or health-food-store counter. One range of supplements even tricks itself up to give the impression that its different varieties of pills are a complete replacement if you aren't eating vegetables or fruit or fish.

In vain do doctors tell us that if we eat a varied diet, we will have no need of supplements. Our passion for lifestyle that is bought in easy packages makes that sound far too boring and difficult. And so you head to the health-food shop to stock up on supplements that cost $20 each a jar, might cost you $60 to $80 a month, and which end up piling up in the dark bit of your kitchen cupboard. If actually used, they'll go straight through your system. Australians now spend about $2 billion a year on the alternative health food industry and the vast majority of that goes on vitamin, mineral and health supplements.

Professor John Dwyer, an immunologist and consumer advocate in the health area, who regularly disparages the consumption of supplements, said to Channel Nine's *Sixty Minutes* programme in 2004: "Like most Australians, if anything, I'm probably over-vitaminised. This whole rip-off industry out there that tries to tell Australians to neutralise an unfortunate lifestyle with vitamins is thriving."[10] He could give only one item a tick for the general population to take: folic acid.

There's another which may have been overlooked in that interview simply because, fifty years ago, authorities took steps to make sure we would never be deficient in it. But now it turns out we are. Someone has dropped the ball. So busy have we been scoffing down our ginseng and magnesium and muesli bars that we have forgotten to look after the basics – what's really vital in our intake, especially with our kids. Almost half of Australian primary-school children, it turns out, are deficient in iodine. Dwyer pointed out to me later that while it couldn't be said that those children would all be clinically deficient, he was concerned that any Australian child would be lacking, that obviously some would be clinically deficient and there would be a danger there may be more. Iodine is essential to the development of the brain. If a pregnant or breastfeeding woman is deficient in iodine, her child's IQ may be lower than normal by ten to fifteen points. There may be problems with hearing, motor skills and growth. Lack of iodine can also lead to thyroid problems later. We used to get iodine in milk because dairies used cleaning solutions that contained iodine. We also used to get it in store-bought bread and we used to use it ourselves in cooking. Now we don't, often because we're watching salt intake or not eating enough fish, and someone forgot to tell us iodine was important. Or we think that the ultra-fashionable rock salts and sea salts contain iodine when it's only iodised salt that has it.

At least and at last, the national food regulator is investigating ways to get more iodine back into our diet.

So much attention to lifestyle and yet it can turn out to have nothing whatsoever to do with life itself.

CHAPTER 7

How to Educate a Goldfish

"General knowledge is anything but general. I was shocked when not one of the 33 second-year university students attending my arts lecture had ever heard of China's Chairman Mao."

SANDRA ECKERSLEY IN A LETTER TO *THE WEEKEND AUSTRALIAN MAGAZINE*, APRIL 16-17, 2005

"A young friend was talking to me in the garden. She's in second-year university. She said to me, 'I wouldn't be able to tell you the names of all the Australian state capitals.'"

DR BARRY SPURR, SENIOR LECTURER IN ENGLISH, UNIVERSITY OF SYDNEY

HOW TO EDUCATE A GOLDFISH

Catherine Runcie came to Australia from Canada in 1969. In the mid-Eighties, she remembers turning up to a Parents and Teachers night at her seven-year-old daughter's school and listening politely, if mystified, as a teacher explained what was what. "She told us that she really didn't care whether her pupils knew when Captain Cook had come to Australia so long as they could do research and hypothesisation. And then she wrote the two words on a whiteboard. She spelt both words wrong," Runcie finishes dryly, asking as an afterthought, "And anyhow, what does a seven-year-old child know about research and hypothesisation?" A little later, she adds, "And, you know, I never did understand why the date of Captain Cook's arrival wasn't important."

The trouble with airheads is that we don't take their nonsense seriously at first. And then it's too late. It's why so many of them have risen as far as they have. We have been far too polite, particularly with those who, at some time in the late Seventies and into the Eighties, decided that the humanities in higher education would be far better administered with an accent. The circuitous postmodern theories of the French philosophers Michel Foucault, Jacques Derrida and Roland Barthes arrived on our shores to be widely misunderstood and misinterpreted. Soon, they were being applied in even more half-baked form to teacher education and then to teaching in schools. The effect on young brains has been roughly the same as what would happen to an assembly line of Rolls-Royces if you poured glue into all the door-locks.

Huh?

"'It's not that we don't want to ensure that teachers are literate, but if you are going to pre-test and prevent people from becoming teachers, then you may well be robbing the profession of some really good thinkers' said Australian Education Union branch president Mary Bluett. 'I would hate to see this debate turn into an absolute prerequisite that all teachers have to pass spelling bees. Literacy is more than just learning how to spell.'"
THE AGE, DECEMBER 9, 2005.

Two generations of experimented-upon young Australians have emerged unable to read, write and think with the skill and clarity they should have been able to assume would be theirs. Economic rationalism has played tricks with maths and the law of consequence, but postmodernism has addled our thinking processes. What the Right did with the economy and money, the Left merrily – or, playfully, as the postmodern crowd might prefer to say – did with knowledge, learning and education.

The irrationalism of economic rationalism – which, if it had flourished any earlier, might have meant man would never have climbed out of the primordial slime to begin with because it wouldn't have been judged immediately profitable – found its outlandish parallel in postmodernism. Pomo took irrationality, turned it into a creed and gave an imprimatur to the now all-pervasive cultural and moral relativism: nothing is better than anything else.

The Right tells us that the individual must be free to pursue his or her economic interests; the Left tells us that the pursuit of self is paramount. Both have done our heads in. Both come down to the same belief: it's all about me, which is the unstoppable driving force of the new airheadism.

Too often, under the postmodern influence, schooling has turned into a hatchery for baby airheads unable to think for themselves or communicate clearly. But, as journalist and editor Luke Slattery has questioned in an essay on the all-encompassing belief in postmodernism and its theory: "How did a minor tradition within continental philosophy come to dominate, to the point where it would brook no dissent, in both teaching and research in the English-speaking humanities? How did a class of people selected for their capacity for independent thought – the PhD thesis is supposed to mark an original contribution to the field – submit to such a stifling orthodoxy?"[1]

Slattery called the takeover one of the great mysteries of Western intellectual life in the late twentieth century. I think clues can be found in the equally mysterious tale of what happened to learning to eat up your green vegetables. Once upon a time, sensible parents always made their children eat their greens. Even if they didn't know exactly why, they did know that it was good for them, and the children, even if they didn't like the greens, which they mostly didn't, knew that they had to listen to their parents because their parents, they observed, were bigger than them. Ergo, everyone ate their beans or spinach, broccoli or brussels sprouts and everyone was better off health-wise.

And thus did we all understand another important lesson as we grew up: sometimes you have to do things that you don't want to do or even understand why you have to because it will pay off in the long run. The same principle used to apply to such activities as learning the date of Captain Cook's arrival in Australia, doing maths in your head, using punctuation, studying grammar or understanding why clear and accurate expression, in writing or speech, benefits everyone.

Now no-one is encouraged to do any of those things just as no-one eats their greens, sees any reason why they should, or why they should listen to anyone who tells them they should. What the education airheads said, and continue to say, with their theory is the equivalent of this: you don't have to eat your greens. You don't have to do anything difficult or unpleasant or boring. Then they started telling us that to do so was actually bad for us. A whole host of behaviours that generations had taken for granted as being normal and/or necessary – from swotting up French verbs to slogging at understanding a poem to receiving grades to being ticked off for being lazy or careless to being taught the names of capital cities – were suddenly on a *verboten* list because they interfered with our self-esteem, creativity, originality, freedom, happiness and rights. Funnily enough, the behaviours newly banned are the same ones that also require rigour, resources and a sense of reality, all of which, in our new airheaded world, have become more and more difficult to muster. How convenient is that?

American academic Susan Ostrov Weisser, a professor of English, points out in an essay[2] on college classroom culture that the study of literature increasingly comes down not to expertise and knowledge, but to feeling. Instead of a student and teacher discussing, perhaps, the biographical, historical and social contexts in which Charlotte Brontë wrote, and researching the evidence, they talk about how the student reacts to the novel, what it personally does or does not mean to him or her. "No-one can then agree or disagree with you – because it's all about you," says Weisser.

Just how different our world has become was encapsulated by one of President George W. Bush's senior advisers in a conversation with *New York Times Magazine* writer and author Ron Suskind in 2002. "That's not the way the world really works any more," he asserted in the face of Suskind's faith in the role of fact in problem-solving. "We're an empire now, and when we act, we create our own reality."[3]

So, increasingly, does everybody.

Really?

"At the [Sydney airport] car rental desk, the clerk spent a considerable amount of time punching keys. My husband handed her his Tassie licence and credit card, and after much more key-punching she looked at us both and asked, 'Is Tasmania in New Zealand?'"
JO ELLIOTT, OF SOUTH HOBART, IN *THE SYDNEY MORNING HERALD'S* COLUMN 8, JULY 2005.

FOR THIRTY years, Catherine Runcie, who taught American, Australian and British literature as well as literary theory at the University of Sydney, watched in amusement, then bemusement, then alarm and finally disgust as she saw education falling apart in Australia. There was, as she puts it, the rise of postmodernism, with its specious jargon, and cultural relativism, with its specious openness; the fall of dead white men like Shakespeare, Milton, Chaucer, Pepys and Pope; the belief that there is no such thing as an objective reality and everything is subjective; that all texts are of equal weight, worth and relevance; indeed, the very notion that the word "text" should be the accepted way of speaking about anything from Proust to the script for a television advertisement to the SMS pumped out via your mobile. The idea everywhere was that it was more important for pupils or students to learn to express themselves than it was for them first to learn the three Rs.

Runcie describes in her laconic Canadian accent how postmodernism and all the other "isms" took over educational and cultural life in the West. "So-called anti-elitism crept into all forms of teaching and curricula. It was mental Maoism," she says. "I'd go back to the Sixties and Woodstock to find the roots of it all. You get into your blue jeans and you are supposed to be equal to all, very democratic. A love-in. But in fact it was just sameness. Like wearing the Mao suit. It was and is dogmatic and tyrannical and has worked towards the lowest common denominator. If you want to do something democratic, then the most democratic thing one can do for a citizen of a democracy is provide the best education." Instead, she watched the basics such as spelling, grammar and learning to read become less important to teachers, and saw in that "a kind of sentimental Marxism, a well-intentioned but daffy nostalgic pining for sameness disguised as egalitarianism, and they wanted this in every walk of life, starting in the classroom. But I cannot see how learning to spell correctly, say, can have any politicisation.

"It came about incrementally; it was tragic. I finally learned to say to my students: 'You are part of the deprived generation. You don't know what a dangling participle is or a gerund or gerundive. Or a verb.' And of course, then they would want to know. But all that should have been done by the age of fourteen or so."

Runcie saw the new ideologues reach critical mass in terms of leadership, saw that happen across university faculties, either officially or unofficially, and then watched their ideology spill over into primary and high school curricula. It must have been like watching water flooding from the top of a layered fountain and splashing down through the levels. Glyn Davis, vice-chancellor at the University of Melbourne, remarked recently that the term "postmodernism" is on its way to meaninglessness. Maybe, but it has done its damage. Postmodernism flushed through the system in the Eighties and nothing will be quite the same again. In the same way, people say that political correctness is finished. That's not true either. Talk to anyone educated after about 1985 and you will find that, with almost every second person, PC is a fingernail scratch below the surface. I doubt they can help it. Postmodernism and political correctness don't have to be in our faces any more: they are embedded in our culture.

An English professor recalls wistfully the time when his field was regarded as a discipline. Now, he says, just the word "discipline" is frowned-upon because it sounds too, well, like, you know, disciplinarian. Disciplines have disappeared into a kind of "cultural stir-fry" so that department letterheads can list a range of studies, and an English department letterhead may cover performance studies, media, visual studies, cultural studies, comparative literature, semiotics and English for the professions – just to name a few. It probably won't be called English any more either, but some amalgam that makes you ponder just which bit of it would signal that if you drilled down in that spot, you might be lucky enough to find a palely loitering Keats. "I don't know why they don't just take in veterinary studies as well," our professor concluded bitterly.

There have been several attack dogs on the traditional notions of learning.

Deconstructionism seeks to reveal the concepts and influences (patriarchal, racial, elitist) that might have led to the creation of a work, so that less attention is paid to the piece, its effect, its beauty, its sweep, its passion, its ability to take us out of our own world and to understand universal themes, than to unpicking its structure, context, unmasking assumptions and so on.

Constructivism argues that learning is really a journey and that education has to be done in the context of the student's own experience, with the teacher a "co-explorer". Everything must relate back to the student. Everything must be relevant, a word that here has all the charm of a vice in the way it has been utilised to take the magic of happenstance, coincidence, growth and curiosity out of learning. "Relevance" condemns students to exist in tiny worlds whose limits they themselves must set. On one American website promoting constructivism in schools, the movement is defined as "a philosophy of learning founded on the premise that, by reflecting on our experiences, we construct our own understanding of the world we live in".[4] It then goes on to argue: "Constructivism calls for the elimination of a standardised curriculum. Instead, it promotes using curricula customised to the students' prior knowledge."

In other words, don't bring exciting new worlds, theories and concepts to the new mind before you. Instead, tailor what you bring according to what the child already knows. Don't look up and forwards; look back and down and inwards. As for exams and assessments: "Constructivism calls for the elimination of grades and standardised testing. Instead, assessment becomes part of the learning process so that students play a larger role in judging their own progress."

The real message: don't aspire, think small. Let the child's existing knowledge be the yardstick of everything he or she is to be taught in future; and then, to top it off, like a monstrous shiny artificial cherry on a cake of fake cream and off-the-shelf sponge, let children be the judge of their own progress and let them be measured by their own ability. (In this particular case, the website is commercial and is run by people who call themselves "product development consultants, specialised in the youth market".)

Not surprisingly, with all this theoretical garble going on, commonsense ran screaming from the room, but such theory is behind the much vaunted "outcomes-based education" that now flourishes in Australia and other "new" countries such as Canada, New Zealand, the United States and South Africa.

Not that it flourishes in France. There has been no deconstructionist or constructivist pawing over of the French school system. Type "France" and "outcomes-based education" into Google and your computer does all but spit in your face. Anastasia, Jeremiah and Alyse, of Perth, Brisbane and Sydney, may be floating along on their educational journey, but you can be sure that Jean-Louis in Lyon is getting his daily dose of maths, grammar and all the other basics. As one Parisian parent of a fifteen-year-old told me, "There is a strong emphasis on French grammar and math, particularly math which is regarded as the foundation of higher education. The end-of-year assessment is rigorous, and any student with low grades is required to repeat the year. More than a third of French kids repeat at least one year at some time in their education."

Trust the French to realise that postmodernism and all the other theories were never supposed to be taken so seriously that you'd actually apply them to your precious children. Whatever the original worth of deconstructionism, constructivism and their like to the history of philosophical thought and debate, here in jumbled form they have brought with them murk, mess, flabbiness and sophistry. They provide a refuge for frauds, for laggards and for the easily impressed. I've done my best with it all and, every time, I keep thinking that Mandy Rice-Davies, the quick-witted callgirl who helped bring down, first, a British cabinet minister and then, the Prime Minister, Harold Macmillan, said it better. Appearing as a witness in the 1963 trial of Dr Stephen Ward, Rice-Davies was told that Lord Astor denied her allegations about sex at his

Que?

Author and foreign correspondent Geraldine Brooks tells a story many years ago about *The Wall Street Journal* during the Iran-Iraq war of 1980-1988: "A sub-editor, working on a piece by me or Tony [Brooks's husband] raised his head and said, 'So, what's our style, boss? Are we making it I-R-A-Q or I-R-A-N?'"

racy house-parties at his country estate, Cliveden. "He would, wouldn't he," she defended herself cogently.

Kevin Donnelly, a former secondary school teacher of English and history in Melbourne, who started his own company, Education Strategies, writes frequently on the iniquities of the modern education system to the fury of the education establishment. He escaped his working-class Broadmeadows background through education and says he'd still be back there if he'd been subjected to going on a personally relevant journey at school. The various teachers' associations and others regularly disparage Donnelly as a right-wing apologist too close to the government of John Howard.[5] In fact, Donnelly had a father who was communist, a mother who was a good Catholic, and he says, "B.A. Santamaria [the Victorian political activist and journalist who was fervently anti-communist] always said I had experienced two of the most powerful forces of the twentieth century."

He was actively involved in the Victorian Secondary Teachers Association for ten years, but was appalled by the moves that brought in continuous assessment where, previously, a child's marks had mostly been determined by a final exam. For him, that was always going to favour kids in comfortable backgrounds who had parents who were professionals. "They could pay for a tutor or even do the kids' work themselves," he points out. Kids from poorer homes with ill-educated parents suffered. He resigned from the union, started writing critically about education for Victorian newspapers and has been regarded as a turncoat by his former union friends ever since.

In the mid-Eighties, Donnelly saw what he believed was "the Left taking the 'long march' through the institutions", referring to a conscious effort on the part of people who were politically active on the Left to change society by changing the institutions of society, especially in education. Left, for Donnelly, in this context, means not the Left of social concern, compassion and humanism, but the radical, social-engineering Left. The purpose of outcomes-based education, remember, is not equality of opportunity but equality of outcome. Huge difference.

Like Runcie, he puts it down to the Sixties revolution, to flower-power and Woodstock. That was how and when it started to get its grip. "There was a very conscious attempt to take control of the curriculum ... that capitalist society could be overthrown and education was the way to do it." It was about changing the way children were educated, and thus, changing the people who inherit and then shape our society. Never mind the Jesuits and "give me the child until he is seven, and I will give you the man"; these new educators wanted the child from babyhood until adulthood. They still do. Reading, that indispensable skill that allows a human being to operate as a member of a civilised, democratic society, with equal ability to question and, even better, to imagine, became the first casualty.

It's worth noting here that political party insiders, who plan election campaigns and put the spin on policies, actions, debate and so on, assume that the average Australian voter has a reading age of twelve and the average journalist can only manage to read to a fourteen-year-old level. This unnerving information is revealed in *The Persuaders: Inside the Hidden Machine of Political Advertising*, by political scientist and media lecturer Dr Sally Young. [6]

COGNITIVE scientist Max Coltheart left Australia in 1969 and didn't return for a couple of decades, by which time the public education system had been turned on its head, the traditional methods that had worked for centuries had been virtually outlawed except in a band of select and selective schools, and university entrants were so ill-prepared it was not unusual for them to have to take courses in how to spell and write before they could start to study and prepare essays.

Not that Coltheart noticed any of this at first. His daughter had attended a conservative private school while he had been researching and teaching at the University of London so she had been schooled traditionally. The ideas that also turned English education upside down in the state-run schools had passed his family by. Back in Australia, the cognitive scientist was not, at first, involved in the learning-to-read area.

Working later, in the Nineties, with some teachers who were already out in the field practising, he was vaguely annoyed to discover they knew little about how to teach reading, writing and spelling. He thought it an aberration, just a few teachers who didn't know what they were doing. Then he met more and more young teachers with the same problem and he started to realise that the reason they didn't know how to teach these basics was because that had hardly been on their curriculum.

He went on the Web to find the syllabuses of different faculties of education at Australian universities and discovered that, all too often, student teachers were being sent out without this most obvious and basic training, although they had had loads of theory stuffed into them. By now, teacher-training had moved from off-campus colleges into education faculties in the universities and that, many believe, was the biggest mistake. Too much theory; not enough practical training. Or as one commentator described it, there is "a broken connection between campus and classroom".

A 2005 survey of teacher education institutions conducted as part of a national inquiry into the teaching of literacy bears Coltheart out. It discovered that half of the faculties were devoting less than 5 percent of course time to the art of teaching reading. Overall, less than 10 percent of compulsory course time for primary school teacher-trainees was spent covering basic literacy skills. The same survey showed that, in a four-year course, practical teaching experience varied from just fifty to one hundred days.[7]

Worse, the educationists in charge, says Coltheart, were preaching something called the whole-word method, and that learning to read was the same as learning to speak. It came instinctively to children, they argued, and all teachers had to do was aid and abet the process, providing a reading environment. Or what they call "reading rich". There was no need to teach the alphabet or explore letter/sound relationships. It was a kind of natural magic, like little children unconsciously picking up foreign languages.

Coltheart knew this was a nonsense, as did numerous other experts in the area.[8] The two abilities are different. "If everyone can learn to read naturally, why is most of the world illiterate?" he asks in exasperation. "Learning to read is artificial. We have to be taught." (As for little children effortlessly picking up other languages, that is a skill

Like, whatever

Sydneysider Tony Keep went into David Jones to buy a jumper. A young salesman showed him one, and Keep asked him if it was wool. The salesman looked at the label and said, "No, it's pure merino."

which, if unused, gradually disappears because of changes in the developing brain.)

Phonics has been around since the sixteenth century. As Coltheart pointed out on an ABC *Life Matters* programme in late August 2005, the phonics method where children are taught to associate sounds with letters has been working very well since 1570. The fashionable method – whole-word teaching – believes that children can learn to read virtually by osmosis; that, by looking at a word, they will gradually recognise and then understand it. As if.

By April 2004, Coltheart had had enough. Along with twenty other distinguished academics, researchers, and psychologists, linguists and educators, he wrote to then federal minister for education Brendan Nelson stressing their concerns about the way reading was typically being taught in Australian schools: "The ability to read is a complex learned skill which requires specific teaching."

They drew on government-funded reports from the United States. "All these reports have come up with essentially the same conclusion: that mastery of the alphabetic code is essential to proficient reading, and that methods of instruction that teach this code directly are more effective than those that do not." The letter also noted, "In cases where children do not learn to read [through the currently fashionable whole-word method which is what teachers are taught to teach], their failure is blamed on their parents or their background rather than on ineffective teaching methods …"

The education establishment retaliated, digging into a grab-bag of statistics that claimed to prove Australia has among the most literate children in the world. Organisations like the Australian Council for Educational Research, a body that supports outcomes-based education, proudly maintain that Australian kids are doing fabulously well, quoting results from the OECD's programme for international student assessment (PISA). But as *Australian Financial Review* columnist Peter Ruehl pointed out acerbically, "PISA tends to be one of those New Age life skills tests, where students are not corrected for faulty grammar, spelling and punctuation … What are you going to do? On your job application at Merrill Lynch, write: 'Look how good I done on the PISA test'?"[9]

Spelling, of course, is not supposed to matter any more, which is stiff cheese for those of us who can spell and who see in it the same sense of security that comes with, say, knowing that cars drive on roads, not pavements. Now, correct spelling is seen as something put on only for special occasions, like people wearing hats and gloves in the Fifties. A smart young woman of good education and in a good job tells me earnestly over coffee one day that she never did learn to spell properly so when she has to write an important email, she'll always use spell-check.

As for a teacher's traditional authoritativeness, that last word, like the word "discipline", has been criminalised. In the fuzzy world of today, where "infer"/"imply", "repel"/"repulse", "procrastinate"/"prevaricate" and "its"/"it's" are regularly mixed up without anyone, even the ABC, batting an eyelid, the word "authoritative" has been blurred in people's minds with "authoritarian", as much of a no-no as "hierarchy" or "disciplines". A New South Wales secondary school teacher, Ryszard Linkiewicz, wrote a piece for *The Daily Telegraph*: "The brutal fact is that the standards have been lowered to such an extent that children who, in former times, would have been regarded as sub-normal are now regarded as well within normal range … No longer are students penalised for errors in spelling and grammar. Any response, no matter how incoherent or insouciant, must get a mark."[10] (Linkiewicz's piece proves that there are teachers, usually older ones educated in more formal times, who are worried about what's happening, but there are penalties for speaking out and so most don't.) In 2005, the Australian Defence Force Academy found that many of 660 undergraduates surveyed were unable to write a grammatical or properly structured essay. A staff member talked of students unable to construct a sentence, use punctuation or spell. A male student complained, "The study of grammar ceased in primary school. Most people have no idea of grammar and suddenly we are expected to know it for tertiary studies."[11] Ten percent of students studying to be teachers at the University of Tasmania had such poor writing skills they had to undertake remedial lessons.[12]

Literals in a major newspaper were considered embarrassing a couple of decades ago. I can still recall the shame of allowing a story to be published in *The Sunday Times* in the mid-Eighties in which the writer had spelt the cigarette brand as Marlborough, not Marlboro, and we had failed to correct it. The mistake was pointed out to us grimly on the Monday. Now we have literals in sixty-point headlines and in stories on page one. There are rogue apostrophes and syntax so bad that I often find myself mentally blue-pencilling a story as I read my daily papers because it's the only way I can work out what the reporter is trying to say. A night editor on a major newspaper goes into regular rants about the stories that plop onto his computer screen at eight at night, seemingly written out in the Russian steppes for all the literacy and clarity and understanding of English sentence construction they display. And these are stories from young cadets and just graded journalists who have been selected, only a few each year, from hundreds of applicants.

Nor are their seniors much better. A West Australian reader writes to *The Australian* about the decline of language on the ABC. "Increasingly, especially on Radio National, we hear malapropisms, neologisms and near-enough-is-good-enough words where the usage is not understood."[13]

A highly literate writer and inner-city mother of two said to me one day that she was thinking of

Totally

"Sir: Allan Massie (Letters, 4 December) asks by whom has Anthony Burgess been forgotten? By my publishers for a start. They commissioned me to write the Magus of Monte Carlo's biography in 1995, and I never heard a word from them again until just the other day. 'Burgess's *Jake's Thing* is out of print in America,' it was unnervingly explained. Perhaps they meant Kingsley Amis's *Clockwork Banana* or Dame Iris Murdoch's *The French Lieutenant's Woman*, the one where Mitzi Gaynor washes that man right out of her hair.

"Secondly, whenever I've told people I'm working on Anthony Burgess, they think I either mean Guy Burgess or Anthony Blunt and so talk to me about the whys and wherefores of espionage. Meantime, Andrew Lownie, who *is* writing a book about Guy Burgess, gets pestered by chaps lecturing him on Stanley Kubrick.

"So it goes. I once published a book on Laurence Olivier. People under 40 thought he was the author of a mucky book on gamekeepers, or maybe that he was that queer in the desert played by Peter O'Toole. My publicity handmaiden at Random House had never heard of Kenneth Tynan, Buckingham to Olivier's Richard III. She thought I was going on about Kenneth Branagh.

"Are these generational mistakes or are people simply plain bleeding ignorant, like the contestant on a television quiz show who believed Albert Camus to be a French detective?"

Roger Lewis

Nunwell Priory, Bromyard, Herefordshire

LETTER TO *THE SPECTATOR*, DECEMBER 11, 1999.

offering her services to her children's primary school: she thought she could provide a half-hour lesson to the teachers on the art of the apostrophe, for instance. She had been appalled to discover that her children, who did mostly know where to put an apostrophe, were having their homework marked incorrectly by teachers who didn't.

Apostrophes, schmopostrophes seems to be the attitude. What has happened here has happened across the world. In Britain, a survey of 250 admissions staff from sixteen universities, including Oxford and Cambridge,[14] found that new undergraduates were less numerate, literate and knowledgeable than ever before. Tutors complained that new students have "a fear of numbers", don't know how to think for themselves and arrive at seminars expecting to have answers doled out to them. One newspaper quoted a physics admissions tutor in the survey's report: "They can't even write in sentences. Their spelling is appalling. They can't be understood. They graduate with a 2:1 but they still can't spell or write English."[15] (Which makes you wonder what their university lecturers were thinking, giving them passes in the first place.) Students were reported to be weaker at reading critically and advancing an argument than they were ten years ago. An over-emphasis on exam success, syllabus and getting a university place was having a negative impact on children's learning as they adopted a tick-the-box attitude. One of the report's co-authors emphasised that the negative comments were not "whingeing or harking back to some golden age but represent genuine concerns about young people and their capacity to benefit from higher education".[16]

When British playwright Alan Bennett was rehearsing his young actors for his latest play *The History Boys*, about a government grammar school in the Eighties, he told journalist James Button he discovered they had no idea who A.E. Housman and W.H. Auden were. Later, he realised one of the actors didn't know what a plural was.

It's all much worse for kids from poor families. As Coltheart and his colleagues have noted in Australia, it is disadvantaged children who are most likely to end up with poor literacy skills because their own parents cannot redress the deficits of their schooling.

I'm grateful to anyone who makes a career out of teaching the young, especially in the public sector, so I take a charitable line with any teachers I meet, presuming they are full of good sense and goodwill, that they will be like Ryszard Linkiewicz, quoted earlier, and that the theoretical nonsense observed by Runcie, Coltheart, Donnelly and various writers of opinion pieces is the exception. But again and again,

I come smack up against a kind of programmed and wilful ignorance, and from the nicest people, too. Discussing grammar with a vital young headmistress of a public high school late one night, I was horrified to hear her dismiss it and say, "Well, just so long as they can do PowerPoint in the home room, that's all that matters." (Such thinking has its influence on young minds. When a senior academic tells his Melbourne honours students that one Ivy League American university, a fervid user of PowerPoint in lectures, was now phasing out its teaching and use of the programme, the students are troubled. They look dubious. They think the students there will be at a disadvantage when they come to look for jobs.)

At a book launch one evening, another teacher chats about word usage, saying firmly that if the kids are using words differently – for instance, "I" when it should be "me" as in the phrase "he sent the parcel to Joe and me" which these days is nearly always spoken and written as "Joe and I" – then we must just accept that that is the new usage.

One day *The Sydney Morning Herald*'s splash on page one carried a headline that was astonishing: "Teachers told: prove you can read and write".[17]

Education was once felt to be a kind of "moral transaction" between parents and children. By the late medieval period, to educate was supposed to be one of the duties of human beings, beyond teaching the young natural processes which all human beings must learn for survival.[18] But what we're seeing now feels like a full-frontal attack on education. No wonder then so many find reading the classics or even a very long novel so impossibly hard that education authorities simply take them off the list or make sure to include much easier books that the children can opt to study. In 1979, the American critic Christopher Lasch wrote in his book *The Culture of Narcissism*, "In the name of egalitarianism, they preserve the most insidious form of elitism, which in one guise or another, holds the masses incapable of intellectual exertion."

Donnelly points out that one of the appeals of outcomes-based education in schools is that it is a natural fit for bean-counters. This is the pincer movement of economic rationalism and postmodern theory at play. "It's very managerial in terms of the bottom line, so, with its accountability and checklists, it appealed very much to the Right," he says. "It's all very output-driven and there's a lot of management speak in it." The two camps have something in common: they love theory and bureaucratic hyper-accountability over commonsense. No wonder many very good teachers are leaving the profession, unable to make head or tail of what they are supposed to be teaching and unable to cope with the jargon and administrative trivia loaded on them. In 2003, the federal education minister calculated that, by 2010, at current rates of attrition, Australia could be short of 30,000 teachers.

UNIVERSITIES themselves have struggled to maintain their special position in civilised society since just after World War II. In post-war Britain, a newly utilitarian class of politicians and bureaucrats who were fixed on the immediate future scrutinised the role of the university. In reaction, political philosopher Michael Oakeshott wrote a series of essays on education, liberal learning and universities over his lifetime. In one of his most famous, *The Idea of a University*, written in 1950, he argued presciently: "A university is not a machine for achieving a particular purpose or producing a particular result; it is a manner of human activity. And it would be necessary for a university to advertise itself as pursuing a particular purpose only if it were talking to people so ignorant they had to be spoken to in baby-language, or if it were so little confident of its power to embrace those who came to it that it had to call attention to its incidental charms."[19]

In 1988, Labor's John Dawkins, who was at the University of WA when I entered as a fresher, was federal education minister and did to our universities exactly what Oakeshott had feared would happen to British institutions. Colleges and tertiary institutions of all kinds found themselves bundled up into the university sector for ease of administration and the whole sector became

---

Huh?

Teachers in the United States have stopped using red ink pens to mark homework and are switching instead to calming shades like lavender. Apparently, some educators consider that red can be stressful, demeaning, even "frightening" to a young person. Many schools also now discourage or prohibit competitive games like tag or dodge ball because they can cause too many hurt feelings. One principal wrote to parents informing them that tag would no longer be played at recess because "In this game, there is a 'victim' or 'It' which creates a self-esteem issue."
AUTHOR AND PHILOSOPHY PROFESSOR CHRISTINA HOFF SOMMERS PLEADS FOR A REALITY CHECK IN *USA TODAY*, MAY 31, 2005.

saddled with the need to concentrate on vocational, measurable skills for the economic good of the country.

In a 1994 essay[20] Simon Leys (aka the Belgian academic and sinologist Pierre Ryckmans) suggested that the best way to protect universities as places devoted to liberal studies rather than glorified vocational colleges would be simply to stop universities awarding degrees. He argued that if people could see that, in practical terms, a university education leads nowhere, the institution would be saved from the current bastardisation in which "we saw a bizarre evolution taking place: these two streams – professional training on the one side and liberal education on the other – which were originally meant to develop separately, began to merge, and today their confusion is complete. To consecrate this glorious muddle, the colleges are now usurping all the titles and trappings that were supposed to be the exclusive preserve of the universities, whereas the universities make pathetic and clumsy efforts to discharge all the tasks that were better performed by the colleges."

A 2002 report[21] into changes in Australian academic life, commissioned by the Department of Education, Science and Training (DEST), summarises what happened after the Dawkins reforms: "Universities became 'industries' and academics 'workers' or 'employees' as industrial laws came to regulate academic work. The efficiency principle was invoked and enterprise bargaining began. Academic staff associations became unions and registered themselves with the industrial Arbitration Commission. The vice-chancellors created a new employer organisation called the Australian Higher Education Industrial Association (AHEIA). These two bodies would bargain: greater efficiency or productivity gains from the workers in return for improvements in working conditions or salaries. Later these central negotiations would be replaced by 'enterprise bargaining' within each institution sharpening the new adversarial roles of academics and university senior administrators."

The report outlined the sharp drop in public funding after the election of the Howard government in 1996 and the rise in student-to-staff ratios as student numbers outpaced growth in academic staff. "Perhaps the most remarkable change in students' circumstances," the report's authors wrote, "is in the amount of outside work that is undertaken. Full-time undergraduates now work on average more than fourteen hours per week during semester, up from five hours in the 1980s."

At the same time, the government's sources of policy advice narrowed from three entities to just one department – DEST. The report's concise sentences reveal dispassionately how one dominant and uncompromising mind-set took over and virtually annihilated another. No wonder its authors couldn't resist including in their preface a wry aside from one academic: "For DEST to do this resembles Yahweh [Jehovah] enquiring into flood damage on Day 40." As the report also noted, in a passage reminiscent of Bradbury, Huxley and Orwell, that with so many younger staff now on campus, fewer than half of all academics can remember what university life was like before the changes began in 1988. Instead, they "regard the present situation, for better or worse, as normal".

The trend now in OECD countries is for the university system not to be academic-driven but to be performance-driven and market-oriented. Australian universities now operate more like large businesses. That has had universities chasing the dollar, doing research for industry, and concentrating on full fee-paying students, especially those from overseas. The sideshows, introduced to raise funds, have ended up changing the main show. Now that overseas enrolments have dropped, several universities are in trouble. Academic standards have fallen because of workloads and lower staff numbers, but they have also been affected by the way students, especially the full fee-paying ones, see themselves as "clients" with a client's privileges and expectations. Academics have come under pressure to give degrees to students who should have failed or to give them higher grades generally. Courses such as business studies that attracted many students who wanted the right letters so they could get the right jobs, boomed, encouraged by newly business-minded vice-chancellors. Other more arcane courses, with less obvious, immediate or fewer monetary rewards, struggled. The move towards the business model has also led to a host of performance indicators and benchmarks being developed and imposed so that managerialism is now entrenched.

One paper[22] on the subject of the market-led university, by James Guthrie and Ruth Neumann, dwelled on "the rise of the self-serving academic", a phenomenon also observed by several other authors they cite. They explain helpfully that what they mean is "an increase in individualism as academics interpret excellence in narrow and more self-serving ways, exploiting for themselves [the new] entrepreneurial culture of the university". They add that managerialism and entrepreneurial activities often reinforced each other.

What hope for Ryckmans's purity there?

Ironically, outside this new university system, important old-fashioned skills such as plumbing, bricklaying, mining, tiling, carpentry and hairdressing, which actually are vocational and which are vital to every country, started vanishing because they kind of, um, got lost in the new economy. First of all, more kids were encouraged to stay at school until Year 12 when they might have been better off going out to learn a trade. More kids went on to university. The kids who did leave school early had often been doing so much "journeying" they hadn't acquired either the basic skills or the discipline to learn a trade. At the same time, the government corporatised or privatised its various utilities and activities and so the main provider of apprenticeships disappeared.[23] Private enterprise certainly wasn't going to pick up the slack and continue paying out for young men and women to learn their trade at their expense. The less they could get away with, the better. Now we're trying to recruit from the United Kingdom but not having much luck because it seems that the Brits – who have had a similar saga in their university system – were too cheap to train tradespeople, too.

So what have we ended up with, courtesy of postmodernism and the market working in cahoots? Talking about the study of English, Barry Spurr, senior lecturer in English at the University of Sydney, says sadly that as a result of the changes over 20 years, it is possible for a student to graduate with English Honours and do a PhD in English poetry without ever studying Milton or reading a line of Dryden or Pope. And while Shakespeare, for all the dead-white-male epithets, has managed to survive in high schools and

---

Ohmigod

"In the past, a WA teacher whose goal was to teach a poem would have done so. This is no longer the case. The same teacher is now required to wrestle with 13 Overarching Learning Outcomes and 5 Values Outcomes from the *Curriculum Framework* (1998); several Learning Area Outcomes; Layer 1 and Layer 2 Aspects from the *Progress Maps*, (2004d). And/Or *Achievements Targets* from the 'New' *Outcomes and Standards Framework* (2004 proposed, DETWA); the *Curriculum Guides* (2004e); *In Phase Scope & Sequence Charts* (2004, in press, CCWA); the *Competency Framework* (Maloney and Barblett, 2004, draft); and information contained within a plethora of 'supporting materials'. To teach a poem?"

FROM A CONFERENCE PAPER BY RICHARD BERLACH, ASSOCIATE DEAN, SCHOOL OF EDUCATION, UNIVERSITY OF NOTRE DAME, WESTERN AUSTRALIA.

universities, even he has had to be made politically acceptable and "relevant". Spurr tells me of an exam question set in the UK for those who had studied Shakespeare's *Julius Caesar* with its wonderful lines: "Men at some time are masters of their fate:/ The fault, dear Brutus, is not in our stars,/ But in ourselves, that we are underlings." And, "Let me have men about me that are fat;/ Sleek-headed men and such as sleep o' nights;/ Yond' Cassius has a lean and hungry look;/ He thinks too much: such men are dangerous."

Instead of being asked to write a scholarly paper analysing or interpreting the play, its characters, its language or its meaning, the examination question set for the secondary school students was: "How have you resolved conflict with your friends in your life?"

Spurr winces. "It's much easier, isn't it, to watch a video of *Pride and Prejudice* and to talk about gender than actually look at the construction of a paragraph and examine how Jane Austen used nouns. The students are in a state of perpetual mystification. Ask them to read a poem out loud and they're reading hesitantly. Ask them to identify a principal verb and 90 percent of them are at sea. So you can't discuss the force, say, of verbs in Austen's sentences.

"It's an awful insult to the students. We're selling the students short by thinking we have to pander to what's easy, what's fun. Learning isn't meant to be fun. It's hard work and often boring, but then one day, something clicks and then it becomes fun. Then the real fun begins, whether it's playing the piano or speaking a foreign language."

Runcie, commenting later on the whole ghastly mess in the humanities, says, "You know, no-one ever wants postmodernism in the disciplines like medicine or astrophysics. No-one in medicine believes that language can't communicate anything. Nobody has ever suggested that doctors or engineers or physicists should espouse indeterminacy.

"Postmodernism only took hold of the 'soft subjects' like arts and you can only get away with it when people are ignorant and lack philosophic knowledge. Of course, what happened was that the arts started apeing the sciences. Absolute hypocrisy! One lecturer used to press the idea that Einstein's Theory of Relativity and the Heisenberg Principle of Uncertainty meant that cultural relativism has scientific forebears. They are all equivalent scientific thought. It was garbage – and he, the last I heard, was still teaching teachers. The student teachers or those retraining could not possibly comprehend it enough to criticise this sophistry."

The paradox is that while postmodernism questions every belief we've had to date, it never arrives at anything. That is the point of postmodernism: there are no objective truths. But the traditional ideal behind the university and knowledge in general is that everything is questioned in order to try and arrive at considered truths by debate, study and research.

Postmodernism's intellectual capering develops a kind of dogmatic scepticism about everything and leaves people adrift. Spurr describes an education system supposedly designed to affirm students, which, in fact, disempowers them. Runcie calls postmodern indeterminacy "junk thinking". She recalls students leaving university because there didn't seem much point in studying if you couldn't reach truth. American academic Susan Ostrov Weisser matches Runcie's observation, quoting an email from a bright and troubled student, which read in part: "I just get so frustrated. Of course there are no definitive answers, so it seems to me that we aren't supposed to argue anything – just merely accept that there are many different sides and nothing can be resolved. I get tired of saying, 'This seems most likely to mean this, because of these examples ... but, of course, it could also mean that, because anything is possible.'"[24]

Weisser asks plaintively: "When everyone is right and no-one is wrong, what happens to the authority of expertise?"

Runcie concludes with this: "You can really only understand Derrida or deconstruction or postmodernism if you know the history of Western philosophy. You can't theorise on an empty stomach. You must have studied what came before. Otherwise it's just memorising the mantras, and that's what the kids do now, they recite mantras. They are chic. So chic now you get *Vogue* magazine talking about how a fashion designer like Akira Isogawa deconstructs his designs."

And we get the teacher who wanted her tiny pupils to be able to "do hypothesisation" – although she couldn't spell the word herself.

AT LEAST Max Coltheart and his colleagues' letter to Brendan Nelson helped towards the national inquiry into teaching literacy. The education minister announced its findings on December 8, 2005, and recommended the use of a phonics-based teaching method for reading. He welcomed the report's insistence on improving teacher education and therefore teaching quality, and he expressed consternation that

Totally

"What is wrong with everyone nowadays? Why do they all seem to think they are qualified to do things far beyond their actual capabilities. This is all to do with the learning culture in schools – the child-centred learning emphasis which admits of no failure and tells people they can all be pop stars, high court judges or brilliant television personalities ... without ever putting in the necessary work or effort, or having the natural ability."
PRINCE CHARLES RESPONDS IN A CONFIDENTIAL MEMO AFTER A GRADUATE PERSONAL ASSISTANT ASKED FOR A CAREER PATH. HE ALSO DESCRIBED THE PA AS "SO PC IT FRIGHTENS ME RIGID". THE ASSISTANT LATER OBTAINED THE MEMO, RESIGNED AND TOOK THE ROYAL HOUSEHOLD TO AN EMPLOYMENT TRIBUNAL. SHE LOST.

"too many of our children are not achieving even minimum standards in reading. In 2003, 8 percent of Year 3 children and 11 percent of Years 5 and 7 children did not achieve minimum national benchmarks. The results for indigenous children are even more disturbing. It is unacceptable that a significant number of Australian children are barely able to read and write."

The findings were greeted with relief by many, although not by the various teachers' associations. Keen to give the teachers' side of the story, television stations and reporters kept rounding up South Australian children's author Mem Fox, a whole-word supporter and former teacher of literacy, who happily took to the media airspace to ridicule phonics with much rolling of eyes and shaking of head. (It must have taken a toll; in an interview about turning sixty a short while later, she confided that she planned to step aside from her role as "whole-word" campaigner.)

The Australian Association for the Teaching of English responded by doing what Coltheart had told me it would do: taking the straw-man route. Coltheart warned me one of the tactics of the "whole-word method" supporters is to claim that phonics supporters insist that only phonics be taught. "And of course, we don't." As with all good teaching, methods are tailored to each child, but the basis is phonics at the beginning. On the same day as Nelson's release, the whole-word proponents, instead of reacting to his recommendations, insisted he really meant "strongly intensive phonics reading programmes" and criticised that position instead.[25]

These tactics work.

I ran into a neighbour on the street, a reasonable man. He was railing against the Prime Minister and the drive back towards "this rigid phonics business". He has no children himself so he was asserting what he had gleaned about the debate from the letters pages of the newspapers and interviews on television. As Coltheart had predicted, the propaganda coming out of the opponents of phonics had had its effect. The conversation reinforced in me the feeling that we are now also in a muddle of our own making, one created out of arguing *ad hominem*, that is, against the man, rather than over the facts. The education wars have polarised us. Phonics, learning dates and getting a foundation in all subjects are strongly identified with the Right; notions like questioning context, listening equally to other voices, in history and the humanities and the arts, are seen as belonging to the Left. Too many people and parents have taken up their own positions on that basis, instead of examining what's really happening or what they really believe. In Australia and the United States especially, where the Left sees leaders Howard and Bush as wilful fools or demagogues, the effect is particularly pernicious. Sensible people like my Left-leaning neighbour are already programmed to distrust whatever the Prime Minister might say about education.

Barry Spurr points out another local factor. Australian study of the classics, history and so on has been affected because we're so busy making sure that we're not being Eurocentric. As he puts it dryly, this is how we can affirm our liberation from our disreputable European past. Best to turn our backs on Milton.

On such confusion do the relativists and the people who have given us today's shocking education system prosper. They work with a kind of sly undermining. The people who now steer education often use the phrase "rote learning" disparagingly in articles and commentary. It's as if those educated before 1975 were taught wearing slates strapped to front and back to teach them good posture, were never allowed to think for themselves, and instead spent hours being drilled in scales, irregular verbs, famous historical dates and nothing else. There is much hoo-ha, for instance, about why students should be looking at Shakespeare, not through his language, but via the messages he sends about race, gender and so on. In an opinion piece,[26] Melina Marchetta, a teacher and the author of *Looking for Alibrandi*, writes that when students have "meaningful debate on issues of inequity based on race, class and gender" they are acquiring valuable skills "of comprehension, evaluation and synthesis in order to participate meaningfully in an increasingly complex world".

The Sisters of Mercy who took me through *Othello* and *The Merchant of Venice* back in the Sixties could never have expressed it quite like that. But guess what? While we studied and appreciated Shakespeare in the traditional way, for his language and vision and plotting, and yes, by rote because we were expected to be able to recite passages as well, we too considered the role of Portia, a woman, as lawyer, the place of Othello the Moor in a white society, the depiction of Shylock, the Jewish money-lender.

If the nuns at a not particularly prominent convent school in Perth were content and broadminded enough to discuss such issues in 1968, I think we can be assured that the current crop of teachers did not invent this particular wheel.

As for being made to learn the basics, and the discipline that demanded of its students, research is emerging that shows that talent and success depend not so much on what you were born with, but how much you practise, how much effort you put into your work, indeed, how much self-discipline you have. Martin Seligman, famous for his research into happiness, is co-author of a paper[27] that claims, after studying more than three hundred eighth-graders in the United States, that the main reason students fall short of their intellectual capital is their failure to exercise self-discipline and perseverance. And yet, too many of our kids are encouraged not to be disciplined because that's not seen as a necessary part of the "journey". Criticism is a no-no. Seligman's paper concluded: "Programs that build self-discipline may be the royal road to building academic achievement."

There's more on that argument. In Florida, K. Anders Ericsson, a psychology professor and expert on the growth of skill and talent, has used the world's specialists to compile a handbook on expert performance. The nine-hundred-page *Cambridge Handbook of Expertise and Expert Performance* was published in mid-2006. Its main finding is that the idea of innate talent is highly overrated, that a specific kind of practice makes perfect, and everyone needs evaluation if they are to improve. That notion about talent has been attacked by bloggers but, over the phone, Ericsson repeats to me that what gives real advantage is something he calls "deliberate practice". This is not simple unthinking repetition but setting goals, thinking about the task and getting feedback. That's what gives the advantage.

"It is very difficult to make adjustments and corrections without feedback," he says. "When you eliminate any kind of evaluation and criteria, that's a world where you've removed the potential for feedback." The biological body, he explains, is made to conserve energy; its basic drive is to minimise effort. Change comes only by exercising some kind of control over what you're doing. "If you're in an accepting world, people don't get any better. The constructivists are so afraid of providing feedback and criticism. It's somehow viewed as stifling creativity, and that's where they go wrong."

The truth is that too much of today's debates is airheaded tosh which covers up the fact that kids are not getting the teaching and knowledge they deserve, nor learning the behaviours that will help them be the best they can be. Nor are they learning the thinking skills that any functioning member of a functioning democratic society needs. The results of the last thirty years are in front of our eyes. Sophistry and propaganda allow scallywags to win, ideologues to prevail and bad methods to creep in through the cracks. Airheads get to run things, and they turn out more airheads.

How convenient is that?

Worse, Donnelly believes that what we have seen so far of the depredations wrought in education is only the beginning, especially now that the teachers going through training and out into the schools grew up in this theory-driven system. This is the only kind of schooling they have ever experienced. He laments the fact that Australia has fewer of the think-tanks and public policy institutions that might have brought the problems to the surface faster. "Debate in Australia tends to be on more practical issues like interest rates, unemployment and mortgages. These cultural ideas haven't been pushed by many politicians or senior bureaucrats. Most of them wouldn't know a cultural idea if it stood up in

Really?

Derrida is "the kind of philosopher who's given bullshit a bad name". UNIVERSITY OF CALIFORNIA BERKELEY PROFESSOR JOHN SEARLE ON FRENCH POSTMODERNIST JACQUES DERRIDA, FATHER OF DECONSTRUCTION, *THE NEW YORK TIMES BOOK REVIEW*, 1983.

their porridge. So, basically, bodies like the Curriculum Corporation[28] and the boards of studies are their own masters and do what they want to do. There has been no real critical analysis of what the edu-crats and the gatekeepers have been doing, no public scrutiny. They're not used to being engaged in political discussion either. At least now I think it's beginning to change because it's out there in the public arena."

Well, there's some hope at last.

In the meantime, if you'd like your child to get a good education, maybe you can move to France.

CHAPTER 8

Management for Airheads

"This opportunity will appeal to a high performing HR professional with several years of solid achievements in a fast-moving business. You will enjoy and be able to example turning policy and systems into constructive and welcome tools. Your style will be positive with a flexible approach to service in a dynamic business where contribution is expected and excellent relationships – including with external providers – ensure quality outcomes."

PEOPLECORP ADVERTISEMENT FOR HR CONSULTANT,
THE SYDNEY MORNING HERALD, OCTOBER 15-16, 2005

MANAGEMENT FOR AIRHEADS

*H*ave you ever seen the Russian film *Burnt by the Sun*, directed by Nikita Mikhalkov? It tells the story of a famous Russian colonel, a military hero of the Bolshevik revolution, who is living with his wife and small daughter at his dacha in the countryside in the mid-Thirties when an apparatchik from Moscow comes to visit. What our hero, Colonel Kotov, does not know is that the times have moved. His heroism, and the courage and independence that fuelled it, is now a threat to Stalin and the central commissariat. His charisma and leadership are seen as being even more dangerous.

In the final scene, the hero is taken off back to Moscow by the secret police in a small black car. He still does not completely comprehend what is happening. He thinks his status and army record make him special and protected.

He questions one of the officials, a small, insignificant man who suddenly reaches out and punches him in the face so that he is bleeding and shocked into semi-consciousness. In that moment, both the colonel and the audience understand what has happened. It's a new order. What has gone before matters no longer.

That's how I think of the rise of Human Resources and that paralysing word of the late twentieth century – managerialism. One moment, there was a pleasant, greying man in a cardigan in Personnel, dealing efficiently with everything from pay to annual leave to hirings and departures, doing it all with maybe one assistant or secretary, and doing it so that we, the workers, could get on

Que?

"The Smithsonian Institution is dismantling Smithsonian Books, a widely respected publishing division of the museum and research complex that dates back 150 years ... The cutback follows the failure of an effort that started in 2002 to make Smithsonian Books profitable."
THE WASHINGTON POST, OCTOBER 16, 2004.

with our jobs. I still have some pay envelopes written out by hand by that man.

The next minute, there were huge carpeted departments of Human Resources people, mostly young women with a slightly menacing air, young women who spend their days briskly handing out forms to be filled in and brusquely telling us how to do our jobs. Interestingly, in my experience few of them ever seem to know quite how to do their own.

Not only was the whole HR profession invented in its current form in the last thirty-five or so years but, with it, an entire language. The very name – Human Resources – sounds as if it might have been dreamed up by one of Stalin's helpful offsiders. (Perhaps because of that, HR departments have since upscaled to vaguely unsettling titles like People Capital or People Services.) There are now more than 60,000 HR professionals in Australia and another 35,300 who are HR managers. An above-average proportion of them are in full-time jobs and they earn above-average salaries. The managers have been having boom years; during the five to early 2006, their numbers rose by 124 percent against an average growth for all occupations of about 11 percent. In the last two years, their growth rate has been just over 40 percent. The Prime Minister's WorkChoices legislation is clearly providing more jobs in at least one area. Meanwhile strong growth is predicted for HR minions. The federal government careers website, which lists all this information, puts employment prospects for HR in its top category of Very Good.

I'll say.

And yet, workplace surveys show again and again that Generation Y workers believe they are not receiving enough training or advice or practical help on career development. A recruitment company reported that, despite our widely publicised skills shortage, one in three employees says the rate of resignations is high. An international survey found that when it came to exhibiting unhealthy behaviours, Australian companies scored worse than their European and American counterparts. Eighty percent of performance management systems in Australia are antiquated, reported another survey.[1] And in March 2005, the Gallup organisation reported that 62 percent of Australian workers were "not engaged" with their work and another 20 percent were "actively disengaged". The levels for engagement were among the lowest in the world.

A 2005 paper for the National Bureau of Economic Research in the United States, using data on 50,000 individuals in 35 countries, put Australians near the bottom, twenty-seventh, when it comes to job satisfaction.[2] Only Japan, Taiwan and the former Eastern Bloc countries had lower ratings. The authors of the study questioned how a country rating third on the United Nations Human Development Index could have such a low score.

HR did not come into those researchers' reckonings, which were mostly to do with the nature of happiness, but, given the above and that HR professionals are breeding like pod people, you'd have to feel safe in saying that one thing HR personnel *don't* seem to do is handle staff very well.

So what on earth *do* these people do?

To read their mission statements is to think that HR personnel are a cross between Mother Teresa and John F. Kennedy with a bit of troubleshooting Red Adair and management guru Peter Drucker thrown in for good measure. In reality, they are no such thing.

"The first thing any HR manager does is hire other HR people," said a University of Sydney lecturer in workplace law. "Then they build walls around their unit and hold meetings. HR these days is a legal risk-management tool and we can trace the rise of HR to the rise in the laws on unfair dismissal and discrimination. But you'd have to wonder what came first. HR is a parasite and, like any parasite, it starts to modify the host."

She cited the example of a law firm that used to handle its own hiring, but then employs an HR manager. "The next thing that happens is the HR people become an obstruction to hiring bright, young graduates." A university vice-chancellor laments the fact that nobody above cleaner level can ever be employed any more unless it is done through an outside recruitment consultancy so that everything is seen to be done by HR rules of fairness and legality. The process takes longer. It costs huge amounts. It also keeps HR personnel in work and makes the HR manager an indispensable cog in the process.

Like smoke, like hot air, like airheads, the HR manager always rises.

At its most basic, HR should be the department that monitors and maintains the health of the social contract between employer and employee. That's the unspoken contract which, in spite of all the workplace changes of the last fifteen years and the advent of the highly mobile Generation Y workers, still exists in our heads and hearts: the notion that if we work hard and well, our company will notice and respond in kind and we in turn will help the company achieve its aims. And this

Ohmigod

"[A corporate governance academic] cited an example of a board which had $1 billion wiped from its market value because of a mistake that arose because the risk committee did not understand what the company's head of risk management was telling them and did not feel able to seek an explanation because of his difficult personality."
THE WEEKEND AUSTRALIAN, NOVEMBER 12-13, 2005.

contract will exist until each goes his or her civilised way. That brief got a bit muddled along the way, however, when HR, self-importantly and with an eye on building HR salaries, staff numbers and indispensability, decided that form-filling was all very well but what it really wanted was a seat at the big table; it wanted to use its shiny tertiary qualifications and stick its nose into what it called "strategising". It wanted to be on a par with the line managers and senior executives. It wanted a say; it wanted to tell people how to behave and work in order to help the company succeed. Unbelievably, that's what then happened. If you consult manuals on HR, the authors talk of this being the time when HR moved into "adding value" to a company, when it started using its skills to give the company a "competitive advantage".

As a result, in most other people's eyes, HR personnel now rank about on a par with standover merchants.

"It's supposed to be about better recruiting and better termination procedures but HR has its own internal logic and discourse," the lecturer in workplace law reminds us. "It actually changes the way an organisation does things to suit HR, rather than the other way around ... It always amuses me the way HR cosies up to top management. That's how you get the best money, a place at influential meetings and the office with a view."

HR loves a number, or better still, a set of numbers and so it isn't surprising that the profession has embraced wholeheartedly, here, in Britain and in the United States, the idea that the worth of a candidate or employee can be told via tick-the-box assessment tests. Another manager recently leaked me a cluster of documents he and his colleagues had been asked to read and fill out as part of a leadership programme. They were supposed to, first, rate themselves on how closely ninety-eight descriptions of behaviour described them. Some examples: "Takes ideas different from their own seriously, and from time to time changes mind", "Capable, cool in high pressure situations", "Creates significant organisational change". Then they were told to get eight (*eight!*) other people to do a similar questionnaire rating their leadership skills, personality, etc. My manager friend had, reluctantly, been about to fill in the form when he noticed that he had to fill it in with pencil. "And then I clicked that this bloody thing was going to be marked by a computer! Stuff that, I thought."

But the real screening comes with psychometric testing at recruitment stage. There are few employers now who don't ask would-be employees to undergo rigorous testing, again often by computer. While some of these tests are for cognitive, mathematical and verbal skills, the controversial chunk is the bit that measures aptitude, behaviour and personality.

Proponents say that psychometric testing speeds up the selection process. Candidates can even try out on-line so they can screen themselves for certain jobs before wasting everybody's time. Type "psychometric" into Google and see how big the testing industry is now. That's odd because researchers acknowledge just how difficult it is to work out whether psychometrics does actually pick the most productive employees. The literature is minimal and mostly critical, which means we have this enormous industry poised on one toe and balanced on ... what? Publicising her new book *Bait and Switch,* about trying to get a white-collar job in middle-age in corporate America, author Barbara Ehrenreich told Amazon.com: "What surprised me most, right from day one of my job search, was the surreal nature of the job-searching business. For example, everyone, from corporations to career coaches, relies heavily on 'personality tests', which have no scientific credibility or predictive value. One test revealed that I have a melancholy and envious nature and, for some reason, was unsuited to be a writer! And what does 'personality' have to do with getting the job done, anyway? There's far less emphasis on skills and experience than on whether you have the prescribed upbeat and likeable persona. I kept wondering: is this any way to run a business?"

A woman tells me about her friend who runs a psychometric testing business.

"She keeps telling me I'm such and such a type, and then gets annoyed when I'm being myself and she says, 'You're an X. You're not supposed to act like that!'"

But what psychometric testing almost certainly establishes – unless the person being tested is wily and wants to fool the potential employer – is how independent or rebellious the candidate is. It must also reveal the candidate's sense of ethics and integrity. A friend going for a job with a financial institution says her testing included a multi-choice question about how she would handle a client who suggested doing something vaguely unethical. She ticked the box with the most obvious, ethical answer, but says, "I wasn't actually convinced that, as far as they were concerned, that *was* quite the 'right' box to tick."

Many people, including me, worry that psychometrics simply weeds out the people who might prove "difficult" or "challenging". When Tom Elliott, now a financial commentator and managing director of his own hedge fund, was wooed by Macquarie Bank to join its private equity division, he found he had to sit a set of personality tests. It became apparent quickly that he might not be quite their ideal candidate. For a start, when he was told the tests were compulsory, he had asked if CEO Allan Moss or chairman David Clarke had taken them. "I received a rather testy reply in the negative." He took the tests and, when it came time to do the complete-the-shape pattern problems, he did his best to imagine what his new bosses might like to see. It didn't help much.

Macquarie asked him to take the tests again because, while his mathematical reasoning had proved very good, there had been "some rather odd results in the verbal and personality parts". Nothing to worry about of course, he was assured, except that, umm, the results had to be "correct" and so Elliott had to sit them again. Whew. This time he did much better and was informed he was "within the curve". That didn't really help much in the end because, over a formal dinner that was supposed to clinch it all – Can he hold his liquor? Can he use a knife and fork? – it turned out Elliott didn't play golf, had no intention of learning and said as much. It was clear the parties were about to go their separate ways.

Elliott says now of such testing that "it's a sign of people not being able to make their own decisions". It's also about "covering your ass legally" because no candidate can then say they've been discriminated against. He wrote a very funny piece about his experiences for *The Australian Financial Review*, but says that, sadly, none of his friends within Macquarie were able to compliment him upon it.

A British research paper on psychometric testing[3] says that high levels of such testing obviously benefit HR departments. The tests can be used and interpreted only by trained staff who tend to be in HR (or are outside consultants contracted by HR). They then end up having a substantial input into the decision-making. In a later paper,[4] the same authors made the point that HR personnel generally have an interest in increasing their involvement in key organisational decisions. Without such testing, HR didn't get to play a substantive role in job interviews outside their own department.

The whole process makes HR sound all too like Vestal Virgins tending the sacred flame and guarding Rome, which may in fact be the fantasy that lulls HR managers to sleep every night.

Political correctness has also helped HR stamp its feet and make people do its bidding. There are umpteen procedures, regulations and team-playing exercises enforced by HR departments that are supposed to eliminate anything that smacks of sexual, racial or whatever-else kind of discrimination. A testy aviation expert whose nephew flies for British Airways complains of the hours pilots must now spend doing "touchy-feely exercises" to improve interpersonal skills. "For heaven's sakes!" he exclaimed, "All that matters with your co-pilot is that he or she knows how to fly!" But heaven help the employee who doesn't co-operate with HR and its politically correct proscriptions, and this particular nephew found himself reported to HR by a flight attendant because she said he hadn't greeted her on arrival for a flight. A producer with one of the public

Like, whatever

"In the spring of 1987, not long after [Tony Ridder] became head of Knight Ridder's newspaper division, he came to visit the [*Philadelphia*] *Inquirer*. The paper had just won three Pulitzers. Ridder told the assembled editors and managers that while he wanted to congratulate them on the prizes, he wanted to speak with them about 'something more important'. 'Next year,' he said, 'I would like you to win a Pulitzer for cost-cutting.'"
COLUMBIA JOURNALISM REVIEW, MARCH-APRIL, 2006.

broadcasters once found himself up against the organisation's head of HR on a series of charges, one of which was displaying "general negativity and disdain" towards the station's other programmes.

HR, in this, its worst and most airheaded manifestation, is simply adopting its employer's cause, peddling all the fashionable gobbledy-gook and empty-headed jargon on ethics and team spirit, while checking every day with the lawyers on how to arrange the latest round of redundancies, how to circumvent dissension and how to fit the legal definition of "fair" (which isn't quite the same as the ethical interpretation). In such a way does such an HR director rise, rise, r-i-s-e, building an empire as he or she goes. It's an empire that has a huge effect on the bigger empire, although not apparently, as the survey results show, in any obviously beneficial way to employees, and therefore, in the long run, to employers if they could only see it.

The legal lecturer laughs about the constant use by HR of the term "team-playing", which too often simply means that HR insists on recruiting people who will stick to the company line and not cause awkward difficulties. The ominous phrase that comes up when HR talks about recruitment is "culture fit". An executive with Australian psychometric testing company SHL tells his audience at a graduate recruitment conference that organisational fit is increasingly the most important selection decision factor for employers in Australia. Too often that really means recruits are picked for their ability to accept the mores of the organisation hiring them. Good organisational fit can just mean pliable, and worse, that an organisation will end up with a staff of clones.

Another business school academic remembers watching members from a prestigious consulting group acting as judges in a business students' competition in which teams competed to produce a strategy for a client. "The prize went to the team that looked and acted like the consulting group's people," she said. "The team's business strategy was bizarre, it was wrong and the consultants knew that but it didn't matter. That team had the polish, and fit was what mattered; the content was actually irrelevant."

L EAFING through Don Watson's excellent *Weasel Words*, his follow-up to *Death Sentence: The Decay of Public Language*, it's quickly apparent how many of his pet entries have sprung from the HR profession: redundancy also meaning *"Efficiency gain output. An involuntary career event. Implementation cost."* Or human resources: "Management *tool* for coercing and manipulating staff and controlling their thought and behaviour. *Downsizing implement.* (See *re-engineering*, etc.)"[5]

The lecturer in workplace law talks scathingly of the turgid prose of HR, too. She's had young HR students who were relieved to discover that studying workplace law was straightforward and simple in contrast to grappling with the thick theory books of HR with its hifalutin language. "Which," she says, "is like wrestling smoke. It doesn't really do anything."

I met my first HR person in the Nineties. She was a neatly turned-out blonde, pleased with herself, dogmatic and almost totally clueless about either journalism or newspapers. Nevertheless, she represented a brand new department at my company, and one that had been given permission to tell us what to do. We were a group of section editors, weary and fraught around the edges from years of trying to corral and tame wayward reporters. (That's not a criticism: a good reporter is naturally wayward and questioning.) But we were still passionate about what could be done with a newspaper or magazine and we did know how to do our jobs.

When the HR official told us that from now on we were to tell our reporters when they could take holidays and for how long, we looked at each other and raised our eyebrows. It was hard enough getting the buggers to co-operate each day to do our bidding so that, each evening, the newspaper could get out on time with good stories, minus mistakes in facts, legals, literals and any of the other disasters that can turn up on a printed page when one human being tells a story about another human being.

The reporters would not like us telling them when to take holidays and, what's more, we wouldn't like telling them. In an ideal newsroom, no-one took holidays. Since the cutbacks of the Seventies recession, after which the in-house cadetship systems on many newspapers virtually expired, staffing was so thin in most places that someone on holiday just meant someone else had to do their job as well. Besides, in this precarious media life, it was taken as read that a slab of saved-up holiday weeks could pay your mortgage or rent if suddenly your magazine closed, or there were cutbacks on the photography desk, or you got into a shouting match with the new editor-in-chief.

We listened in barely polite disbelief, asked some patronising questions ("So *where* have you worked before?"), told the new official gently that we really couldn't see the reporters responding very well to this new order ... And by doing all of this, only proved, first, how useless we were at the new management and, second, how little we understood the changes already well in place generally and beginning to infiltrate newspapers. Like Colonel Kotov, we hadn't noticed. Probably because we were working from 10 am to 10 pm each day, fussing over stories, fighting and competing with each other, in short, trying to get our newspapers out to the best of our ability.

To an outsider, it would have been like watching the Goths occupying Rome while the Romans were still busy fiddling around with civilisation and forgetting to bar the gates. The same thing was happening in all kinds of companies.

After my original essay on the triumph of airheadism appeared in *The Weekend Australian Magazine* in early 2005, a reader from Queensland emailed. Barry Wells had worked in IT most of his career. He, too, had had an early-warning moment, but his had occurred back in the mid-Seventies. "It was part of that whole up-titling thing when secretaries were becoming PAs," he remembers now. "We used to have someone called a personnel officer who facilitated decisions on manpower made by management and he was content to do the job with a couple of clerks. What happened overnight was that job turned into HR and HR gathered more and more power over manpower decisions while line management got less. Industry at the time was faced with this wave of sociology and psychology graduates and they were all looking for employment."

Wells's original email had been terse. "Some years ago, I arrived one morning at my middle-management job in a high-tech company, now mercifully defunct, to find yet another amazing

Really?

"A Scottish executive stripped naked for an interview with a 25-year-old female job applicant and requested she do the same. Saeed Akbar, an interpreter and respected boss, told a Glasgow court at first that it was 'part of his tough interviewing technique' but later confessed he'd just been bored."
THE MIRROR, MAY 4, 2005.

memo from HR. Their latest wheeze was to announce that, in the light of falling sales, we would have to sack even more sales people. While digesting this nugget, I read the second epistle from HR proudly announcing their newly augmented organisation chart with considerably more bodies than the sales department had in the entire country.

"I found myself another job within the month."

Good on Barry.

But let's look at it another way. Who had to find another job? Who stayed?

TODAY'S management is invariably driven by the new managerialism and you can be certain that wherever a company boasts a lusty, strapping HR department, there too will you find managerialism showing its muscle.

In the early Eighties, an interest in managerialism for me meant reading a handbook called *Strategies for Women at Work* each night before I went to sleep so I could work more fruitfully as a deputy for my English editor the next day. Neither of its authors, Janice LaRouche[6] and Regina Ryan, had been near an MBA: one called herself a career strategist and the other was a veteran of publishing, an excellent forum in which to learn practically how to distinguish between the baddies and the good. After all this time, it's still the simple, commonsense book I'd recommend to anyone who wants to work hard and well but is flummoxed by office politics, complications and predicaments.

By the end of the century, though, things were very different. Managerialism was now a vast semi-cult, taking up metres of space on bookshop shelves, commandeering hours of course time in universities and infiltrating organisations the way legionnaire's disease goes through air-conditioning systems. In this environment, anyone who was an editor or a semi-executive on the up and up would get regular phone calls from HR, demanding to know if they were going to attend a managing-staff away-day or a leadership seminar hosted by one of the top executives and run by consultants. There was a problem with this. It was called work. The seminars and away-days were almost always in work-time. If you suggested that you might be interested so long as you could go outside work hours, in your own time, you would be met with puzzlement. HR wouldn't respond. Perhaps they looked at each other and went: huh?

That wasn't playing the game. Managerialism is not about work, for heaven's sakes, it's about the appearance of work. It's about business degrees and remembering who wrote what book of management theory. God forbid that anyone should put their daily workload and company business ahead of doing leadership exercises that didn't even apply specifically to their field (but would allow plenty of time to brown-nose and/or impress the bosses and the ever-alert HR guardians). Such exercises are parcelled up to work across all industries and are supposed to replace the old way of learning one's craft by watching good people do it.

The exercises are produced by the same managerial thinking that claims a CEO with an MBA, or some other degree that means he or she is well-versed in management technique and theory, can run a soft drink company as easily as he or she can run a pharmaceutical outfit. That is, that a man like Mark Scott, a former education bureaucrat who went into journalism with Fairfax newspapers in 1994 and who has no radio or television experience, can be appointed as managing director of the ABC. Scott has a degree in public administration from Harvard and it's reported that his shelves are stuffed with books on management theory.

A few days after his ABC appointment was announced in May 2006, he was interviewed on the public broadcaster's *Media Report*.[7] The programme also spoke to a management consultant, Tony Golsby-Smith, who had worked closely with Scott for the previous six years and saw himself, the programme reported, as something of a mentor.

Golsby-Smith had written his PhD thesis on pursuing the art of strategic conversation. I reproduce verbatim from *Media Report* his words on the subject and what he has taught Scott about it: "Well, Mark did one of our courses years ago; the course was on how to facilitate the strategic conversation. We have a model called the ABCD model, which creates an intellectual architecture for how to frame the conversations of change. We don't just have meetings, we have creative workshops where people actually map conversations and capture them and synthesise them. We have a process of involving what we call the voices of change, three voices of change, which are important in any big system, that is, the voice of intent, the voice of design and the voice of experience. There are a lot of toolkits there, as well as quite a bit of theory, which I just alluded to briefly. You can sum up my doctorate as: the Western world bought the wrong thinking system from Aristotle, which was a bummer of an investment. And I think Mark's across all those ideas, and I'd have to say we've trained lots of people as facilitators, it's probably the hottest, it's the toughest gig you can get, standing in front of a group of people without preparation, trying to guide and facilitate their ideas, and he's certainly among the most talented people we taught at that. He's a natural at it."

I apologise for the length, but better to hear it from the man himself than for me to try and describe these thoughts. I'll leave it to you to judge.

Meanwhile, my favourite quote about the rise of the ubiquitous MBA is this one from the head of Sydney Grammar, Dr John Vallance, who, in a speech at the University of Sydney in 2002, predicted: "When someone comes to write the history of institutional life in the late twentieth century, I think it likely that the cult of the Harvard Business School, the MBA, the idea that management is a science and that its practitioners can turn their minds to running anything, even universities, will be roundly discredited."

Managerialism has dressed itself up in jargon and double-speak and woof-woof language as well as expensive clothes, high-powered cars and BlackBerrys. It does a very good job of looking much, much smarter and cleverer than it is. When PricewaterhouseCoopers investigated the $360 million foreign exchange currency scandal at the National Australia Bank and reported in early 2004, it found in the bank's culture "that there was an excessive focus on process, documentation and procedure manuals rather than on understanding the substance of issues, taking responsibility and resolving matters".[8] Managerialism may be spoken of with scorn in speeches, in the media, in books and in commentary, and is the butt of cartoonists and comic strips like *Dilbert*, but that has not stopped its spread. Like the people who do well out

Huh?

Thirty-year-old New Zealander Sam Morgan sold his online auction site TradeMe to the John Fairfax newspaper group for $620 million. After being exposed to high-level management- and business speak at Fairfax headquarters, he said on radio that the meeting was full of "stuff I don't really understand; half-yearly results ... I feel as though I've been through a washing machine."
THE AUSTRALIAN, MARCH 9, 2006.

of something-nothingness, these spanking new managers have been able to claim they have a rightful home anywhere they choose. They will not give up such fantastic privilege easily.

Web-logger and economist John Quiggin spells out how companies under the influence of managerialism work: "The main features of managerialist policy are incessant organisational restructuring, sharpening of incentives and expansion in the number, power and remuneration of senior managers, with a corresponding downgrading of the role of skilled workers and particularly of professionals."[9]

Before I read that, spoke to Quiggin and understood it was all part of some well-theorised *über*-plan, I had already put together for myself a summary of what I thought had happened to professionals in companies over the last fifteen or so years. I had watched, in my own business, twenty-six-year-old marketing managers talking over the top of editors, and noted, with amazement, the failure of a newspaper company like Fairfax, for instance, to appoint anyone with editorial experience to its board. When young Lachlan Murdoch moved to Sydney in 1995 to become, first, publisher of *The Australian* and, then, deputy CEO of News Limited, his arrival coincided with that of tribes of spunky little people in neat suits. I don't know if he'd had them packed away in his suitcases or what, but overnight, they were everywhere – although not anywhere any time after 6 pm when the real, frantic work began on the company's newspapers. But then, there they'd be first thing next morning, ordering their lattes from the newly installed barista bar.

It wasn't just in the media, though. I started seeing a hangdog look on all sorts of people who used to think their creative efforts or their skills meant they mattered to their bosses. Slowly and surely, the people who perhaps had once helped create and grow companies (or a university or a library or a government department's reputation) either by creating an exciting product or researching or developing a new process or just doing the skilled professional work necessary, started losing their status and power. Their work, naturally, could sometimes be a hit-and-miss thing, troublesome and unpredictable. It took staff. It took time. It took resources.

In short, their efforts always needed money. The failures (there is no successful creation without failure) didn't look good on annual reports either, or in board meetings. And because they knew their stuff, they also had an annoying habit of being wet blankets about guaranteed whiz-bang, cost-cutting bonanzas.

The new darlings became those who used to be in support roles. These were the accountants and financial officers who could cut staff and/or costs and whose positions, always strong, became stronger and stronger as the markets, concentrating on short-term share value, responded to their profit-boosting quick fixes. As the fortunes of research and development and the denizens of what is loosely called the shop floor sank, those of accounting, marketing, corporate communications, finance, legal and human resources all rose.

Within just a few years, this has had a remarkable effect. The expression "on the line", which means being accountable, comes from the notion that there were certain employees in "line jobs". They were demanding high-pressure roles and their success was easily measured and apparent, and they carried rewards because it was understood that without the right people in those "line jobs", the company, gallery, museum or department wouldn't exist.

Now it's the administration areas, it's HR, marketing and so on, which have seen massive recruiting. While those areas bulged out of their floor space and took up ever more of a company's budget, the budget and floor space allocated to the creators and the skilled shrank. At Fairfax, for instance, an analyst complained in late 2005 that of 5,000 staff, only 900 were journalists.[10] The real figures turn out to be closer to 4,000 and 900, but those 900 keep the whole shebang on the road; meanwhile, 500 Fairfax staffers are devoted to such non-journalist areas as HR, marketing, finance and IT.

It's power and money and the promise of both that drive the new airheadism. No wonder then that it has so many recruits willing to turn a blind eye to the kind of managerial nonsense that even Blind Freddie should be able to spot.

In September 2004, the Commonwealth Scientific and Industrial Research Organisation (CSIRO) flew seventy science "communicators" to luxurious South Stradbroke Island for a two-day conference. These communicators were part of the huge staff the CSIRO employs to handle media, internal communications and so on. The conference cost $70,000, and a magician – *que*? – was flown in to take part.[11]

The story broke nearly a year later, and within two months of it, the organisation announced it would cut up to a quarter of its research support staff, that is, about 200 of the total of 780 jobs in that unglamorous but vital area. (The CSIRO employs about 6,500 full-time staff – about 1,000 fewer than it did ten years ago.)

Earlier that year, 2005, Labor senator Kim Carr had hopped into CSIRO chief executive Geoff Garrett at a senate estimates hearing over revelations that the

Totally

"I was also surprised – and disgusted – by the constant victim-blaming you encounter among [career] coaches, at networking events for the unemployed and in the business-advice books. You're constantly told that whatever happens to you is the result of your attitude or even your 'thought forms' – not a word about the corporate policies that lead to so much turmoil and misery."
AMERICAN AUTHOR BARBARA EHRENREICH ON THE TRIALS OF WHITE-COLLAR WORKERS TRYING TO FIND A JOB IN CORPORATE AMERICA.

organisation's media manager, Donna Staunton, was being paid $330,000. She had handled corporate relations in the tobacco industry as well as once heading the Tobacco Institute of Australia. Mid-level CSIRO scientists were earning $67,000 and senior scientists about $100,000. Garrett himself is on a salary of $479,000, according to figures released in mid-2006.

Under Garrett, who started in 2001, the CSIRO was pushed firmly into the world of economic rationalism and managerialism. Executive-sounding titles multiplied. Complicated reorganisations were announced. It went from being "a research-based institution, generally perceived as working for the public good"[12] and funded by taxpayers, to being an institution that had to make money to fund an increasing portion of its scientific research. That is, it was supposed to become a business and operate like a business, and this at a time of real national need for the best possible scientific advice, without fear or favour, on matters such as sustainability, fossil fuels, water usage and global warming. In 2003, the CSIRO restructured so it could pursue six "flagship" initiatives, designed with federal government priorities and commercial partnerships in mind.

Before Garrett's arrival, the CSIRO, which had been taking budget cuts since the early Eighties, had been comfortably earning between 20 and 30 percent of its total income from doing targeted research on contract. Garrett's role, according to his federal minister, was to be a "change merchant". He told a delighted federal government he would need less funding because he would get the CSIRO to generate much more – 50 percent more – of its income from external contracts. The original target, which soon became wobbly, was an extra $400 million in income.

The CSIRO soon began to post regular deficits and to receive constant negative national media coverage. In its annual report for 2004-05, it showed a loss of more than $9 million, up from $5 million the year before. For 2006, the government approved a predicted deficit of close to $15 million. As for the promised increases in external earnings, there is an hilarious exchange between Labor senator Penny Wong and the CSIRO bosses during the May 2006 senate estimates committee hearings.[13] She wanted to know how three years of deficits could indicate an organisation in a "robust financial position", as the bosses in front of her were putting it. The senator clearly felt she was in Humpty-Dumpty territory.

Senator Wong: "So you have a position where your deficits are increasing over the last three years, yes?"

[Chief financial officer for the CSIRO, Mike] Whelan: "Mathematically, yes, that is correct."

Senator Wong [who could have been excused for thinking she was starring in *The Office*]: "What do you mean by 'mathematically'?"

And so on.

One of Garrett's favourite sayings to explain his revolutionary approach to management used to be: "If it ain't broke, break it." Hearing that made me feel much the way the senator probably felt as she worked her way through the CSIRO's finances. In the end, the CSIRO didn't record a deficit for the 2005-06 year, but a wee profit of $300,000, reportedly due to a sudden surge in intellectual property revenue. That must have surprised many concerned, given that as late as May 31, 2006, at the senate estimate hearings, even Whelan, the CFO, was anticipating a deficit, albeit a lower one than approved.

Announcing the profit to staff in late August, Garrett said, "We have continued to make solid progress across the range of dimensions against which our performance can be tracked." He also congratulated staff on their splendid efforts. The staff association's secretary, Pauline Gallagher, responded snappily the next day, pointing out in an email to members that staff were getting a raw deal in a number of areas, from the rearrangement of research resources to a rise in the proportion of staff on fixed contracts, to site closures, unexpected job losses and uncertainty over the futures of support staff. She wrote, "In such a successful year, it is disappointing that the trust staff have placed in the Executive has not been returned."

Funnily enough, as the CSIRO under Garrett had launched itself into the market like an emu trying to fly, the numbers of staff on super-high salaries had just kept growing. The 2004-05 annual report revealed that where there had been five staffers earning more than $320,000, now there were nine. In the six years to June 2004, corporate management positions more than doubled, while 316 people were dumped from research projects (and whereas back in 1989, administration used to take up nearly 30 percent of this country's expenditure on research and development nationally, now it takes up just under 50 percent).[14]

"The mechanic has become more important than the creator," Michael Borgas, president of the CSIRO staff association, said to me. As for managerialism, the $330,000 media manager's most memorable moment, before stepping down in mid-2006, was being involved in a move that effectively banned access to freelance journalist Peter Pockley, an outspoken expert on the troubled and struggling organisation. The ban lasted nearly a year, and a senate committee questioned Garrett vigorously over this "peculiar" decision.[15]

There were also serious allegations that scientists were being "gagged" by management from publicly discussing issues like climate change and energy research, a story carried first by ABC-TV's *Four Corners* programme and then by the prestigious *Nature* magazine in February 2006. A CSIRO chief denied scientists were being censored, but said staff needed to tread warily. By mid-2006, after much public criticism, Garrett had announced a more open policy on public comment.

Borgas wrote in early 2006 in *Australasian Science*: "A business model, or even the appearance of a compliant, unquestioning, propaganda-driven organisation, is not an acceptable strategy for CSIRO." But, as he had written in *The Age*, almost all CSIRO appointments in the 2004-05 financial year were either fixed-term or casual, leading to a culture of insecurity, where people simply kept their heads down.[16]

Science journalist Julian Cribb, a former head of public affairs at the CSIRO, puts it all in historical context: "Part of the original rationale for the CSIRO was a serious attempt to understand the nature of this country. It produced the knowledge we need so we can live here for the next thousand years."

If it can happen at the CSIRO, one of Australia's most loved and trusted institutions because of its once pure dedication to science and the good of the nation, it can happen in any corporate or institution. "Line-people" have been turned into the pointy bit of an inverted pyramid. A culture of expertise has been turned into a culture of managerialism, which means the experts and creators now have to work harder and harder to support the huge edifice above them. Even a ten-year-old who can add up can see the problem and what will happen eventually.

But "eventually" is the key word because it can take such a long time to arrive. By then, almost everybody prominent will have moved on, from the CEOs and top management to begin with, and then the swarms of HR personnel, consultants, spin doctors, company doctors, accountants, marketing managers, product managers, all those people who rose to power while the "producers" and "creators" saw their numbers cut, their budgets sliced and their influence wane or vanish.

HR people often claim that on this managerial totem pole, they rank lowest (although above the line-people, of course). But HR is what actually allows the totem pole to operate at all, for it's HR that regulates everything that has a pulse.

MY ORIGINAL 2005 essay on airheads attracted plenty of email, including one from an HR professional who works for a global management consulting company. She was obviously put out by my comments on her business. Not that she told me so. I picked it from the slightly bullying tone of her email, couched in just the right "do tell" language. She wanted details of my research, my "related work", so that she could understand how I had "made the link with HR and airheads".

I was able to reply in serious detail, giving my

Que?

"[BHP Billiton boss] Chip Goodyear has decided he can't live without a 'chief human capital and excellence officer' … We think the job used to be called Group Vice President Human Resources and before that, Head of Personnel but really, how yesterday."
CBD COLUMN,
THE SYDNEY MORNING HERALD, SEPTEMBER 5, 2005.

sources and citing the work of academics here and in the United States. Ms HR, who by the way, didn't at any stage reveal she was in HR – I learned that only from her employer's switchboard – then wanted me to refer her to an electronic version of my story to circulate, but I wasn't able to help her with that. I did ask her for an interview, though. Clearly, she was someone who knew the subject well, had hands-on experience, very likely had a different point of view from mine and so would make a good and valuable interviewee. I didn't hear from her. I sent her a follow-up request four months later, but again, no reply. Finally, seven months after my first request, she acknowledged that, yes, indeed, she was still alive and promised to think about an interview. A week later, she declined the invitation.

That's HR as I know it so well. Bullying and then retreating. Refusing to take part in thoughtful discussion. The iron hand in the velvet glove with its grip so very often around the wrong neck. And of course, in these cost-cutting times, it has to be expected that sometimes the velvet is pretty thin or is never there at all.

Under former CEO David Murray, for instance, the Commonwealth Bank aggressively restructured, so that during his 13 years at the top ending in September 2005, 20,000 staff lost their jobs and 600 branches closed. Murray's programme, instituted as the bank privatised in stages, produced strong financial results and a share price that went from an initial float of $5.40 to about $38 just before he stepped down. But in late 2005, CBA management copped a vigorously worded serve from a federal court judge. It was over a case in which some 250 bank staff had been asked to resign so they could be re-employed on individual contracts by CommSec, another company controlled by the bank. These staff managed the accounts of the bank's more affluent customers. The CBA and the Finance Sector Union, which brought the case, now disagree point-blank with each other's details of what disadvantages would or would not have been involved for the workers but, in the federal court, Justice Merkel described the bank's action as "essentially an industrial regulation-avoidance scheme [which] possesses an ingenuity that is reminiscent of the tax-avoidance schemes of the 1970s". The bank had operated "solely in pursuit of its self interest and profit ... without proper regard for the legality of its conduct".

Justice Merkel ordered the bank to offer re-employment with CBA to the 73 staff who had agreed to transfer and to pay $750,000 to the union, a record fine. The CBA immediately issued a press release saying it disagreed with the court's reasoning and believed the penalties were excessive. It also said it took its employment obligations very seriously. The bank's appeal against the judgment was heard by the federal court of appeal in Melbourne in mid-August 2006. The decision had been reserved as this book was going to press.

About the same time as the Merkel decision, the CBA released a grooming guide to staff to accompany the arrival of new uniforms, provided free to those who served customers directly. Advice ran from staff being told to get regular haircuts, wear flesh-coloured knickers preferably and to trim their nose-hair. Women were advised not to wear shiny stockings because they made legs "look larger". The media fell with pleasure on the story and the embarrassed bank was quick to apologise and to say the guidelines were just that, a guide.

In early 2006, CBA's new CEO, Ralph Norris, made customer service a top priority.[17] You'd have to think that would involve making the staff happier as well. A few months earlier, the union had expressed the view that outgoing CEO Murray hadn't got it quite right when he cited a Gallup survey that showed good staff satisfaction levels. An independent survey, conducted by McNair Ingenuity Research for the union, found 20 percent of staff said they had been encouraged to be positive in the staff survey and another 50 percent said they'd felt pressure to be falsely positive. Not surprisingly, as Murray bowed out of the bank – with his retirement payout of between $22 million and $28 million – he made a point of targeting the union. He said it had let its members down.

Since Norris's arrival, a bank spokesperson says, staff satisfaction levels have continued to rise. The truth is that the CBA has had a history of tension between a once highly unionised, ex-public sector staff and management, and the bank, for whatever reason, has been touchy and aggressive about that in the past.

In November 2005, Nine's *Sunday* programme[18] ran a piece about John Howard's industrial revolution, mentioning the move of top management and HR personnel from the mining industry into organisations such as Telstra and the Commonwealth Bank. One thrust of *Sunday*'s story was that the ideology that drove the tactics used in mining to break tough unions and get workers onto individual contracts was now being used elsewhere. John Ralph, former CEO and deputy chairman of CRA, went to the board of the Commonwealth and later became its chair. In 1996, Les Cupper, who had run HR at CRA, now Rio Tinto, joined the same bank to run human resources, or rather, People Services. By all accounts, he is an exceptionally charming man. I would have liked to talk to him about all this, but was told by the bank that Cupper's background wasn't relevant. In any case, in early August 2006, Norris announced Cupper's retirement, although said he would continue to consult to the bank. At the time of Merkel's judgment, a union rep had plaintively hoped the bank would have another look at the way it handled its staff, although CBA maintains it has always treated employees correctly. In June, the bank's new CEO had announced a range of additional well-being initiatives for staff, including flexible leave alternatives and child-care places. Norris described them in a press release as "some of the most significant to support bank staff in the past decade". He said later, "If we get staff right, we get the customers right and therefore get the shareholders right."

Ohmigod

When HR is applied with too much force and rigour, its jargon, its forms and its legalism may operate as effectively for crowd control as a private

---

Managers of a new DIY warehouse in Scotland, part of the B&Q chain, decided staff would be much happier if, instead of wishing each other "good morning", they sang lines from a song called "Mahna Mahna", from the first *Muppet Show* series screened in 1976. After hearing the first line, the staff were to be encouraged to reply with the chorus: "Do doo be-do-do". One worker told *The Scotsman*, "The staff had just returned from lunch and all the managers were in a training room, sitting in a semi-circle and looking really pleased with themselves. Then one of them blurted out 'Mahna Mahna' at us without warning. We just stared blankly back at them. Then another manager repeated the phrase, and asked what our first reaction was when we heard it. When someone mumbled back 'do doo be-do-do', they all burst out laughing and were nodding at each other, saying, 'Told you so.' " When other staff in existing stores got to hear of the proposed morning routine, they refused to transfer to the new store. A spokesman defended the team-building exercise, saying it was part of making the warehouse chain a fun place to work.

police force. Just before Christmas 2005, journalists at John Fairfax went on strike over a round of redundancies. The strike was declared illegal, and the Industrial Relations Commission told the strikers to return to work. Fairfax HR got to work with the zeal of immigration officials doing a raid in Chinatown. So assiduous were they in rounding up the recalcitrants that they rang a woman who hadn't been employed full-time at Fairfax since 1991. Her last job with the company, as a casual, had ended two years before. (She had hoped that job would become permanent, but there had been a job freeze on.) But this time, HR staff were not to be dissuaded from their belief that she belonged with them. There was a phone call during which she was informed that, according to their records, she was still on the payroll and that she was a senior section editor and she must get back to work. News to her, and to her bank account. In some bemusement, but taking it in good spirit, she said that of course she'd co-operate but they might need to find her a job and could she please finish her Christmas shopping first. The next day, there was a stern text-message and a message left on her answer-machine.

Given that her husband, now an executive at News Limited, had also once worked for Fairfax, I guess it was just luck that they didn't both get chivvied. Delightedly, her husband's newspaper ran a report on this little saga of ineptitude.

NONE OF this, of course, is what HR and people management are supposed to be about. There are many in the profession, and also in fields such as organisational behaviour, who lament what is happening and point out the invidious position too many HR professionals now find themselves in.

The profession does have its clear thinkers who can see exactly what's going on and what should be done. HR expert Thomas Kochan, of the Institute for Work and Employment Research at the Massachusetts Institute of Technology, explains that while the old contract that promised long-term job and financial security might no longer be viable in the modern economy, a new social contract at work has to be rebuilt.

In an address[19] to the University of Sydney in 2003, Kochan was blunt. His theme was that the HR profession faced a crisis of trust and a loss of legitimacy, and that "HR professionals [have] lost any semblance of credibility as a steward of the social contract because [they have] lost their ability to seriously challenge or offer an independent perspective on the policies and practices of the firm". He argued that

HR, too often "perfect agents" for chief executives, had a responsibility to balance the needs of the firm with the needs, interests and aspirations of the workforce, to build an employment system that was fair and equitable to all.

If my experience and that of my friends and colleagues is anything to go on, Kochan is whistling in the dark. Does he really think HR will risk all its perks and powers for the sake of ethics, the community and the long term? Fat chance. Jo Mithen, head of the Australian Human Resources Institute, based in Melbourne, is fervent in her defence of HR and what good HR can achieve, but she also feels a little beaten by what she sees happening around her. "They get overly caught up with being HR professionals and forget they are part of the business first. There's all this mucking around ticking boxes with too much focus on what can't be done instead of providing solutions to enable the things that should be done." She talks of the necessity for good systems to be set up to protect transparency, decency, honesty and respect, and to look after both the short-term and the long-term interests of the company. If such systems are in place, companies can only benefit, she says. She believes HR should always be alert, warning against incentivisation share-based packages for CEOs that reward short-term thinking, for instance, and counselling against wholesale downsizing. To me, she sounds first, like the ideal person to be running an HR department and, second, like very, very few practising HR people I've ever met.

In a paper on Kochan's theories and the role of HR in the Australian workplace,[20] Sydney University academics Russell Lansbury and Marian Baird also worried about the profession. Australian researchers had noticed emerging problems in the workplace which many in HR have chosen to ignore, especially those to do with greater inequity between workers and employers. Citing a number of research papers, Baird and Lansbury wrote, and this was in 2004: "Australians who are in full-time jobs are generally working longer and more intensively than previously, and many have less secure jobs than in the past. Much of the growth in employment over the past decade has been in jobs which are casual and part-time or for a limited duration. Australia currently has one of the highest proportions of 'atypical' or non-full-time employees in its labour force in the industrialised world. A more decentralised regulatory system of work and employment relations has removed many of the safeguards and protections for workers which existed under the previous system of awards and collective agreement … The Australian Workplace Industrial Relations

Survey (AWIRS) in the mid-1990s revealed that approximately half of the workforce reported increases over the previous 12 months in work effort, the pace of work and stress levels. Extended working hours have been shown to have health and safety risks for individuals as well as negative effects on family relationships, children and communities. Long hours lead to fatigue, stress and undermine social relationships, particularly when they are irregular, unpredictable and workers are poorly paid. Workers' compensation data in New South Wales shows that stress claims were the fastest growing and largest single cause of occupational disease during the 1990s, particularly among white-collar workers."[21]

Kochan already recognises that HR in the United States certainly can't be doing its job, given the massive leaps in CEO compensation. (It's worth noting here that studies are gradually trickling out proving that CEO salary often has no relationship to a company's performance.[22] There is also strong criticism of a corporate buddy-buddy culture that basically allows CEOs to influence decisions on how much they're paid.) In his address, Kochan quoted a survey of HR professionals that confirms pretty much what most of us observers and critics know.

When a bunch of them in the States were asked in the late Nineties to rank their profession's most important goals and priorities, the first six of just seven points they cited were all to do with the needs of either their organisations or themselves. The workforce didn't get a look-in until the seventh point and even then it was the anodyne aim of "addressing the diversity challenge". Other

Totally

"Performance targets are open to considerable manipulation. As is well recognised, carefully timed announcements of staff cut-backs can also serve as a powerful share price stimulant and it appears to be far from coincidental that past and present Business Council of Australia CEOs with the most to gain from share options and rights have also been among the most committed practitioners of workforce downsizing. Accounting-based hurdles are also open to manipulation. For instance, with profit-based targets, the executive may artificially inflate paper profits by postponing infrastructure investment or cutting back on research and development."
ECONOMIST JOHN SHIELDS IN A PAPER ON AUSTRALIAN CEO SALARIES, "SETTING THE DOUBLE STANDARD".

priorities ahead of that included such uplifting concerns as "reinventing the HR function to be a more customer-focused, cost-justified organisation" and "attracting and developing the next generation of twenty-first-century leaders and executives".

Not much room for the little fellas there. Do they even realise they are there? Seems not.

CHAPTER 9

Accountable (Or Not)

"Are you a complete fool, Mr Lindberg?"
"No, I am not a complete fool."

EXCHANGE BETWEEN SENIOR COUNSEL AND AUSTRALIAN
WHEAT BOARD CEO ANDREW LINDBERG DURING THE 2006
COLE INQUIRY INTO KICKBACKS TO SADDAM HUSSEIN

I am the first person to complain about anything. I know this only because whenever I do complain, I am nearly always told that no-one else has complained. "You're the first person to complain about that," says the voice on the phone from the call centre, sounding like a slightly ruffled hostess at a Fifties Tupperware party who has spotted the cheese cubes being disturbed. It doesn't matter if I am complaining about the lack of ATMs, a lid that is impossible to remove or a mail-order website, I am Robinson Crusoe or so they would like me to believe.

When, in late 2004, I complained to my bank that I was sick and tired of the way they kept closing down branches, I got the same reaction. Even cranky me, ready to acknowledge my easily aroused crankiness, found that hard to believe. Between 1996 and 2004, Australian banks went down by almost 1,600 branches. Nevertheless, Ms Westpac Call Centre wanted me to believe I was the first human being to have raised a peep to her about it.

"We haven't had any other complaints," she said stoutly, prissing up the Jatz biscuits thrown into disarray by my rude and sweatily angry phone call. I had trudged across two suburbs in early summer heat, from the closed-down branch in one to the now unexpectedly closed-down branch in the other. I wanted to deal with real live humans so another slog was obviously ahead. Now I was being asked to believe that Australians hadn't noticed their local branches closing down while bank profits in the same period doubled or tripled and the salaries of their chief executives hiked up by even more.

Really?

"Customers who rang the helpline of one of Britain's biggest cable television companies were shocked to be told to 'f*** off'," the Press Association reported. A disgruntled customer, who had been kept on hold for an hour by the company, had worked out by chance how to change the recorded message on NTL's customer service line. So he did, turning it into a tirade that basically told NTL's customers that the company didn't give a f*** about their complaints, so "just f*** off and leave us alone!" Better still, magistrates dismissed charges against the customer, deciding that although the message was offensive, it wasn't "grossly offensive".

A bit later on, I asked the same bank about its ATM policy. This is the bank that paid its CEO $7.5 million in the 2004-05 year but is so stingy with its branded ATM machines that in my whole inner-city suburb, there is only one. If I must use another bank's ATM to access my funds, my bank socks me a $2 fee. You can't get much more of a twenty-first-century airhead paradox than being charged by your bank for not using a service that the bank tries not to provide.

It's strange that in a society where you and I are so answerable for everything we do and must fill in countless forms and provide endless numbers in order to do almost anything, the powers that be are strangely unaccountable. Pinning them down on anything can be like trying to swat your way through mosquito netting. There's a muzziness abroad that paralyses the capacity for linear thinking. Westpac's call centre explains to me that of course I have to do without their ATMs because there are so many shops that dispense cash with Eftpos in my inner-city area. I can feel logic and commonsense evaporating like a haze in the desert. Were they ever there in the first place? Sometimes it just seems impossible for the average person to get a grip on what's actually happening around them. That's not by chance.

If, like my bank with its all-but-non-existent ATMs, you have enough power or money, you don't actually have to give rational answers. Or any answers at all.

In late 1996, Alan Bond, the man who won the America's Cup for Australia and then gave the country its largest case of corporate fraud, pleaded guilty to siphoning off $1.2 billion. His trial had had the nation rolling its eyes because of his continual memory lapses. A psychologist finally declared that the fraudster didn't have the brain power to run a corner store. Sentenced to four years in jail, increased on appeal to seven, the vague-minded bankrupt got going with a High Court challenge on a technicality, was out of jail by early 2000 and soon back in business.

Bond continues to maintain that both his IQ and memory had suffered because of stress, depression, medication and tiny strokes. In one media outing, he managed to pull off sounding both very vague and very definite at the same time. Defending himself to Andrew Denton in an interview on ABC-TV for *Enough Rope*,[1] he said: "That's a standard joke around town: 'Got your memory back?' But the reality is that I was, and I'd had enormous pressure and the system was … er, had stopped. I was on heavy medication. Um, I was … I had been in a, um … in with a psychologist and I'd been hospitalised for a week prior to this and I was in a pretty difficult position, quite frankly."

Bond proved to be a trendsetter. More than a decade later, at the Cole Inquiry into the Australian Wheat Board scandal over $300 million worth of kickbacks to Iraq leader Saddam Hussein, the board's CEO, Andrew Lindberg, used the terms "I don't know" and "I can't recall" 250 times in his first three days. This from a man with a base salary package of almost $900,000 with bonuses taking him close to the $2 million mark. Counsel finally asked in exasperation: "Are you a complete fool, Mr Lindberg?"

Within two months, everyone from various Wheat Board officials to the Foreign Minister and on up to the Deputy Prime Minister and the Prime Minister had appeared before the inquiry and, according to crikey.com, between them, had answered questions 1,757 times with phrases such as "I can't recall", "Not to my knowledge", "I don't know", "I'm not across that detail", "I'm not sure", "I'm not certain" and "Not that I'm aware of". (The PM, reported AAP, put it this way: "I believe that I did not receive or read any of the relevant cables at any time during the relevant period.")

A few months earlier, on November 23, 2005, Rupert Murdoch's son Lachlan confessed in the New South Wales Supreme Court that his memory banks were also empty when it came to recalling what had happened in various crucial meetings associated with the collapse of telco One.Tel, which went down in mid-2001, owing $600 million. Murdoch had sworn in an affidavit that he had been at a crucial meeting in January 2001 on the telco's finances and the minutes recorded him being there via telephone conference call. Now he wasn't sure. A diary note had been found that conflicted with that. "I cannot say with confidence whether I was at the meeting or not," he said.

In all, as *The Australian Financial Review* calculated, the younger Murdoch uttered the words "I don't recall" 205 times on his second day in the stand when being questioned on One.Tel board meetings and other discussions that might have taken place on management and financial issues.[2] By then, even the presiding judge was getting tired of it: "Mr Murdoch, could you listen carefully to the questions before you answer them? Sometimes the answer 'I do not recall' is not an answer to the question asked."

Astoundingly, what Lachlan did admit in the Supreme Court was that when he and his father invested $380 million followed by another $200 million of shareholder funds in One.Tel, they did so without News Limited conducting any formal due diligence.

The collapse of One.Tel coincided with the decision by News Limited management to close down *The Australian's Review of Books*, a monthly giveaway with *The Australian*. Begun with Australia Council funding in 1996, the review had provided a rare space at the time in Australia's mainstream media for long pieces on ideas and books.[3] Management's decision to close it was a blow. A sub-editor, coming back from having a fag up in the roof garden of News's Sydney headquarters, found herself sharing the lift with Lachlan.

"You're the bloke who's made me lose my job," she said upfront. "Are you sure you don't want to change your mind about closing the *ARB*?"

"We had to close it," said Lachlan. "It was costing us a million dollars a year."

"Really," replied the sub quickly. "Well, if you hadn't put your money into One.Tel, we could have kept it going for another 500 years."

YOU WOULD think an airhead world would be the last thing in simplicity but it's the very opposite. Sometimes it feels as if we all went to bed one night in the mid-Nineties and woke up next day living inside a quadratic equation, and trying to make sense of it. Things don't add up. Nothing is ever quite what it seems. Nor is it easy to find anything out. To paraphrase the Bush adviser at the White House: that's not how things work any more. Reality is what you want to make it. (Well, at least if you have the clout to pull that off.)

Once upon a time there was a principle that people explained themselves. Sometimes other people disagreed with the explanations, raising

Que?

Channel Seven suffered a power surge that blacked out fifteen minutes of mid-evening television viewing in April 2005. In spite of the fact there was nothing on screen, ratings figures showed – or purported to show – that more than 600,000 Australians were watching, *The Sydney Morning Herald* reported.

their eyebrows or reacting with displeasure. Sometimes the explanations just took everyone further down the route that leads at last to the bitter realisation of what a tangled web we weave when first we practise to deceive. But it was accepted that explanations, of some kind, had to be given. Then politician-speak caught on and the mantra "Never apologise, never explain" went from being a sure sign of an arrogant bluffer out for his own ends to apparently acceptable everyday behaviour. You don't exactly lie, you just don't say anything or you leave things out. You fudge or you deliver propaganda or even just plain bull-dust. You protect yourself. You also call it something else so that it sounds as if it's right for our times. Spin. Realpolitik. Good management. Looking out for the bottom line.

Or you declare it a matter of national security. By July 2005, the Bush administration was classifying 125 documents a minute to keep them out of the hands of interested parties. *The Guardian* reported that 15.6 million documents were classified in 2004, twice as many as in 2001. New classes of classified documents were created with vague titles such as "law enforcement sensitive" and "homeland security sensitive".

The odd, chilling thing, though, in this new airhead universe is that when bad things happen, and are found out, they're allowed to, somehow, just keep on happening. This isn't like American Ralph Nader blowing the whistle on dangerous cars in 1965 and thus, through public outrage, forcing the massive American car industry to produce, at higher cost, safer cars. This isn't like the media discovering the Watergate burglary and so a president is forced to resign to avoid impeachment. This isn't like the horrors and devastation of World War II after which world leaders emerged to agree that they should set in place programmes and legislation, checks and balances, and establish international organisations to get people and countries back on their feet and to prevent such events from happening again.

American journalist Mark Danner, who writes for *The New Yorker* and *The New York Review of Books*, has even come up with a name for what we're now seeing. He calls it "frozen scandal", which means, as he described in an interview,[4] that the expected steps in a scandal no longer happen. That is, we are used to seeing revelation, followed by investigation and then by expiation: the courts or government impose punishment so society can believe that the wrongdoing has been corrected and thus be reassured, and can go back to doing whatever it was doing before the scandal was revealed. Now, says Danner, there have been revelations in the United States of torture, illegal eavesdropping, domestic spying and cronyism, and, in Iraq, corruption, but no official investigation follows.

Here in Australia, we had the children overboard scandal of 2001 that saw lying and cover-up in the very top layers of government. The Prime Minister and the ministers for immigration and defence falsely accused refugees of throwing their children from their rickety fishing boat into the sea in order to get asylum. In early 2006, journalist David Marr, co-author of a book on the case, sharply picked up the PM when Howard casually remarked to *The Age* that "and they did after all sink the boat, didn't they?" No, said Marr, "wrong again, Prime Minister" and he outlined in print for the record, and for what must have felt like the umpteenth time, what had really happened and what the refugees had done and how the overloaded boat had begun to break up as it was towed by HMAS Adelaide.

In his interview, Danner remarked on the way the US government did not properly investigate scandals or, if it did, it was the little people who got punished, not the policy-makers, who remained in their jobs. In Sydney, the same thing happened with the disastrous state-government-approved cross-city tunnel in 2005. With the city in a furore over the toll set by the private tunnel operators, it was the head of the roads department who found himself forced to resign, not the various ministers who had approved and overseen the money-grubbing project. Danner described a process with which we are getting too familiar: "… it's as if we're this spinning wheel, constantly confirming facts that we already knew, so the revelations become less and less effective in causing public outrage. The public begins to become inured to it, corrupted in its turn."

Journalist William Greider, who writes for *The Nation*, examined what happened when Citigroup paid $US2 billion compensation to Enron investors.[5] Financiers at Citigroup and other banks had helped Enron pull off its accounting tricks. Citigroup had already had to pay out $2.65 billion for its role in the WorldCom shemozzle, the largest accounting fraud in history. But, revealed Greider, the Wall Street bank had set aside $9.8 billion for such contingencies and, as it was earning $5 billion every quarter, the costs would be easily spread over years and attract tax deductions anyway. "No contrition required; pay out some money, get on with business … criminal behaviour is defined downward into a manageable cost of doing business," Greider wrote. He called the process "a huge, all-service, guilt-free money machine", the creation of "modern bankerly imagination".

As for when the PM seemingly vagues out over the precise details of the children-overboard case, what he's really saying to us is: whatever.

People in the hot seat confidently take the ostrich position – head in sand – without worrying too much about a kick in the rear. This spreading tendency to vague out is a massive undermining of the principles of accountability on which our society is based. But people in a variety of jobs at a variety of levels now regularly retreat to the looking-blank defence.

In the midst of the furore over the Australian government's $50 million spend to promote the new industrial relations legislation of 2006, WorkChoices, a lucky doctor confided to the media that he had been paid a very handsome few thousand of taxpayers' dollars to appear in one of

Huh?

"Fourteen percent of Australian students had more than 500 books in their home, about a fifth had each [sic] of 201 to 500 books and 101 to 200 books; about a third had 26 to 100 books; about a tenth had 11 to 25 books and five per cent has no more than 10 books in their home ... On average, students from the Northern Territory had the lowest number of books in the home and students in the Australian Capital Territory had the highest ... Figure 6.4 shows the positive relationship between student performance and the number of books a student has in their home by indicating the mean performance in *mathematical literacy* for each of five categories of books in the home. The correlation coefficients between performance and the number of books in the home were approximately 0.30 for each of the three literacy domains and for problem-solving. On average, a student whose home had between 201 and 500 books scored 76 points higher in *mathematical literacy* and *reading literacy,* and 89 points higher in *scientific literacy* than a student who had between 11 and 25 books in their home. On average, students scored about 16, 15 and 13 points higher in *scientific literacy* performance, *mathematical literacy* performance and *reading literacy* performance respectively per increase in each category of the books in the home variable."

FROM *FACING THE FUTURE: A FOCUS ON MATHEMATICAL LITERACY AMONG AUSTRALIAN 15-YEAR-OLD STUDENTS* IN THE OECD'S PROGRAMME FOR INTERNATIONAL STUDENT ASSESSMENT (PISA), 2003.

the IR commercials – and he hadn't even made it to the screen in the end. When journalists attempted to speak to the head of the advertising agency involved, a spokesman simply responded by saying blankly: "We can't say anything."

On Australia Day 2006, someone at the ABC thought it would be a wheeze to air a send-up version of the national anthem during prime-time. The anthem was a clip from a mockumentary series and featured male comedian Chris Lilley dressed up as schoolgirl Ja'mie King soulfully turning the words and music of *Advance Australia Fair* into a joke. It screened at least twice during the evening. It was a massive misreading of the public, who reacted pretty much the way you might imagine the French, the Americans or the English might have reacted if an airhead at one of their public broadcasters had decided to send up *La Marseillaise*, *The Star-Spangled Banner* or *God Save The Queen* on July 14, July 4 or the Queen's Birthday.

The ABC got it in the neck and ABC-TV's media people assumed the ostrich position. My calls to the publicity department to find out more simply weren't returned, which is an interesting position for a taxpayer-funded organisation to take. Then I saw that an explanation of sorts had been given to a Sydney newspaper. Defiant to the end, the ABC's arts and entertainment chief, Courtney Gibson, told television reporter Michael Idato that "Ja'mie King is a very beautiful girl and a charity-minded citizen who gave our anthem her all on Australia Day. The ABC is sorry she has been misunderstood by some of our viewers."

Do you know why people in official capacity now respond like this? Because they can. Because they know we will wear out before they do. Whatever.

Good numbers in the market-driven economy, for instance, are supposed to justify anything from the presence of a reality television show full of boofheads showing their genitals to the spread of the Botox forehead. Bad numbers, conversely, are supposed to prove something shouldn't exist because the market isn't there. But then there are sagas like that of Sydney's cross-city tunnel, a classic huh? moment for the twenty-first century. Sydney, of all cities, bursting as it is with billionaires, millionaires, fledgling millionaires and wannabe millionaires, and tarred as it is with a convict history and a reputation for crass money-making, has been studiously swallowing the lessons of the market-driven economy for decades. Then came the privately run and funded tunnel, which was supposed to provide a fast and easy way for people to get across the city from east to west, west to east, bypassing the city's congested centre. The charge was steep: $3.56. People rebelled and refused to use the tunnel. Then it was discovered, way after the fact, that actually not that many cars had been in the habit of making those trips anyway; most just went into the city. Worse, residents from the areas around the new tunnel discovered that they could no longer easily use certain roads to get quickly to their destinations because those roads had been narrowed or closed-off to force motorists into the tunnel. This was in spite of the fact that these local residents couldn't access the tunnel without going kilometres out of their way to reach an entry point. They jacked up, too, especially when everyone started referring disparagingly to perfectly good routes as "rat-runs", as if the residents had, overnight, turned into vermin trying to evade well thought-out government policy.

The tunnel, which was supposed to teem with 90,000 motorists a day, was lucky if a third of that number used it. Meanwhile, a taxi trip between Darlinghurst and Double Bay that used to cost $11 went up to $18 because of the traffic jams above ground caused by changed road conditions. Overnight, the tunnel turned into an outrage. Scapegoats were sought. A range of government ministers and local politicians blustered through headlines and devastating media coverage that kept unearthing more and more signs of apparent collusion between government department and private operator at the expense of Sydney people.

Finally, nine months of fury and traffic jams later, the New South Wales government announced it would reopen thirteen closed roads. It was estimated the compensation to the tunnel operators might go as high as $100 million.

What I kept thinking through it all was: so where is a market-driven economy when you really need it?

By all the rules of market forces, the tunnel was a failure. People did not want to use it. The numbers revealed it, and would have done so in the earliest stages if anyone had cared enough to collect or assess them properly. That's when the real truth about market force and accountability in our new world was pushed, unwillingly, bad-temperedly and ungraciously into the light.

Market force is what benefits people who make money from it. Accountability is what you can get away with.

There are many such paradoxes around now. It all works brilliantly for some and not at all for others.

For the last decade, for instance, since the election of Prime Minister John Howard, the Business Council of Australia, whose CEOs control the largest and most important companies in the country, has campaigned loudly and self-righteously for more "competitive" labour costs. But here's the thing: between 1990 and 2005, the average full-time adult salary went up annually 4.2 percent (or 1.4 percent after adjusting for an average inflation rate of 2.8 percent) but the BCA's CEOs' salaries went up 13.5 percent (or 10.7 percent in real terms).[6] These CEO salary figures only reflect the cash component too; when long-term incentive plans are factored in, the annual rises are much higher. John Shields, senior lecturer in work and organisational studies at the University of Sydney's school of business, is the researcher responsible for this number-crunching. He says: "To reiterate, over the same period, for ordinary wage and salary earners, the real annual increase has been just 1.4 percent."[7] But it's the CEOs who are stomping around crossly on wage control. Just so long as it doesn't apply to them.

American billionaire Warren Buffett, revered for his commonsense and tough attitudes to business, put his finger on something when he wrote tersely in his annual letter for 2005 to his Berkshire Hathaway shareholders about CEO salaries: "Too often, executive compensation in the US is ridiculously out of line with performance ... The upshot is that a mediocre-or-worse CEO – aided by his hand-picked VP of human relations and a consultant from the ever-accommodating firm of Ratchet, Ratchet & Bingo – all too often receives gobs of money from an ill-designed compensation arrangement ... Huge severance payments, lavish perks and outsized payments for ho-hum performances often occur because comp[ensation]

Totally

"I was proudly involved in this very fine project, right up to my little, fat neck." FORMER NSW STATE TREASURER MICHAEL EGAN BOASTING ABOUT HIS ROLE IN SYDNEY'S UNPOPULAR PRIVATE-PUBLIC-PARTNERSHIP CROSS-CITY TUNNEL. EGAN LATER SIGNED ON WITH AN INVESTMENT GROUP THAT SPECIALISES IN SUCH DEALS.

committees have become slaves to comparative data ... yesterday's most egregious excesses become today's baseline."

How do they get away with it?

You are finally left with the distinct impression that those up there know something we don't. They do. This is the new way of things. Customers, staff and the public are out of the loop. Expecting answers, expecting service, expecting that someone might actually want to do the right thing by you or your money, custom, vote or employment can be seen as a bit of antiquated, fuddy-duddy, old-fashioned nonsense. So is expecting public officials and people in power to be accountable. To keep on as you are, trying to meet vagueness, blankness and illogicality with precision is to find yourself thrashing around for nothing. Vagueness takes us over the way ectoplasmic gloop envelops its victims in space monster films. If you fight back, you work yourself in deeper.

IN ANY CASE, we've got enough to occupy us. If life is airy at the top, in the more mundane levels of the atmosphere, people labour under a huge weight of regulation and accountability like Hebrew slaves hauling slabs for the Egyptian pyramids.

Documentation, for instance. Nothing happens easily any more. When I notify my house insurance company that they need to note on my policy that I no longer have a mortgage on it, I'm told this can't be done over the phone; they have to sight the original letter from my bank stating this. (Why? What effect does this have on my insurance? Do they think I'm lying and that I'm going to run away in the dead of night with my house tucked neatly into a robber's large suitcase?) To renew my yearly residential parking permit with the council, I have to produce a number of documents to prove that I am still who I was twelve months ago. And as anyone who has applied to renew a passport knows, it is virtually impossible to get all the accompanying documentation right in one go. Sorry, says the official when it turns out you have omitted to include one tiny but vital proof, you'll have to go away and make another appointment. A close friend, born in Britain while his Australian parents were there on sabbatical, tells me that after living here all his life he's realised he must apply for Australian citizenship. I feel as if I am about to farewell Scott on his final trek to the Antarctic.

This is as nothing compared with the documentation required every day at work. Your bit of the office needs a new photocopier? The bureaucracy and time involved in making sure all forms have been filled out and signed, that all approvals have been got, that all costings have been done and compared, that all other avenues for acquiring the equipment without outlay have been explored, will make you sometimes wonder if you should just go out and buy the photocopier yourself on your own credit card.

A friend joins a university as a casual lecturer and is told that she must have an employment number before she can access the university's intranet to post assignments. But she can't get that until she's been paid. And she can't get paid until the university has agreed on her payment method, and how and when she is to bill. Ergo, she cannot post work for her students. Another friend joins a huge organisation and then disappears from view. It is impossible to reach him via the switchboard which claims he doesn't exist. No department has heard of him. I imagine him being found in five years time behind a row of shelves, with his legs curled up in the air like a dead cockroach. It turns out that HR must let the switchboard know of his arrival, but HR will not do that until some vital piece of paper is signed and released. This also has to come from HR.

The metres of red tape are supposedly there for transparency and efficiency but, according to ethicist and political philosopher Onora O'Neill, insistence on such micro-management of objects leads to micro-management of people. "The new accountability has quite sharp teeth," she said in "A Question of Trust", her 2002 Reith Lectures series for the BBC. She also talked of new systems of control by which she meant the audit culture. "The idea of audit has been exported from its original financial context to cover ever more detailed scrutiny of non-financial processes and systems. Performance indicators are used to measure adequate and inadequate performance with supposed precision. This audit explosion … has often displaced or marginalised older systems of accountability." Conjuring life as mathematics, she said, "The new legislation, regulation and controls are more than fine rhetoric. They require detailed conformity to procedures and protocols, detailed record-keeping and provision of information in specified formats …"

Anyone who has done any managing lately, even if it's looking after chickens or school-children, will recognise what she's talking about and the enormous effect it can have on a job, how long that job takes and how well the real bit of the job – that is, doing the work rather than the numbers and reports and forms – can be done.

Privatisation has played its role here. Privatising institutions and organisations is supposed to minimise the role of the state but regulatory theory shows that the very opposite happens. The state imposes more regulation and more duties of compliance because the risk factor goes up once a body is in private hands. And so there will be new regulations on privacy, probity, occupational health and safety, and freedom of information. Then there's the constant threat of litigation, which means every institution covers its ass up to its neck with extreme and convoluted rules and signs aimed purely at protecting it from massive compensation suits.

It's all a bonus for the many lawyers involved and there are mutterings everywhere about what came first – too many lawyers or too many regulations. The law has, unfortunately, never been just about commonsense, so now that we've entered the age of the airhead, lawyers are everywhere.

Meanwhile, governments forever fret over what we might get up to if left to our own devices. In early 2005, I spoke to Casper Conde, now an adjunct scholar at the Centre for Independent Studies in Sydney, just after he had published a paper there called "Smothered by the Security Blanket: Risk, Responsibility and the Role of Government". He said at the time, "The argument is that the risks of modern life are so great – climate change, nuclear power – that they need an anticipatory reaction from government. But when that seeps into everyday life, it's disastrous. It leads to loss of liberty; it generates a learned helplessness and it means there are big costs associated with the sheer size of government." Thus the security blanket gets bigger and bigger, tighter and tighter.

Ohmigod

Walt Disney shareholders took the board to court for allegedly wasting money after the board paid group president Michael Ovitz $US140 million severance pay. Ovitz worked for the company for just fourteen months from late 1995. In 2005, a Delaware judge ruled against the shareholders, declaring the board and its then chairman – Ovitz's one-time friend Michael Eisner – had acted properly and in good faith. In 2006, the Delaware Supreme Court upheld the judgment. Ovitz blamed Eisner for his departure, saying he hadn't been given enough time to learn the job.

Conde and his colleagues "decided it was a situation not dissimilar to Stalinist Russia. The managers would have their targets and they had to cover their backs, otherwise they'd end up in the gulags. So they'd always have another plan if a target wasn't met, and on it would go. People don't go to gulags now, but they don't want to lose their jobs. Or their consultancies. In the last forty years, the amount spent on the public sector has almost doubled as a proportion of GDP. The amount of Commonwealth legislation has gone up eight times in the last hundred years."

Two CSIRO staffers caught the overall mood when they wrote this in *The Age* newspaper about the decline of their own organisation and of scientific research: "As a nation ... we have become captured by a bureaucratic audit-and-control culture that affects everyone and everything, often unintentionally."[8]

Australian universities suffer more than most because of extra federal government requirements accompanying funding. Monash University vice-chancellor Richard Larkins has complained about the countless hours taken up with "seeking to satisfy requirements which are arbitrary and imprecise".

The administrative workload has burgeoned, too. With the drop in university funding, academic staff are now more dependent on grants and accessing other funds, and so they must produce reports to accompany their applications. Then, if they get the grant, more reports have to be written on their progress. An administrator at one major university describes what might happen if, say, the Australian Research Council gives a university $5,000 to buy a computer. "It has to be tracked as an asset over the next five years and then, if you want to use the computer for another purpose, you have to get written permission from the federal minister."

He says of all the micro-regulation, "You just can't breathe."

You can't help feeling that that's exactly what the authorities want. Keep us busy with all this documentation and accountability and it's harder for us to notice what else is going on. It's so much easier to get away with things when everyone is too busy, too frantic, too over-burdened and hemmed in, to ask questions.

SOME OF the very best sleight of hand now occurs with numbers, which have taken us over, migrating from the business pages to dominate newspaper coverage, infiltrate every political speech and turn up as the star of any PowerPoint presentation.

Numbers are used to corral us, convince us, influence us, bamboozle us and keep us under control. Ever tried to compare superannuation funds or Broadband sign-up agreements? Mobile phone companies, investment funds and credit card firms and spruikers use numbers to promise us they can get us a better deal.

All these numbers at a time when, I can't help thinking, fewer and fewer of us even know how to add up or subtract in our heads. Dr Nick Coates, senior policy officer at the Australian Consumers' Association, points to the way banks now make their money out of retail customers. "Increasingly, it's moved to penalty fees: if accounts are overdrawn, or if an incoming cheque is dishonoured, or a cheque you write bounces. There is this broader trend to move towards slightly underhand fees, things you don't necessarily check when you open a new account. There might be a $40 or $50 penalty charge and this really affects lower-income people." Noting how numbers bewilder consumers trying to choose between two types of bank account, he says, "Financial products are extremely complex and the penalty fees assume the customer won't understand they're there."

(Ethics columnist and social researcher Hugh Mackay came across the example of Citibank customers who had signed up for what many obviously thought was a fee-free credit card. What they didn't realise was that there was a fee and it was a whopper. A whole $160 if they didn't spend to a certain figure within a set time. Citibank called it a "fail to spend" fee. An Australian Securities and Investment Commission investigation decided the law hadn't been broken, but that promotional material might have misled.)

Banks tangle us even more, Coates says, by making it virtually impossible for customers to compare different financial products between banks, different mortgages or different accounts all wrapped in complex fees and conditions: "They try and create oranges if someone else is offering apples."

Then there are the numbers dealt out by economists to prove to us that life is getting better all the time, even for sweatshop workers. It's now virtually impossible to win any argument without numbers, which is why I've used so many of them in this book. Without numbers, a statement is shoeless. Not for us any more the rousing speeches of a Wilberforce, a Macaulay, a De Gaulle or an Emerson, with their vision, their calls to a cause and their imagery more important than any stray numbers. In William Pitt the Younger's speech urging the abolition of the slave trade, given to the British House of Commons on April 2, 1792, he relies on just one set of numbers "seventy or eighty thousand persons", which later becomes just "eighty thousand", and that is that. There is no barrage of figures on just how many slaves there were, had been or would be, or calculations of English pounds to be gained or lost. His argument instead gains its power and effect through his language and through his calls to his listeners to imagine themselves in such a scenario and to remember that, under the Romans, Britain had once been thought to have no better future use than as a supplier of slaves, so barbarous did the Romans think its society.

When, by comparison, Prime Minister John Howard gave his Australia Day address in 2006, it was like hearing someone recite his times tables. He began with a list of numbers and statistics: Australia is now third in a list of 177 countries on the United Nations Human Development Index; our income per capita is eighth highest in the developed world; 80 percent of Australians surveyed profess pride in our economic achievements; in the last decade, private sector wealth per capita has more than doubled; and our level of general government outlays is 36 percent, second lowest in the OECD.

Howard knows his audience. Rhetoric is what used to make people listen and take note. Now it's numbers that make us feel safer, and rhetoric is very likely what we distrust. People also like certainty, especially in these insecure times, and numbers start off looking very pure and unbiased. They aren't at all though and so we end up with the current problem: there are so many numbers that they whiz towards us like *shuriken*, those lethal, spinning blades from the Samurai ninja movies.

Figures on the workforce, poverty and other such indicators turn up every day in the news as

Like, whatever

The July 2005 rail and bus bombings in central London caused major disruption to traffic and public transport. But figures are figures and hours are hours. One company, Trailfinders, still docked staff for being late. *The Sun* newspaper reported that one employee who rang in to work after starting to walk because the tubes had stopped was told: "Get in or don't get paid."

quarterly results are released or monthly job movements are listed. They're bewildering just because there are so many of them. A closely watched set of numbers, with every minute fluctuation noted every month, means we often forget to look at what's really happening in the long term. Like most people, I rely on anecdote and observation, reminding myself all the while of the maxim that "the plural of 'anecdote' is not 'data' " (but also noting the equally savvy retort on one website that "the plural of 'datum' is not 'proof'").

Newspapers are full of statistics that, if not at war with each other, certainly seem to indicate fundamental disagreement of some kind. In a July 2005 speech, the Prime Minister claimed that real wages had increased 14 percent since the first workplace reforms of 1996. Unions NSW, citing research from the Workplace Research Centre, formerly the Australian Centre for Industrial Relations Research and Training (ACIRRT), responded that the high salaries of managers had distorted the figures and most working Australians received a real wage rise of just 3.6 percent in the six years to 2004. The Prime Minister's office bit back the same day, August 29, with a press release claiming the union report was flawed.[9] This time the PM, quoting the centre's own tables, claimed they showed that average weekly ordinary time earnings had actually increased by 20 percent in real terms. A week later, there was Don Edgar, author, policy adviser and foundation director of the National Institute of Family Studies, pointing out in print, as the centre's own people had done, that the government figure was due to it being the mean (that is, averaged out), as opposed to the median, "which is actually a 2.6 percent pay rise". The bottom 20 percent had received just 1.2 percent.

For the statistically challenged (and also for those who are more than a little squinty-eyed about what might really be happening in our economy), the median is the figure in the exact middle. It means there are as many people above that figure earning more as there are below earning less. In this situation, where salaries at the top are so very much higher than those at the bottom, and where jobs are now clumping at either end, an averaged or mean figure, rather than the median, is distorting. When figures are distributed evenly, the mean can be very similar to the median, but if there are large disparities between top and bottom – as in this case – the median will be quite different from the mean or average.

After fifteen years of prosperity in Australia, the job market has changed, but not always for the better. We are turning into a society with two kinds of workers. As

The Australian's George Megalogenis put it, we are changing to "a more radical order where jobs are divided between those who run the open economy and those who answer their phones, cut their hair and serve their lattes".[10] You can leap up the ladder or slide down it; it's the comforting middle that is disappearing. One in six full-time jobs disappeared from the middle in the two decades to 2001, Megalogenis writes. Of the male full-time jobs, half went to the top; half slipped down one or two rungs. Twenty years ago, nearly 50 percent of working men and women were clustered around the middle. Now the figures show about 37 percent of those men in the middle and 44 percent of the women. Two out of every three newly created jobs are now in management or the professions. Pity about that middle which Robert Menzies once called "the backbone of the country".

Can we measure what a comfortable, egalitarian, secure middle class achieved for Australia? For all the derision the middle class scores – too bourgeois, too sanctimonious, too conservative, too safe, too Ikea, too concerned with appearances – that was never the whole truth. Have a look at who turns up for the protest marches on anything from Iraq to the new IR laws. See who writes in to the letters pages of the newspapers. Just as women are supposed to civilise men, so the middle classes civilise a society because, traditionally, they're the ones with the education and comfort zone of stability, security and decent income which gives them room and know-how to worry about schools, health, their kids' future, other people, a country's future, peace. Democratisation and a strong middle class go hand-in-hand. It's also the middle that provides the necessary connection between the poor and the rich, says Megalogenis, author of two books on Australia's economic and social revolution. However, it is the middle that has been most buffeted by the economic reforms of the last two decades and the recession of the early Nineties.

The new prosperity is covering Australia in a stupefying haze. Wrote former Liberal MP Michael Baume in mid-2005, "This period [of prosperity] has reduced Australia's unemployment to the lowest level for almost 30 years, has massively increased workers' real incomes and lifted the number of Australians in work to a record 10 million as 370,000 new jobs were created over the past 12 months, 70 percent of which were full-time."[11]

But the new jobs aren't necessarily like the jobs we remember. Between 1992 and 2004, 1.5 million extra jobs were created in the Australian economy. Impressive, until the figures are dissected, as they were by Sue Richardson, professor of economics at

Flinders University, who discovered a long-term trend among men towards semi-employment. Only 12 percent of those new jobs created were permanent full-time and taken by men.[12]

Nor does "full-time" mean what it used to mean and what we instinctively take it to mean. Full-time now can just mean you are on contract to work full-time for a set period. Or you could be a casual working full-time. There are full-time positions that come without the safeguards of sick pay, annual leave, superannuation, continuity, security, stability … Casuals made up only 12 percent of the workforce in 1982 but, by 2000, the figure stood at 27 percent and it's now about 28 percent. We have one of the most casual-ised workforces of any advanced economy in the world, which means we have, pro-rata, more workers than any other developed country who will go to work when they are sick because they fear losing their shift; who don't take holidays because they're not entitled to them and they again fear losing their shift; who can't get mortgages or credit or, if they do, it's at higher rates; whose hours can be as irregular or as regular as an employer desires; who can't plan child care and who can be got rid of simply through the employer giving them fewer and fewer hours until they can't survive on them. How does that fit alongside the triumphant economic numbers constantly delivered to us?

In his reporting and books, Megalogenis has drilled down and down through ABS data to come up with findings that echo those of the Workplace Research Centre (previously ACIRRT) and Sue Richardson. His findings show what a very

Totally

"All along the opposition has taken the wrong tack: it is not about whether the government knew [about kickbacks from the Australian Wheat Board to Iraq dictator Saddam Hussein], although this is important, but about it *not* knowing. At the moment, the three amigos – Howard, Downer and Vaile – are dancing around like village idiots saying with puffed-out chests that they did not know. This is not a defence. That they did not know, if true, is a damning indictment of their managerial competence."
SIMON BARTHOLOMEW, IN
A LETTER TO *THE AUSTRALIAN*,
APRIL 11, 2006.

different country we now inhabit. Back in June 1982, with a recession just started, men made up 63 percent of the workforce (3 percent in part-time work; the remaining 60 percent full-time). That's how many of us still think of Australia, but the mid-2006 figure shows us what's really happening with men's jobs. Now men make up 55 percent of the workforce, and nearly 47 percent of that workforce are men in full-time jobs. Eight percent are men in part-time jobs. Job creation for men is at the top or at the bottom.

Meanwhile, women now make up 45 percent of the workforce, with almost half of them in part-time work. This swing towards women is becoming entrenched. Of the full-time jobs created in the six months to June 2006, 56 percent went to women. But women get paid between 10 and 15 percent less to do the same jobs as men. That is "the dirty secret of deregulation", writes Megalogenis in his latest book, *The Longest Decade*.[13] "The price that capitalism has placed on the heads of women, and their willingness to take the work despite the short-changing involved, has helped to underwrite the boom."

Yes, as noted, there are jobs opening up at the top of the tree – 66 percent of the half-million or so jobs created in the last two years were for managers and professionals – but in two decades, men who could be termed either battlers or on the bottom rung have gone from 23 percent to 28 percent of all people in full-time jobs.

Nor do welfare benefits help much now that, as Megalogenis has shown again, they go increasingly to a group of the population that is declining, families with dependent children, while welfare funds available for the aged and for those on the dole or disability support are less. "Welfare today has become a marker of prosperity, not disadvantage," Megalogenis concluded.[14]

Sue Richardson was particularly interested in what all these changes in male employment mean for families. For years, she has been charting the growth in numbers of men aged thirty-five to forty-four who aren't married and who don't have full-time, secure jobs. In 1978, that described only 20 percent of those Australian men. By 2003, in this run of fabulous economic growth the world has enjoyed and Australia particularly, the figure had risen to 35 percent. These were men who were no longer needed in industries such as manufacturing (and, it seemed, Australia's government had no need of them either). Richardson sees in those figures the rise of a severely alienated group of men whose presence could undermine our settled way of life. Marriage, families and setting up home are expensive. Women don't want to partner low-income or unemployed men, and so more and more men are being priced out of the market.[15] The Australian Family Association has come out with similar warnings,[16] stressing that, unlike the impression created by television, it is not the wealthy who are divorcing. Higher incomes and job stability enable people to hold a family together. The lower the income, the lower the marriage and partnering rate and the higher the divorce and separation rate. "The critical condition for marriage [for a man] is a full-time job," said the association. It also cited research by ACIRRT (now the Workplace Research Centre) that 87 percent of new jobs created in the Nineties paid less than $26,000 a year and nearly half paid less than $15,600.

I wonder who in politics is working out the figures on all this – in particular, the cost to all the kids who are going to be brought up in these circumstances. That is, future generations of Australians. Politicians already seem to be so completely surprised by everything: oops, honey, we forgot to train teachers; oops, honey, we forgot to train doctors and carpenters; oops, not enough scientists either. Why be surprised to discover that, oops, we also forgot to look after the children.

As for the unemployment figure, now standing at about 5 percent, it's worth noting that, statistically speaking, you are counted as employed if you have worked for an hour or more in the week for pay, profit, commission or pay in kind. Or if you have worked for an hour or more, even without pay, on a family farm or in a family business. (Officially, an unemployed person is someone over fifteen years of age, who has not worked at all in the week counted, has actively looked for work in the previous four weeks and is available to start work.)

Numbers, as we know from the meticulous statistics kept by the Nazis, can keep thoughts of humanity and ethics, of living people, at bay. When Jung Chang and Jon Halliday published *Mao: The Untold Story*,[17] the result of ten years of study of the Chinese tyrant during whose reign at least seventy million died, they came under attack. One biographer criticised them for "denying [Mao] his complexity, his perversity, his genius …" Halliday replied: "Saying we are too negative … is a bit like saying [that] in writing about Hitler you should devote space to the recovery of the German economy between 1933 and 1938." Another of their critics, University of Chicago academic Lee Feigon, who has made a film about Mao, did virtually that. He claimed that, under Mao, literacy rates rose from 15 to 80 percent, industrial output went up thirty-fold and life expectancy doubled.[18] Just a pity, I guess, that that last one didn't apply to the twenty million to thirty million alone who died in The Great Leap Forward.

In our working world, where the number is the new God, various employers are lobbying the federal government to make it easier to bring in immigrant workers on temporary visas. The numbers must look good on paper. A Perth manager unwittingly revealed the thinking behind it to the ABC's *PM* programme,[19] saying of the Filipino guest workers his building company employed: "We found that by using this migrant labour we could show them what needed to be done and they'd just follow it and do it the way we wanted. They wouldn't sort of put their own influence on how they thought it should be done ... I'm not saying that they are at a lower level of intelligence or anything like that. It just seemed that they can do one task and not want to do something different until they're told to do something different."

The workers for this company accepted less pay than their Australian counterparts, who, in turn, were being offered more money by rival companies because of the labour shortage. The guest workers, though, can't change local employers without great difficulty or, alternatively, going home first; that means they can't pursue the dollar although that is supposed to be the point of a market-led economy.

For some.

In the four years to 2006, almost 200,000 temporary skilled migrant visas were issued, wrote *The Age*'s Michael Bachelard in July 2006. The numbers issued each year almost doubled in that time. Newspapers now regularly carry stories of immigrant workers being treated unfairly although the federal government insists the skills shortage

Really?

"Clumsy typing has cost a Japanese bank £128 million and staff their Christmas party and bonuses after a trader mistakenly sold 600,000 more shares than he should have. The trader ... fell foul of what is known in financial circles as 'fat finger syndrome'."
The trader had actually wanted to sell just one share for 600,000 yen but ended up selling 600,000 shares for one yen each.
THE TIMES,
DECEMBER 9, 2005.

means the visas are needed. That small snapshot shows what happens when you put globalisation and numbers in the same room. Remember Hobbes: "The value or worth of a man ... his price ... is so much as would be given for the use of his power ... And as in other things, so in men, not the seller but the buyer determines the price." As Stanford economics professor Dr Frank Wolak reminds us: for markets to be successful, both sides must be able to adjust to the changing conditions.[20]

AFTER IGNORANCE, an airhead's second-best friend is numbers because, while they give the illusion of being the very opposite of vague, the truth is that you can do anything with them, prove anything with them. Just the way questions are asked in a statistical survey has an effect on how people answer them. In 1999, *American Journalism Review* ran a crisp piece on focus groups and debunked polling.[21] In the reporter's words, a group of Germans was asked: is tennis more or less exciting than soccer to watch on TV? Thirty-five percent said tennis was more exciting, 65 percent said less. Then the researchers posed the same question to a second group of Germans, but this time reversed the wording: is soccer more or less exciting than tennis to watch on TV? Guess what? Only 15 percent found soccer more exciting, down from 65. Seventy-seven percent found it less exciting, up from 35 percent. (And this time around, 8 percent were undecided.) "Which sport these people would really rather watch, God only knows," the reporter commented.

We live in an age of science, and science is all about numbers and that now extends to the social sciences. Surveys, statistics and research projects can, of course, provide us with the numbers to guide us towards better decisions. As one student of mathematics says to me, "Numbers are an important tool for how we assess a society. Now that we are globalised, how would we be able to compare countries without numbers? For the International Monetary Fund to do its job and know where they are going, they need scientific statistical basis. Numbers are a sign of a sophisticated civilisation trying to establish an ability to understand itself better. And that is all completely consistent with a society that wants to have a discussion about principles and values."

Quite right. The problem, though, is how humans behave around numbers. It's all too likely that we can end up with those at the top knowing the figures on everything and the meaning of nothing.

Despite an acknowledged rise in numbers of administrative staff in Australian universities the ratio of such staff to academic staff has remained stable for two decades, at roughly 55:45. That defies commonsense. But here's the trick: while HR staff may have increased their numbers, for instance, overall figures will be the same because all the cleaning staff might have been outsourced.

When notable McKinseyite Fred Hilmer was CEO of Fairfax, he decided that journalists' mistakes in print had to be classified into different categories – grammatical, spelling, factual, errors in hindsight and so on – and that a total limit would be set on acceptable error rates. It was decided – by God knows what criteria – that 3.1 errors per broadsheet page was the benchmark, as Hilmer announced at a conference on media ethics in June 2002. While he was going about this extraordinary exercise, two prominent academics, infuriated by the increasing numbers of literals and such in *The Sydney Morning Herald*, a paper of record, started keeping their own account. They eventually sent their results to Hilmer and waited for a response. There was none, even when one of the pair fronted him at a function later on.

Perhaps Hilmer had sent their research to his own counting department and it had come in at fewer than 3.1 per page in which case all was hunky-dory.

When a team of time-and-motion experts whipped through *The Sydney Morning Herald* in 2005, working out how to save a minute here, a team of staffers there, they asked the newspaper's sub-editors to fill out a form. One of the questions was: how long does it take you to think of a headline? There is no answer to that one. Probably about as long as it takes you, or anyone, to work out what to have for dinner, what to call your cat, how to start a letter to the bank, what to title your next presentation …

This obsession with statistics, measurements and numbers can make it feel as if we live in a world with a government decree that all important things be painted yellow. Except that important things like horses or cows or flowers can't be painted. Ah, say the people at the top, squinting through their prisms, if it cannot be painted yellow, it cannot be important. This is the odd and potentially terrible side-effect of this obsession. Anything that can't be put into numerical form is somehow regarded as immaterial or ephemeral, even though we should all know that the most important things in life can never be measured.

It is commonsense to understand that happiness, love, a sense of security, commitment, loyalty, honesty, duty, creativity cannot be assigned numbers or measured in purely mathematical terms. We can only measure the consequences of what happens when such motivators are disregarded or disappear. Divorce rates. Job movements. Crime rates. Depression. Youth suicide rates. British psychiatrist and author Raj Persaud, talking of the difficulty of measuring something as crucial as motivation, said, "Scientists have a natural tendency to be drawn towards studying things that are easy to measure and the problem is that sometimes the things that are easy to measure are not that important."[22]

Now it seems that too many have been drawn into the convenience of believing that a number will tell us everything. If I pursued my bank on its no-show ATMs, what numbers would they persist in giving me? The number of small stores where I can use Eftpos? The executive responsible for the bank's ATMs has already gone on ABC-Radio to whine about the cost of his ATM network. Perhaps I could provide a cost analysis of how much time it takes me to buy groceries whenever I want cash; perhaps I could supply the number of minutes it takes me to find a store that doesn't mind being used as a bank.

Like, whatever

Eight thousand students with cancelled Australian visas suddenly had valid visas again after a federal court decision. The court decided that a standard form letter sent to a Bangladeshi student asking him to attend a meeting with immigration officials was defective and did not fit migration regulations. Officials had cancelled the student's Australian visa after he had failed to attend half his classes and then didn't turn up for the meeting. The student successfully sued, *The Australian* reported in September 2005. The 8,000 other failed or truant foreign students who had received the letter and not turned up to their appointments automatically had their decisions reversed as a result of the court decision. The Department of Immigration had to immediately launch a worldwide search for them. There could also be compensation claims, it was reported. The letter was defective because it asked the students to report to a Melbourne immigration department office and officer rather than *any* office or officer.

"How do I love thee, let me count the ways," wrote Elizabeth Barrett Browning, proving with her poetry that there are just some things that should never have to be argued in figures.

Concepts and numbers cannot always belong in the same universe. When they are forced to do so, disaster looms. On Australia Day 2006, a school leaver with top scores in advanced English and cosmology explained why so many bright science graduates were disappearing overseas: "One worry more specific to prospective science researchers is the greater emphasis in Australia on goal-oriented work, rather than pure research. Although this is practical and can provide immediate benefits for the country, the concern is that future advancements can only go so far without more input from the blue-sky half of pure research."[23]

It's never been easy to measure blue sky. It is even harder to measure bull-dust. That is increasingly the problem for everyone trying to live like humans in an economically rational society, irrationally driven by numbers.

CHAPTER 10

The Something-Nothing Problem

"Can I say this? I think there's a kind of class-based issue here as well because, you know, I mean upper-middle-class women who spend thousands of dollars on an Armani suit and wear subtle but classic make-up and nice pearl earrings, that's okay to pay that kind of attention to your appearance, but if you want to put on a pair of white cowboy boots and kind of a lamé bikini and get a boob job, then that's white-trash stuff. So I wondered to some extent whether we are introducing an unstated element of class into ideas about what is appropriate self-enhancement and what isn't."

CATHARINE LUMBY, ASSOCIATE PROFESSOR OF MEDIA STUDIES, UNIVERSITY OF SYDNEY, ON SBS *INSIGHT* PROGRAMME, FEBRUARY 28, 2006

The challenge of the twenty-first century is not how to turn a sow's ear into a silk purse; it's how to make sure we can get away with pretending that nothing is actually something. This is the age of empty-speak and empty-think, which is the only way an airhead society can get itself up out of bed each morning and keep going. We are busily creating and promoting a culture where things *look* as if they signify something, or *are* something or *should* be something, when, if you get a chance to look more closely, there may not be much there at all.

Something-nothing is speech or activity that is designed for show, not wear. If you have ever been in a meeting of twenty people that has lasted two hours, involved five PowerPoint presentations from outside experts and a rallying speech from your CEO, and then left, with the colleague next to you whispering, "So what was *that* all about?" you have experienced something-nothingness. It takes up time; it gets you nowhere. It is often illogical, like Catharine Lumby's argument, which is clearly well-meant but which, if taken to its conclusion, would have someone in a lamé bikini and cowboy boots conducting a business meeting and no-one would be able to say boo because that would be elitist.

There's plenty more of this around. A seminar on ethics *looks* as if the company means well, but overall, ethics has never been more on the nose. If your company brings in a troop of expensively clad management consultants, you can be pretty sure you're in for a dose of very high-priced something-nothing. Kids *look* as if they're busy as they amble

Totally

"Our main consulting strategy is to convince clients that we do stuff they can't do themselves, and that we deserve lots of money for it. The best way to do this is to always look good, and always sound like we know something you don't. Because we do. Are you confused yet? Of course you are. And that's just how we like it. Our marketing professionals are constantly coming up with new ways to make you feel inferior and stupid. Because you are. And we're not. We're new-age, eMoving, marketing consultants."
SPOOF WEBSITE HUHCORP.COM, WHICH SENDS UP CONSULTANCIES.

down the street, texting their friends and arranging to catch up, immersing themselves in PlayStation – but what is actually produced from all that endeavour? Newspapers have taken to running stories that *look* like news stories, but aren't. A paper reports that a new study reveals that anti-depressants can stop people committing suicide. Goodness gracious, who'd have thunk it.

Something-nothingness has so infiltrated the way we are conditioned to react and think that not thinking things through to a logical conclusion is becoming a habit with us all. When parents are asked what they want their children to grow up to be, nine times out of ten they answer as a reflex: "I just want them to be happy."

Really? How novel. Let's see if we can find any parents who want their children to grow up *unhappy*.

A big, tough businessman, used to issuing orders in his CEO role, sent an abrupt email to the principal of one of Sydney's top schools. The man had seen the mission statement for an elite private school in Melbourne. It had promised parents and students that the school was devoted to the pursuit of excellence.

"Where's your school's mission statement?" he demanded.

The principal thought for a while before derailing him by emailing back: "Of course. Here it is. We are not devoted to pursuing excellence."

Something-nothingness can be a harmless laziness of mind or speech. But at other times, it has to be recognised for what it is: sophistry or plain bull-dust. It can be highly profitable when it's sold to corporations, posturing as the latest management theory. (Anyone remember re-engineering? Or all the people who were let go because of it?) It can also let us off the hook by allowing us to blather and obfuscate. Politicians are especially fond of something-nothingness. On the day the Bureau of Meteorology officially declared 2005 Australia's hottest year since records began, federal minister for the environment Ian Campbell announced there was no point setting targets or timetables for reducing the gases that cause global warming. "Targets are a proxy for not doing the hard work,"[1] he pontificated.

When the US Supreme Court ruled, in late June 2006, that the military commissions set up to try alleged terrorists in Guantanamo Bay were illegal, the Australian government did not immediately make plans to ship home David Hicks, held without trial for four-and-a-half years. His lawyer said, "It no longer passes the commonsense test to keep David Hicks further imprisoned." But the Prime Minister responded that now the Americans would just have to come up with some *other* way to try Hicks. "He should be brought to trial," John Howard said firmly on radio. The statement looks like something – but it's nothing. It avoids the key issue: why is an Australian citizen, captured in Afghanistan, sitting in an American naval jail? Hicks cannot be prosecuted in Australia because there is no law under which he can be charged. On that basis, the federal government insists he stay in Guantanamo to face trial. Trying to debate this circular reasoning is, once again, like fighting gloop.

The single most important thing to understand about something-nothingness is that it's actually about doing nothing. Or nothing meaningful. Something-nothingness, as practised by an expert, always means that the buck stops somewhere else. And yet, it now takes so many forms and has achieved such respectability that we unquestioningly accept that it has become the way of doing things.

It even plagues young romance today. Dating between two people is considered old hat. Instead, people go out in groups and, if they feel like sex, they hook up with "friends with benefits". Or the girls give the boys oral sex. No strings. No commitment. No hearts broken. Or so they say. But when the something-nothing disease infects two human beings who would normally be going about the business of being attracted or not to each other, learning about each other, getting close to each other, the consequences can be debilitating, if not lethal: a deadening nihilism of the heart.

The latest scam on our emotions is a plethora of articles and columns either commenting on, or extolling, the art of relationship by technology. "Text-messaging is the latest technology for hooking up," announced *New York* magazine[2] before quoting a number of automatons who seriously believe that someone using their thumbs to tap out a text to them on a mobile – "DRUNK. SEXSEXSEXSEXSEXSEX SEX. XO, M" – is more arousing, more stimulating, more erotic than the exquisite caress of a lover on the most delicate parts of your anatomy. Said twenty-four-year-old Madeleine, "There was not a lot that compared to the charge I would get when I'd feel my phone vibrate in my pocket during my medieval-art-history lecture and find a message like, JUST THINKING ABOUT YOUR FANTASTIC TITS."

Madeleine, if you truly believe this, then I can only repeat what Harry said to Sally in the famous Billy Crystal–Meg Ryan romantic movie of the late Eighties: "Oh, I get it. You've just never had great sex." Unfortunately, the way we're all going on, acting as if this nonsense is for real and as if text sex is something, poor old Madeleine will probably never get to find out what she's missing.

Ohmigod

"I don't mean to sound like I'm an A-list celebrity because I don't think that, but when I'm on the front of a magazine, I sell more copies than Victoria Beckham does. That is an amazing thing to be told, and I think it's a massive achievement for, I dunno, doing nothing."
BRITISH *BIG BROTHER* 2002 CONTESTANT JADE GOODY WHO WENT FROM BEING EVICTED FROM A COUNCIL FLAT FOR UNPAID RENT TO A FORTUNE OF MORE THAN £2 MILLION BY 2006.

The New Age has done very well out of something-nothing. For all our hard-headed rationalism, it is flourishing. Its branches and sub-branches have set up shop and practice in every highway and byway of Western life. As the world becomes more complex, frightening and fragmented, less understandable, we beat a path to the magician's door. The New Age, of course, is centred on the word "I" so it's perfect for these airhead times. I know of what I speak; I've been there. One afternoon, in counter-culture Byron Bay on the northern New South Wales coast, a clutch of us sat around a table engrossed in books about feng-shui, astrology and Chinese horoscopes. "Gosh," said one of us, without a trace of irony as he read out a character description, "don't you just hate people who are self-obsessed?"

I once relaunched a small New Age magazine for friends. It was good fun for a couple of months as I had intense and complicated talks with a range of contributors about numerology, tarot, chakras and the position of Jupiter in a chart. What it meant was that we were able to talk about ourselves a lot. There were occasional glitches. As part of the relaunch, the magazine had been repackaged into a long, thin, rectangular shape, which meant that all the artwork for the advertisements had to be re-sized from the more usual A4. Re-sizing is expensive, though, so many of the ads ended up just being squashed and manipulated into the new shape. When the magazine was finally printed, all the people spruiking in them – the psychics and clairvoyants and people who communicated with angels – came out looking as if they had long pointy heads.

Fortunately for me, something-nothing will out in the end if you keep your wits about you, and came the day at the New Age magazine when a writer from Los Angeles suggested a thousand-word piece on a moon ceremony on a beach. The piece came in late and about three thousand words too long. By about the seventeen-hundredth word, the writer hadn't even managed to get us outside the house and down to the moonlit water's edge because we were still wrapping or unwrapping specially bought candles in specially folded silk cloth. At that stage, I decided life was too short for moon ceremonies.

Years later, I had another New Age huh! moment as I watched a former colleague, Ruth Ostrow, on television. Ruth had made her name with raunchy, barrier-breaking sex columns and a radio show about sex, but had gravitated towards the New Age. She had thrived, writing about the universe, friends, life experiences, spirituality, honouring the self and the search for meaning. On this night, she was interviewed by Peter Thompson for his ABC-TV series *Talking Heads*. The most telling bit of the show came at the end when a warm and friendly Thompson suddenly asked Ostrow, who was sitting perched like an elf: "So what do you teach?"

It wasn't a surprising question given that throughout the programme we had seen Ostrow doing her life-coaching, or facilitating, as she calls it, escorting numerous clients or friends around her home base of Byron, lecturing them, going about her day, answering emails from her readers ... But she looked flabbergasted. Her mouth opened but nothing came out; a cloud of doubt crept into her shiny brown eyes. She stumbled and said ... "Umm ... Well, that's a very deep question. I think that's one of the deepest questions I've ever been asked actually because I can't answer it, I try not to teach ..." It eventually emerged that she hoped to teach people how to ask the right questions – not that she had any answers, she readily admitted.

Hardly anyone does these days, although we all crave them and are sure they are to be found somewhere, under a rock, in a manual, on a whiteboard, in someone's supposedly wise head. This is why something-nothingness has become so ubiquitous and so very useful, particularly in two areas. The first is business. (Natch. If you're in business today, you're going to need something magic in your knapsack to justify what is going on out there.) The second is in education, of which, more later.

My first inkling that the day of something-nothing had dawned came in the mid-Nineties when advertising reps at the newspaper where I worked kept asking us to produce advertising-driven supplements on something they called TQM.

Que?

TQM stood for Total Quality Management, a concept that gave an edge to Japanese industry in the Fifties and gathered favour elsewhere in the Eighties and especially in the Nineties. Like many something-nothings, it isn't talked about that much now, although it still has a grip. As one pro-website puts it: "TQM is a set of management practices throughout the organisation, geared to ensure the organisation consistently meets or exceeds customer requirements. TQM places strong focus on process measurement and controls as means of continuous improvement …" Another site says, "Important aspects of TQM include customer-driven quality, top management leadership and commitment, continuous improvement, fast response, actions based on facts, employee participation and a TQM culture."

The same site admits: "Many companies have difficulty in implementing TQM." It is, of course, just a fancy brand name for commonsense management skills dressed up in fancy-schmancy language, and of course it's hard to do because good management always is.

A lot of people have made careers and a fine living out of TQM. Since then, there have been other crazes such as re-engineering, quality circles and participatory management, each with its own language and catchphrases. Canberra University academic Jenny Stewart, a specialist in public sector organisations, has what she calls a little museum of hand-outs and goodies from various practitioners. Her prize souvenir is a laminated tablemat with "Best Practice" inscribed on it, although, she wonders aloud, "I'm not sure what you're supposed to eat off it."

"The current fetish is corporate governance," she continues. "It's like a magic ritual, or a St Christopher medal that you wear on your rear window. There's this idea that if you have 'corporate governance', everything else will be fixed. As humans, we have an innate ability to ignore inconvenient facts."

In 2004, her own book *The Decline of the Tea Lady*[3] came out. Its subtitle was "Management for dissidents". A current favourite phrase of hers is "organisational regeneration". She says, "That's consultant-speak for how do we fix up the joint now that all the good people have gone."

Then there's "spiritual intelligence", or SQ, which I heard about from a professor at a business school. First there was IQ, then EQ, the idea of emotional intelligence, and now SQ. It is supposedly a hot business topic in companies from hamburger chain McDonald's to Shell, while at least one of the senior directors at McKinsey, the elite international management consulting group, is a vocal fan. The concept of SQ is the brainchild of Danah Zohar, a UK-based management consultant who studied physics and philosophy at Massachusetts Institute of Technology, and then theology, philosophy and psychology at Harvard. Spiritual intelligence is a New Age way of looking at wealth and power. It takes current feel-good fad words like "vision", "meaning", "values" and "service", and phrases like "holistic collaborations" and looks to a future where we have all harnessed the wisdom of our inner selves so that we understand our common purpose together. Other major corporations who have expressed interest in pulling up their spiritual socks at some stage include Coca-Cola, Starbucks, Unilever, Nokia, and Hewlett-Packard. According to the website for Zohar's 2000 book *SQ: Connecting With Our Spiritual Intelligence*, SQ "is linked to humanity's need for meaning". It is "the intelligence that … gives us our integrity".

"Oh, bullshit," said one local workplace consultant.

"Spiritual intelligence? It's an oxymoron," scoffed the professor who teaches at one of Australia's top management schools.

But Zohar's book on SQ is a world best-seller, has been translated into eighteen languages and now has a sequel in *Spiritual Capital: Wealth We Can Live By*. Oxymoron or not, Zohar claims science is behind her theory; that is, quantum physics as opposed to Newtonian physics. She sees the latter as encouraging a world view of individualised atoms,

Really?

"I cannot recall the last time I heard a bride promise to love unto death. People are more realistic now, especially if they are on their second or third marriage."
US ASSOCIATION OF BRIDAL CONSULTANTS SPOKESWOMAN, *THE SUNDAY TIMES*, JULY 31, 2005.

whereas "quantum systems, on the other hand, are thought to be concretised balls of energy that take on different forms as they relate to each other through participating in the system together. When two quantum systems meet, they overlap and combine their total identity."[4]

Zohar's studies in physics and her constant use of scientific terms to explain SQ do their work well. British magazine *Personnel Today* declared earnestly: "Zohar's background in physics ... may help to dissuade sceptics from dismissing SQ as a woolly, feel-good idea and leaving it to languish on the margins of management thinking."[5]

Reading *Personnel Today*, why am I not surprised to learn that, according to an enthusiastic Zohar, the boys and girls in Human Resources have been instrumental in getting this SQ-speak into companies and central to getting its initiatives up. On her website's home page, she advertises her six-month training course (after which, she says, graduates will be qualified to run SQ workshops and design SQ interventions in organisations). Given the course includes such topics as understanding the systems dynamics of organisations in terms of IQ, EQ and SQ energy flow, I am fascinated to think what ruckuses might erupt when Zohar's trainees hit the office floors. I fear SQ, for all its well-meaning phrases, is to the inhabitants of the business world what the happy drug Soma was to the populace in Aldous Huxley's *Brave New World*. Most managers I know would be happier if they had more, and better skilled, staff and had to watch less PowerPoint.

People with a weakness for this kind of lucrative New Age woo-woo tend to gravitate towards each other so there are now all sorts of surprising alliances across very different layers of society. Capitalism, as one commentator noted, has become increasingly complicated. Does anyone really understand what is going on and where we're heading? In late 2000, the ANZ Bank brought in McKinsey & Co to introduce EQ to all staff. The cost for the first two years was a reported $16 million. By ANZ accounts, the strategy has worked. Staff satisfaction levels have climbed from 60 percent to more than 80 percent. Engagement levels are high. A major part of the programme's initial work was in deciding on a set of values the bank and its staff could share. The values turned out to be putting the customer first, leading and inspiring each other, earning the community's trust ... Am I the only one who thinks it's seriously weird that a major bank and about 25,000 people needed someone else to work out that these were their values? It makes me want to talk like an airhead.

Like, duh? Is this what thirty years of market forces and postmodern, value-free relativism have wrought? And what about the other tangible improvements ANZ introduced meanwhile? Better staff benefits, for instance, the option to work part-time for staffers over fifty-five – I bet that helped satisfaction and engagement levels.

McKinsey, of course, has also shown interest in SQ, as mentioned earlier, although oddly its local spokesman was not keen to talk about that.[6] McKinsey was also the consultancy that was favoured by Enron, the huge power company seemingly run by airheads (who were very good indeed at deal-making and making nothing look like an enormous something). In 1997, in the consultancy's own journal, *The McKinsey Quarterly*, this blasé opinion appeared: "Enron was not distinctive at building and operating power stations, but it didn't matter; these skills could be contracted out. Rather, it was good at negotiating contracts, financing and government guarantees – precisely the skills that distinguished successful players."[7] And in a 2001 entry, there was this: "Enron has built a reputation as one of the world's most innovative companies by attacking and atomising traditional industry structures."

Enron was held up by fraud; its complex accounting meant that it was able to hide billions of dollars of debt while making the bottom line look good. When its two top executives, Ken Lay and Jeffrey Skilling, the latter formerly a partner with McKinsey, finally went on trial in early 2006 for defrauding investors while helping themselves to vast riches, the American newspaper chain Cox Newspapers called the court case "the most important in business history". It ended with the two being found guilty of fraud and conspiracy. Lay died of a heart attack a few weeks later.

The Wall Street Journal noted in 2002 of McKinsey that "the celebrated consulting firm was a major force at Enron almost from the company's birth in the mid-1980s ... McKinsey was instrumental in advising Enron during its decade-long transformation from a natural-gas-pipeline company into a massively complex trading operation with far-flung interests in water, timber and high-speed Internet."[8]

The journal wondered in print about the firm's liability over Enron, given its long and close relationship. In the conclusion, McKinsey denied involvement, saying that suggestions that it was a "decision maker or a necessary review body on Enron's asset investments are flat-out wrong". The firm continued to deny involvement in the financial structuring and other issues that had brought Enron down. In a cringing there-but-for-the-grace-of-God-go-I moment, one McKinsey senior partner even had a book published just months before the final collapse, in which he extolled Enron.

Even more unfortunately, the book was entitled *Creative Destruction* although it wasn't Enron's the author had in mind.

A former Wall Streeter, a woman with a fierce imagination, once described McKinseyites to me as "the devil's spawn". It's a description that can't stand the test of truth or logic (Is there a devil? If there were a devil, could he/she be bothered spawning a management consultant?) but its passion captures how all too many feel. It is McKinsey, more than its rivals Boston Consulting, Booz Allen and Bain and Co, which has been held responsible in the public imagination for the spread of the idea that management is all about theory: just join the dots. It was McKinsey that pioneered the idea of hiring graduates from business schools rather than getting in older managers with experience in the field. Such graduates then earned far more than their salary for their employers by being hired out to clients. Not surprisingly, other consultancies soon jumped on that idea like a bunch of used-car salesmen spotting homeless ten-dollar notes on a sidewalk. Some of the less scrupulous took it to extremes. Confessed a writer for *Forbes* who had joined one of those consultancies two weeks after graduating and found herself sitting before executives from Pfizer and Lucent, "I had no idea what revenue meant, what EBIDTA[9] stood for or whether growing margins was a good thing ... My benchmark rate: $US10,000 a week. Though I didn't walk home with the cash, my firm's top brass enjoyed it."[10]

Meanwhile, McKinsey itself has powerful links throughout the international business community.

Totally

"It's hard to get on [US TV show] *Jerry Springer*. But now there's infinite space for people to indulge this narcissistic hunger to be seen. [The Internet gives everyone] an opportunity to put themselves out there."
PSYCHIATRIST ARMOND ASERINSKY, SPEAKING TO *THE NEW YORK TIMES*, JUNE 3, 2004.

Its alumni often take up CEO roles and Enron is but a painful memory that only the ill-mannered bring up. That's in spite of other embarrassing bankruptcies among its clients (Kmart in the United States and Global Crossing, although McKinsey denies final responsibility). It's in spite of the fact that, back in 1984, McKinsey told US telco giant AT&T there was no future in mobile phones. In 2003, it also reassured eBay that Google wouldn't get into online commerce. McKinsey's continued profile is also in spite of critical articles in places like *The Wall Street Journal* and *BusinessWeek* that raised the possibility the firm had kept its mouth shut to preserve relations with Enron when it might have been better to voice concerns. But still, in 2002, reported *BusinessWeek*, seven months after the Enron collapse, McKinsey was serving 147 of the world's 200 largest corporations, charging them each upwards of $US275, 000 a month for its services.[11]

McKinsey has a clever recruiting and seeding programme. If graduate recruits decide, after an initial training and further study period, that they don't want to continue at McKinsey after all, they can be offered out-placements with McKinsey clients. It's a smart ploy, like planting pre-programmed agents.

It works in reverse, too. In Britain in the early Nineties, for instance, the then director-general of the BBC, John Birt, hired McKinsey to sort the place out. The result was that, four years later, the corporation ended up with fewer staff, more red tape and a staff bill that, confoundingly, was £140 million higher.[12] On top of that, management consultancy fees, many to McKinsey, had run to £20 million a year. As various critics noted sourly, the public service broadcaster became hemmed in by a new market-based bureaucracy based on "business units". After Birt stepped down, he went to work for McKinsey as an adviser in media at £100,000 a year, a relationship that ended in uproar in 2005 because Birt had also been working as an unpaid adviser to Downing Street.

And so it goes. Something-nothing has friends all over the place, and especially up high. But if anyone had bothered to listen or learn, the cat was let out of the bag early on as far as holus-bolus management theory goes. In 1982, then McKinsey consultant Tom Peters co-authored *In Search of Excellence*, studies of various companies which the authors deemed excellent examples of management, innovation and profitability. The influential book made Peters, an ex-engineer who had studied organisational behaviour at Stanford University, into the world's foremost expert on management. Unfortunately, about two-thirds of those companies he cited later ran into trouble.[13]

Peters wasn't fazed, sticking by the basic principles (which were pretty much fundamental commonsense) and saying later in business magazine *Fast Company*,[14] "...when a bunch of the 'excellent' companies started to have some down years, that also became a huge accusation: 'If these companies are so excellent, Peters, then why are they doing so badly now?' Which I'd say pretty much misses the point."

With that kind of bustling confidence, no wonder Peters is still The Guru. McKinsey consultants, with a similar self-belief, are still considered The Elite. Management consultancies generally grow ever more powerful, so powerful that *Forbes* estimates the global worth of their business to be $US100 billion a year. Which is odd because estimates give management consulting a success rate of only about 30 percent; the same success rate that applies to new projects.

I wondered aloud to an enthusiast for these consultancies if maybe there would be less antipathy from the public if consultants just charged much less, especially given those low success rates. But then I realised that the high fees are the very point of it. If a corporate is paying *that* kind of dosh – and in 2002, McKinsey's largest client was shelling out $US60 million a year – then everyone's safe. No-one, not the client, not McKinsey, is ever going to say: gee, well, that sure was a waste of money.

Knowledge, ability, experience and a certain healthy scepticism are no friends to twenty-first-century airheadedness. Something-nothingness is much better. As Jenny Stewart points out, "People do sense that something is wrong, but there's a real reluctance to look at the cause of it. Also, it's a power thing. There are a lot of people with power who have done very well out of these conditions and they want to hang on to that power."

THE MORE we carry on like this and the more we encourage the something-nothing experts, the more we undermine what *is* knowledge. Unfortunately, at the very moment when clear thought was most needed, the universities went the way of business and fell to the forces of something-nothing, too. I asked an academic why the postmodernists, the critical theorists, the politically correct and the other various and varied babbling naked emperors had been able to first take over university campuses and then the education establishment to such an extent in the Eighties and Nineties. "Didn't you fight back?" I asked. "Yes," he replied tersely. "We did, and we suffered. A colleague and I were involved some ten or fifteen years ago in a campaign against 'Language Guidelines' issued by Human Resources here, to prevent people using 'inappropriate' language, gender-specific, etc. Big Brother had nothing on Big Sister from HR. We were regarded as pariahs as a result. I've always been true to my principles and it has cost me promotion. The people who have got on are those who have toed the party line in everything – HR, political correctness – but this would be true in most places."

A university student tells her father, an academic and a professor, one of the old school, that she doesn't believe a word of what she has been taught in cultural theory for her English studies, but she has to be able to regurgitate it in her papers or she won't pass. There's someone who, at the very beginning of her thinking career, has been taught not to search hard for truth but to dissemble to get ahead.

The New South Wales high-school syllabus for final-year English exams, introduced in 2001, divided texts into how they fitted into a student's "journey". Poetry could not be read in the raw; it could not be approached with an open and questioning mind. Instead, it had to be treated in a pre-arranged way. The poetry of Bruce Dawe had to be studied for what it revealed about consumerism; Shakespeare's *The Tempest* had to be approached only for what it revealed about the imaginative journey. No starting here and ending up somewhere altogether unexpected and remarkable.

This kind of learning is rigorous, but it's not about intellectual rigour. They call it a journey, but to me it looks like travelling to a tight timetable and with not much choice of destination. It's about squeezing minds, reining in young men and women so they learn quickly that thought processes and

Ohmigod

"The AFP [Australian Federal Police] says it appears its members were not aware of their legal obligations to cetaceans, and it has counselled them about their duties under Australian law ... Sue Arnold, an animal activist, said ... the swim was inexcusable. 'It's a bit like state police going on picnics with bank robbers.' "
THE SYDNEY MORNING HERALD, JULY 23-24, 2005, AFTER POLICE SWAM NEAR BOTTLENOSE DOLPHINS OFF GAVUTU ISLAND IN THE SOLOMONS.

inquiry must only proceed obediently along expected lines. A Ph.D student wrote longingly of crossing boundaries instead, of the science teacher who might quote Wordsworth or an English teacher who might bring up Darwin. He concluded that none of it was about "broadening minds and encouraging thought, it only permits thought within strictly defined parameters".[15]

This is how knowledge becomes "knowledge" and, this time, I'm the one being ironic. What we are really seeing here is the demeaning of real knowledge and learning and the rise of something specious and controlling in their place. Human beings like to laze – we are designed to operate with minimal effort – but what has helped stir us over thousands of years of civilisation has been the notion that it's the hard-working and hard-thinking among us who do well and that what a good society thrives upon is commonsense, fairness, hard work, originality, decency and truth. How bloody fantastic then for the lazy and unscrupulous and weak-minded to find that suddenly they could dress themselves up in the new intellectual fashions sweeping the campuses, stick their trousers on top of their heads, put their shoes on their hands, and parade into the top jobs in schools, universities and education departments while continuing with their incomprehensible intellectual habits.

It's my experience that the kind of academic or lay-person who believes in the worth of studying Virgil, Chaucer, Shakespeare or the Brontë sisters is also reasonably sanguine about the argument that film scripts, television shows and websites might also be studied at some stage. Their argument is only that there should be foundation study first. Those in the opposing camp, though, are contemptuous of the idea that the older works might be regarded as important at all. That's what gives them away, for it tells us that this is not about learning at all; it's about pushing the cult of something-nothing. If someone has only been exposed to that and nothing else, it will be so much more difficult to judge that it's a lot of tosh. When you have only seen parading naked emperors, it's that much harder to understand what you're seeing. Or not seeing.

A prime example of what the last twenty years has produced with the rise of "knowledge" is gender studies. The discipline had its birth in the pro-feminist Seventies and is now established in hundreds of universities. But why? What has gender studies achieved in a world where rape is still used as a weapon in war and for preserving tyrannies, and where feminism isn't just in retreat, but has become an irritating irrelevance to young women? In Australia, the numbers of women in senior positions are going up, but at less than the speed of rising damp. No-one can think now that only time will fix the problem. In 2002, 8.4 percent of senior executives in the top 200 companies were women. By 2004, it was 11.4 percent, reaching 12 percent by 2006. Women occupied not quite 9 percent of board seats at these companies.[16] And on mid-2006 ABS national figures, just 28 percent of managers and administrators are women. In the booming finance and insurance industries, women, often kept in subsidiary or supporting roles, earn a little less than two-thirds of what the men earn. (Note, though, that in cafes and hotels, women, always so very good at serving, earn about 95 percent of the male wage.)[17]

To wade through the promos for gender studies at different universities is to get lost in a world of words made to perform functions for which they were never designed. The theory crowd has a habit of turning words into the equivalent of painfully dancing bears. There is "gendered social movements" for a start, at the Center for Gender Studies at the University of Chicago. It's hard to trust a discipline that puts together such pretzel phrases as "the gendering of labour force participation" and "the study of gender and/or sexuality as historical practice, scientific concept and site of representation".

The website for undergraduate study in the Department of Gender Studies at the University of Sydney lists the areas examined. In 2006, they included pop and consumer culture, Australian identity and race, globalisation, feminism, violence, images and ideas of masculinity, love, intimacy and friendship, pop music, bodies and nature ... It seems horizon-less. Are there any areas that the department *doesn't* consider suitable for the gender studies net?

The prospectus for gender studies at the University of Melbourne has the same grab-bag mentality. Basically, as long as a subject involves men or women or both, it's in. And so "Scandal, Sex and Sentiment", "Reading Sexuality" and "Sex and Gender in the Ancient World" are there as optional units, and "A History of Sexualities" and "The Body: History, Sex & Gender" are core subjects.

As far as I can see, several of the gender studies degrees I check out here and overseas seem to promise that they pave the way for yet more gender study at honours, masters and doctorate level. All this knowledge and studying and dissertation-writing, but for what? At Rutgers, the state university of New Jersey, the "women and gender studies" website proudly boasts that back in 1973, the university offered just a handful of such courses. Now, it has become "one of the strongest interdisciplinary graduate and undergraduate programmes in the United States". The department faculty now consists of "27 core, 104 graduate and 68 affiliate members".

That's one of the main reasons for studying gender; that you'll never be out of a job, not with that ballooning body of students. It's the academic world's version of a pyramid scheme: the more people who join in, the bigger it gets and the bigger are the rewards for the people clinging on to it.

If it seems mean to pick on gender studies as opposed to, say, the diploma in surfing studies offered at Southern Cross University (so popular it turns away students) or the courses in ethics at any business school, it's because the very broadness of gender studies is what makes it so inescapable, so enveloping, so gloop-like. So perfect for a century that is addicted to information and data, but not to understanding.

Occasionally, someone who is considered an expert on gender will be brought into a national debate, or to apply a band-aid to some stinking mess created by the failure of men and women to understand and respect each other. In March 2004, in Australia, the National Rugby League, embarrassed by allegations of rape and inappropriate sexual behaviour against some of its players, signed up academics Catharine Lumby and Wendy McCarthy, and NSW Rape Crisis Centre director Karen Willis, to research the attitude of League players to women and to do additional international research to determine "best practice in education and mentoring programs and codes of conduct". It cost the NRL a million dollars, and the

---

Really?

"Asked if he had any insight into the book's [*Eats, Shoots and Leaves* by Lynne Truss) popularity, Andrew Franklin, whose tiny company, Profile Books, published it in Britain, appeared to give the question extended thought. 'I have a theory,' he finally said. 'It's very sophisticated. My theory is that it sold well because lots of people bought it.'"
THE NEW YORK TIMES MAGAZINE, NOVEMBER 20, 2005.

outcome? A document, called *Playing by the Rules* was produced nine months later. It contained such illuminations as this, the first under Key Findings: "Players were unequivocal that sexual assault of women is always wrong."

Where is Mandy Rice-Davies when you need her?

I'm trying to imagine the expressions on the faces of the thick-necked men who run the NRL when they read this material, purchased for seven figures. The NRL declared in the document that its "stated rationale for commissioning this research was to ensure that the organisation does everything in its power to ensure that women are treated with respect and fairness across the League". Goodness, as Mandy might say. The report recommended educational programmes for the players, among other things. I am sure it was all well-intentioned and the research was thorough – but did anyone really think this was going to work? Or that we would find out something we didn't already know? Within a flicker of the report being released, another NRL team was enthusiastically disgracing itself. Change in the League will have to come from the top, at the level of the people actually running those clubs. If that were ever bluntly suggested – I believe it was – I would like to have seen the expressions then.

Gender studies, though, and commissioning earnest studies of what footballers really think of women are just another manifestation of what has overtaken us. Once truth became "truth", we were well on the way to words and phrases simply becoming carefully chosen objects, picked not for their meaning, but for their emotional impact and how that might be used. That move opened up a vast, gaping chasm into which anyone with commonsense is liable to fall, legs flailing and spinning, as feet try to connect with solid earth.

Those of sense and some learning, for instance, wouldn't ever have felt drawn to defend the fact that the moon is not made of cheese. Nor would they have thought, a few years ago, that they needed to remind everyone that the theory of evolution was accepted as scientific fact long ago. We all knew that, didn't we?

Well, no, as it turns out.

Creationism is now called intelligent design, which is the belief that life is so complex that a highly intelligent being must have created it. As a result of the name-switch with its emotive use of "intelligent" – it's still, at heart, the same belief as creationism – President George W. Bush and others ranging from British Prime Minister Tony Blair to United States Democratic presidential candidate Al Gore, our former education minister Brendan Nelson and at least one prominent Sydney headmaster have felt safe keeping the creationists on side and declaring that intelligent design should be discussed in schools. This is the equivalent of telling astronomy students that they should not just study the findings of Copernicus – who calculated that the sun must be at the centre of our planetary system – but that they should continue to discuss the merits of Ptolemy's earlier theory which held that the earth was at the centre of the system and all the planets revolved around it.

It's not far-fetched to suggest that when the postmodernists and cultural relativists decided in the Eighties that the works of the "dead white men" were no more worthy of being studied and read than a film script, they paved the way for the return of such ideas as creationism. Their belief that everything is up for grabs and any hierarchy of knowledge should be disregarded; that all writing and thought is of similar value, and truth is "truth" reduces everything to sludge.

Once truth has been mugged and robbed of its rightful value, it's just about getting out the cudgels, flexing the biceps and seeing who has the loudest voice to decide who or what is right or wrong. Or "right" and "wrong". In this battle, don't be surprised if the creationists and their like turn out to have the most powerful muscles.

It's not about who is really right any longer, but who is enough in the ascendancy to be able to insist, if they want, that yes, the moon *is* made of cheese.

IN THIS time of something-nothingness, economics, the discipline that the nineteenth-century Scottish historian and essayist Thomas Carlyle called the dismal science, has also fallen on good times. The study of real science is in decline but economists after all are about money and figures, the drivers of our age; scientists belong to the old world that centred on manufacturing and finding out more about what's around us.

Svein Sjøberg, an academic from the University of Oslo, is involved in an international research study into why student numbers in science and technology are down. In the United States, more than half the students awarded doctorates in 2004 in physics, engineering, maths and computer science studies were recruited from overseas; there aren't enough American students.[18] Science, as Sjøberg puts it in one of his papers,[19] invades all realms of life in modern society. "Scientific and technological knowledge and skills are crucial for most of our actions and decisions, as workers, as voters, as consumers … Science and technology are major cultural products of human history, and all citizens, independently of their occupation 'needs', should be acquainted with them as elements of human culture."

He has speculated on thirteen reasons for the decline in science students, including that the curricula may be "dull, authoritarian, abstract and theoretical", that there is a lack of qualified teachers, that postmodernism has had its effect by rejecting notions of objectivity and rationality and that vigorous scientific debate in the media about such issues as global warming has confused students who have only been used to the certainties of school science. There is also the possibility that scientists are now often seen to be in the service of the big corporations, the military or the state rather than being "neutral defenders of objectivity and truth". The media's attention to rich football players, film stars and pop artists means that not very well-paid scientists in white coats working away in laboratories aren't role models. And of course, science requires hard work and intellectual effort. Sjøberg remarks soberly, "Concentration and sustained hard work do not seem to be a dominant feature of contemporary youth culture."

He also discusses the upsurge in "alternative" beliefs, in the supernatural, spiritual and metaphysical. Which takes us back to almost where we started this chapter. A philosophy professor in Melbourne remembers holding a seminar with his undergraduates during which the discussion got hijacked by an enthusiastic recounting of an experiment in Washington. According to the students, a group of people had meditated and thus

Like, whatever

"Mr Barnes [Queensland coroner] also labelled 'preposterous' the practice of psychiatrists refusing to admit patients for treatment because it may infringe their human rights."
THE AUSTRALIAN,
APRIL 11, 2006.

brought down the level of crime in the city by 25 percent. What's more, they told their professor excitedly, the meditators had originally believed the meditation would result in a reduction of 26 percent and "so, they were almost spot on!"

The beleaguered professor said later it was impossible to get his students off the subject. "It was just very embarrassing. They seemed to think it was appropriate to keep discussing this and treating it as if it could possibly be true."

A gentle man, he was too shy and flummoxed to tell them it was a lot of nonsense, thinking that *of course* they must know, deep down, it was nonsense.

Not at all.

The scientist Carl Sagan once told the story of a taxi ride in New York.[20] The taxi driver was entranced to have a real live scientist on board and wanted to talk about science. Except his science consisted of questions about the lost city of Atlantis, the shroud of Turin, Nostradamus, crystals, astrology and so on. Sagan was in misery. There was so much real science that was truly exciting and yet here was a well-read man who knew nothing of it. The myths fed into the taxi driver's precious inner life but there was no rigour there beyond the same fascinated fixity that comes with listening to Gothic fairytales.

If the world fills up with non-readers, non-learners, non-knowers, as Bradbury wrote, who will even care that we think the moon is made of cheese? The erosion of test-able knowledge, in business and education, leaves us as exposed and vulnerable and ultimately useless as a decayed tooth in a rotting mouth.

The new non-knowledge has worked its way into every facet of society, masquerading as knowledge and freakily displacing real knowledge as it does so. We feed on bites of knowledge, grabs from talkback radio, snippets from television news, condensed dot-point pars in the news and business magazines. News organisations themselves are ever more dependent on the information doled out by public relations people, media officers or spin doctors. So postmodern have we become about something-nothing non-knowledge that in Sydney, ABC local radio has a regular weekly segment in which a panel of spin doctors assess the news in terms of its spin and commend good spin-doctoring. The segment appears in the heavily news-based morning show, which is hosted by Virginia Trioli who has a good and strong news background. If anyone at the ABC has spotted the logical fallacy, they're not saying.

Access to real knowledge gets harder all the time. Science journalist Leigh Dayton complained in an opinion piece[21] that she is besieged by PRs pushing stories they want to flog. However, if she ever has to go through these same PRs to get access to someone she actually does want to interview, maybe a geoscientist on earthquake monitoring, she has to turn into a performing seal. Questions must be answered, letters written. Dayton's experience is that of any other journalist trying to tell the real story these days. The media officers could be simply covering their accountable asses. Or making access so tediously difficult that the journalist gives up and starts writing about handbags instead. Probably both.

As for the rest of us, television channels run reality shows based around the word "clever" or "brainiest". The idea is that these reality quiz shows, often featuring celebrities, will ask questions that demand answers of intelligence and learning. In fact, most of them do no such thing. But just as the lecture circuit teems with celebrities who let us go to the equivalent of a talk show but think we have listened to something profound, these quiz shows take the word "clever" and apply it to something that isn't so clever.

At the same time, anyone born since about 1980 has been taught that it is his or her right to have a voice on everything. Witness the phenomenal growth in blogs, particularly overseas, which, as one observer noted, are now the equivalent of elevator Muzak when they are founded to discuss such subjects as what to do if you take too much luggage on holiday. But those untried voices will insist on being heard, whatever the topic. Whether it's a reality television show, a radio programme or a church service, there's a demand for involvement. The equivalent of idle pub chat has become talk that demands the imprimatur of a public hearing via blogs and any number of other interactive spaces. A pastor with a Pentecostal church says of its popularity with youth: "Young people relate … they wanted to be involved in a service; they don't just want to be a spectator."[22] Elsewhere, the young are egged on by their postmodern relativist elders – and by any number of other hard-nosed elders from the television, computer and entertainment worlds. The main motive there, though, is not to hear what these energetic young voices are saying; it's to make a wad of money out of them. For all the pious championing of *Big Brother* – this is what kids are really like today and we have to give them a forum – the only reason the show exists is because it's a massive money-maker for its producers and television network.

The insistence on having a voice dogs today's classrooms and lecture halls. In her essay[23] for the American journal *Academe*, Susan Ostrov Weisser wrote poignantly of her role as professor of English: "I believed in my education: now students believe in themselves, or say they do." When she suggested to a first-year writing student ways to improve her essay, the student replied: "I don't agree with your personal preferences."

Weisser delicately exposes the central contradiction and what the student is really up to. It's another version of something-nothing and in this case the student wants something for delivering nothing. Weisser continues: "When I heard those words, I saw my many years of graduate training and even more years of teaching experience dissolve before my eyes. It's as if my student and I live in parallel academic universes. In mine, I am the expert who shares my expertise and evaluates student performance from the position of that expertise. In hers, I am not more likely to be right than any eighteen-year-old student; on the contrary, I don't know anything worth knowing better than she does. It's all about personal opinion anyway, so why am I troubling her with my 'opinions' when she has her own perfectly good ones already? My intellectual authority as her professor is equivalent to a useful fiction, a semi-ironic game she agrees to for a short time for pragmatic reasons, with the understanding that we both know it is faintly ridiculous. She believes in herself, and that belief is quite unshakable.

"Yet it is mandatory that I give this student a grade; moreover, she herself wants an evaluation of her performance. Not just any evaluation, however; she demands – *insists* – on a good one, because she *believes in herself*. My job is to confirm what she already knows; in other words, to give it the institutional stamp that will enable her to get the

---

Ohmigod

"Finally, in August 1996, Christopher telephoned me and told me that Bloomsbury had 'made an offer'. I could not quite believe my ears. 'You mean it's going to be published?' I asked rather stupidly. 'It's definitely going to be published?'"

AUTHOR J.K. ROWLING, NOW A BILLIONAIRE, REFLECTS ON HOW LONG IT TOOK TO GET HER FIRST HARRY POTTER NOVEL ACCEPTED.

job she desires or entrance to the grad school she covets."

Sydney academic Joellen Riley says students now expect a lot of bland compliments: "They won't want to take on anything that might make them feel inadequate." She remembers trying to tell one law student, who objected to criticisms about her lack of knowledge, that what she was copping now would be as nothing compared with what she would suffer if she later revealed her ignorance in front of a judge. The girl, fed on something-nothing all her life, was impervious. The truth is she couldn't see the difference between something and nothing.

The persistent culture of "personal relevance" and its tight control has also produced in many of the under-thirties a profound disdain for anything or anyone they've not heard of before. Their internal thinking, programmed into them by years of the education I've already lamented, seems to go like this: I have been taught all my life that I must only know about things that are personally relevant to me, and the implication behind this is that *only* things that are personally relevant to me are important. This new person/concept/fact/event is something I have never been taught about or been asked to learn about. Ipso facto, it/he/she is unimportant. It is nothing.

This is the ultimate triumph, and revenge, of the something-nothing age: when it finally convinces us that something that really is something is nothing.

There's a cost to all this pushing forward and me-tooing and braying over the top of everyone else. Sometimes, the only way to acquire knowledge is to listen and watch and read. This is happening all too rarely anywhere, as you can see in CEOs ignoring their own staff so they can hire consultants and in New Age gurus preaching New Age intelligence – but you can see it best on the Internet. This remarkable, stupendous invention has changed our world completely and made knowledge available to all; it gives us something *for* nothing. Gradually, though, it is being taken over by one huge chattering, swarming, opinionated mass, muttering, spouting and swapping muzzy details, data, gossip and uncooked arguments with the certitude of a Carlyle or Gibbon.

"Shut-up" is a helpful term that leaps to mind.

CHAPTER 11

Stuff Happens

"*An outgoing personality combined with a healthy self-regard is also a must, say employers, because investment bankers spend a great deal of time charming clients and negotiating deals.*"

A STORY IN *THE AUSTRALIAN FINANCIAL REVIEW*, JULY 11, 2005, EXPLAINS WHY "ONLY BRIGHT AND BOLD NEED APPLY"

"*What's been happening in the United States for about twenty years is a long-term trend to differentiate compensation ... We've moved into a star system for some reason which is not fully understood.*"

SECRETARY OF THE US TREASURY AND FORMER CORPORATE CEO JOHN SNOW EXPLAINS TO *THE NEW YORK TIMES* THE RISE OF THE TWENTY-FIRST-CENTURY MEGA-RICH

Sunday. Friend's house down the street burns down.

Monday. Friend, who has been away and uncontactable, taps diffidently at my door. "What happened?" he asks.

Tuesday. Friend is standing outside his house with his assessor. He reveals he hasn't yet seen the young woman boarder who accidentally burned down his house. She has lost all her belongings and apparently she is now at work. My friend is very understanding about it but I'm not. His large and once meticulously restored terrace is a gaunt grey shell, blackened and lurching towards the sky like a ruin in a Victorian gothic novel.

I stomp back upstairs to ring another baby-boomer friend, a Scotsman who lives up on Sydney's northern beaches. "Don't you think you'd come around pretty quickly and apologise face to face if you'd just burnt someone's house down?" I say to him.

"I've got a story just like that," he says. "A friend was walking along the beach and suddenly a girl in the waves got hit right on the lower back bit of her skull by a surfboard. He and a few others got her ashore and called the ambulance. She was unconscious and they were keeping her immobile because they had no idea how much damage had been done. My friend said to one of the guys who'd got there before him, 'So where's the surfer, the one who did this?' He looked blankly at him and said he didn't know. He added, vaguely, that the guy must have left."

The new ways of behaving can leave us speechless

Huh?

Cherie Blair, wife of the British PM, decided to hold her fiftieth birthday early so it wouldn't conflict with the launch of her memoirs. Her actual birthday is September 23. She chose to celebrate it instead on the third anniversary of 9/11.

but we're going to have to get used to it. When I began writing this chapter, I was listening to the radio news about a young man questioned over the death of cruise passenger Dianne Brimble. He had complained to police that finding her body in his cabin had ruined his holiday. Then the latest *Big Brother* scandal broke, two young men were evicted, and I had to listen to various cultural, media and gender-studies experts poncing on about how if we wanted *BB* off our screens, then we were, like, you know, totally missing the point. A show that I thought was about a group of show-offs competing for money and hoping for easy fame turned out to be essential and important viewing for all of us, but especially young people who were unsure about sex and how to fit in with a group. The season before, *Big Brother* had introduced these young things to the practice of "turkey-slapping", that is, a man flapping his penis in the face of a woman. This was the behaviour that led to the 2006 evictions when two contestants held down a female housemate for a fine spot of turkey-doo-dah. Not that the experts seemed to spot any incongruity. "As a device for giving us an insight into young people, it's more effective than a number of studies of that kind. It's much more immediate and personal," argued one lecturer who sounded as if he'd packed his normal, decent, thinking self off on sabbatical too early.

Host Gretel Killeen, lamenting the fact the two young men had to leave her show, described them as "fantastic" housemates. The young woman concerned was both tearful and mortified that she might have been to blame for the evictions. As for the two blokes, they protested they had only been joking and the mother of one of them discussed whether her son should sue the television station for defamation.

Neo-liberalism, aka economic rationalism, is all about the rights of the individual to compete freely in the market for his/her own interests, never mind anyone else. The fatal flaw in the argument, though, is that it ends up producing some not very pleasant people at the top who then create a rather unpleasant world everywhere else. What happens up there always affects us down below. What's acceptable behaviour among people with a public face becomes our accepted behaviour. If lack of accountability, ruthlessness, callousness, self-centredness and greed are what we see, that infects us. We are equally influenced if popular idols, icons and reality TV guests reveal themselves to be acquisitive, heedless, vain and empty-headed. Or if they turn up on sex tapes.

Ever since Kenneth Anger released his seamy exposé *Hollywood Babylon* in the early Sixties, we've known what the rich, beautiful, famous and selfish can get up to when they think the public isn't watching. Anger's book and its Eighties sequel were full of scandal, gossip and innuendo about Hollywood's most famous names, and readers were shocked. Now we hear the same kinds of sleazy tales or see them playing out in full view, but something odd has happened. It's like, you know, whatever.

Celebrity magazines crowd newsagents' shelves clamouring for our attention. The experts tell us we are riveted by starry gossip because the stories are like contemporary morality tales. Discussing J-Lo's triple marriages or what Jude did to Sienna and what she then did to him in the infidelity stakes is supposed to allow us to reflect upon and talk about the problems in our own lives. It seems much more likely that the antics of the famous will simply make us think their behaviour is normal. And that if, with everything they have going for them, it still doesn't make them good and contented people, what then? As journalist Jacqueline Maley commented in a satirical media column at the height of the Ange-Brad-Jen triangle saga: "Ange is worried Brad will cheat on her, *NW* reports, and is devastated because the entire planet thinks of her as a man-stealer. Cruel, cruel world. If La Jolie – superbabe, humanitarian and lady-pilot – is worried about her image, what chance do the rest of us have?"[1]

Instead of good behaviour being on one side and bad on the other, we now have a slippy-slidey continuum. One minute actor Lindsay Lohan is supposed to be Hollywood's latest bimbo car-wreck with her drinking and partying and eating problems; the next *WHO* magazine is putting her in its "Sexiest People, 2006" issue, giving us a sultry and flattering black-and-white portrait of her and describing her thus: "This is what you get when Hollywood innocence grows up: a party-starting, man-eating vixen."

When a British tabloid photographer catches model Kate Moss snorting line after line of cocaine, there is a frenzy and a few of the more sedate conglomerates drop Moss's services, but overall the tone is best caught by this quote from the *Times* fashion editor: "The reason they [the big brands] love Kate is the danger she brings. As long as she gets up in the morning and looks beautiful, they will still love her." *Vanity Fair* confirms this by putting her on the cover less than three months later, and running a series of sexy pictures inside.

Then there's hip-hop, with stars like 50 Cent, Snoop Dogg and Sean "P. Diddy" aka "Puffy" Combs, and its run of murdered rappers. A lifetime ago, poor, malnourished black kids escaped the ghettos only by studying or through sport. Now

Ohmigod

Viewpoint 1: "The audience that does watch [Big Brother] is very capable of observing the behaviour and making judgments and engaging with the show on that judgmental level."
ERROL SULLIVAN, FORMER EXECUTIVE DIRECTOR OF THE COMPANY THAT PRODUCES BIG BROTHER, TALKS TO THE AUSTRALIAN, JULY 2005.

Viewpoint 2: "As Spike previously revealed, 27,800 5-12-year-olds and 81,000 13-17-year-olds watched a recent episode of Big Brother Uncut which featured dangly bits, a frank discussion of rectal exploration and the imaginative use of an electric toothbrush."
THE SPIKE COLUMN IN THE SYDNEY MORNING HERALD GAVE THE BIGGER PICTURE IN JUNE 2005.

it's through music which takes all the violence, murder, guns, pimping, sex and savagery of everyday gang and ghetto life and drums it into our heads. In the process, something weird happens. It becomes glamorised, and this at a time when the American under-classes, especially blacks, are worse off than ever.

Australian war artist and filmmaker George Gittoes made *Soundtrack to War*, which showed American soldiers in Iraq creating their own rap music to give a rhythm to their disjointed days. Then he made a semi-follow-up with the documentary *Rampage*, which told the story of one family, whose soldier son Gittoes had met in Iraq, living in a murderous Miami ghetto called Brown Sub. The family is devoted to hip-hop, and the youngest, dubbed "the rising star", might actually crack a recording contract, which Gittoes tries to help deliver. When studio executives in New York flinch at a fourteen-year-old delivering his lines about death, guns, drug deals and poverty, we're made to think they're being weak and hypocritical for worrying about "age-appropriateness". (I was on their side and I also would have liked to hear one tell Gittoes to make sure the kid got schooling as well as stardom.)

The ABC told Gittoes, he said, that hip-hop wasn't its demographic, so instead he got *Rampage* screened at the 2006 Sydney Film Festival to grateful praise from its first audience. The documentary is long and full of the kinds of scenes you'd expect to see on the wrong side of Miami – teenagers toting guns, kids showing off and smoking dope for the camera, broken-down housing, a funeral and a lot of rapping. It is hard to forget. Many of the people in it – from the Miamians themselves to the recording bosses – are hard to like, although that is not always what the voice-over is leading you to think.

I couldn't help thinking of writer Tom Wolfe as I watched the audience's reverent reaction and its acceptance of the film's key propositions: that Miami is more dangerous than Baghdad; that the only way out of a ghetto is via drugs, the army or becoming rich and famous through music. If there has been any movement in the understanding shown by the white middle classes to politicised blacks since Wolfe had fun writing *Radical Chic & Mau-Mauing the Flak-Catchers* in 1970, it seems to have been in the wrong direction.

Wolfe's two title pieces both sent up the same thing: educated white society's guilt and unease about black Americans and, at the same time, its awareness that there was apparently something, you know, just so fashionable, funky and liberated about being black. Wolfe described a cocktail party at the Park Avenue penthouse duplex of conductor Leonard Bernstein. Some Black Panthers had been invited, along with about every acting, directing, producing, composing, writing name in town. A woman says excitedly to a *New York Times* writer, "I've never met a Panther – this is a first for me!" One of the Panthers has just been arrested in an "altercation with the police, supposedly over a .38-calibre revolver ..." For the evening, the finely tuned Bernsteins have made sure that the serving staff aren't black but South American.

Gittoes is a passionate and well-meaning man who says he has put his house on the line to finance his film. Nevertheless, to me his documentary has a whiff of the Bernsteins about it. The nearly all-white festival audience's unquestioning embrace of the film, that this is what "poh black" people have to do, their seeming fascination with and approval of what they're seeing, grated. (How did these Miami kids finance their lifestyles? Gittoes slipped over that. What would an ill-educated fourteen-year-old rapper who gets lucky do with his life except make a bucketload of money? What then? If the audience had been watching a film about a "poh white" suburb, would they have been as ready to accept that only drugs, the army or music could save its inhabitants?[2])

Earlier, at the Berlin film festival, Gittoes had said, "[The Brown Sub boys] have got nothing and yet the whole time I was with them, I felt that I was poorer than they were. I felt that they were in a culture which was much, much richer than mine." When that comment appeared in an interview by Los Angeles reporter Jeffrey

Wells on website hollywood-elsewhere.com, it drew a tetchy response from a young photographer who used to live on the border of a ghetto in Baltimore and knows how rotten and desperate ghetto life is for anyone. Wary of sounding cantankerous, he wrote: "Their culture is richer than yours? You must be dead in the grave then ... I've been all over the city and the 'culture' Gittoes is talking about is one of macho thuggery, irresponsibility, misogyny, short-sightedness, ignorance, and generally not giving a shit about anything." He emailed me later: "My anger is at an establishment that keeps [ghetto inhabitants'] situation static, and the white majority that keeps them in place while having this bizarre adulation of them at the same time."

BEING BAD, as we know from wicked Lord Byron, has always been much sexier than being good. But the above cameos from today's world are not so much about being bad as being foolish, thoughtless or irresponsible. We seem to have landed ourselves in a moral slurry, courtesy of thirty or so years of political correctness, relativism and something-nothing non-speak. There is now a strong sense among the hip, the clued-in, the media-savvy, that holding on to what used to be called traditional values, especially when they get in the way of fun or entertainment, is old-fashioned, repressive and, worst of all, judgmental. A cultured, middle-aged American friend remarks, "It seems that the worst thing you can call an Australian is 'wowser'. Why is this?"

Nothing seems to have changed since I was a gawky fresher at university explaining to a group of sardonic, superior third-year students that I didn't want to smoke dope because I was worried about its unknown side-effects and what it might do to my brain. (Well, sorry, things *have* changed: I turned out to be right and attitudes that were once entrenched in a protected pocket of middle-class counter-culture are now everywhere.) People who object to the sexual antics on *Big Brother* are pooh-poohed for not living in the real world where *of course* even 15-year-olds have regular sex. Don't even think of having an intelligent, open-minded discussion about gay marriage and its various ramifications. It's appropriate, right! Question acceptance of dope-smoking and Ecstasy among the young and it's like, *helloooo!* Whaddya want them to do? Take heroin? Then there's the sanctimonious, politically correct response that alcohol is much worse anyhow. An unprecedented study[3] of cheating at universities reveals, to the shock and surprise of academe, that students have a high tolerance for cheating, plagiarising, copying and falsifying research results. The authors of the Queensland-based study sensibly argue that students who do not respect academic integrity while at university are less likely to respect integrity in their future professional and personal relationships; dishonest behaviour is not situation specific. A follow-up study[4] found neither students nor academic staff were inclined to report such misconduct. The students didn't want to be dobbers and staff members were hamstrung by what would be needed to make the case against a student, and a feeling that management wouldn't want to support them anyway.

Humans are fascinating creatures. Put us in stable circumstances with clear values and we may still give in to the baser instincts, but we will understand what we are doing. However, once the moral compass disappears or starts to disappear, and the most basic lines on behaviour and expectations are stepped over, humans lose the plot. Like pilots in storms who become disoriented and can't find the horizon again, we lose our sense of what is up, what is down, where we're going and how to get there.

The advertising slogan of Enron was "Ask why". The trouble, of course, was that too few ever did.

A *Newsweek* magazine piece[5] on psychopathic behaviour in the workplace notes that qualities such as charisma and being "hard-charging" are increasingly valued in politics and business, leaving everyone vulnerable to the slither-tongued snake whose ruthlessness and deviousness are rewarded.

It's never been easy for the shy and retiring, and now it's much, much harder. Reality television shows have made instant stardom, and sometimes

Really?

"*Good Luck*, a short how-to-get-it guide knocked up by two Spanish writers in eight hours, has recorded one million sales worldwide in 30 languages."
THE WEEKEND AUSTRALIAN, OCTOBER 16-17, 2004.

instant wealth, possible for unknowns, but the qualities producers look for in would-be participants are not those that would win you prizes at Sunday school or plaudits from your head teacher. The numerous fast ways to skedaddle up the ladder to undreamt-of wealth – hip-hop, talent quests, modelling, investment banking – all require massive front and an unshakeable belief in yourself. If you need to make a choice between ego and brain, it's likely that rampant ego will get you much further than a brain and a conscience that both tick like Swiss clocks.

Likewise, ethics can be a distinct disadvantage to healthy career progress. When the young National Australia Bank rogue traders, who had lost their employer $360 million, had their various days in court, one defence counsel told the court his client had been under increasing pressure to "gamble hard". Profit targets had been raised tenfold in a few years. In spite of the fallout at NAB after the losses, are we to believe that such pressure isn't going on in a million other offices around the globe? Indeed, at the committal hearing for two of the former currency dealers, the court heard how one senior NAB executive, now in a high-ranking job at the ANZ, had panned suggested reforms to the foreign exchange options desk two years before the scandal. The bank's internal auditors had been concerned at the willingness of the traders to take large risks. The executive allegedly told top management at the time that the auditors didn't understand what it takes to run a bank.

Further, if our current position, for all its upside-down-ness, seems to be delivering advantages to at least ourselves – although maybe not to our fellows – we tell ourselves that it's really okay; we're just part of a revolution. Alternatively, we may have been made so unsettled and insecure we don't dare draw attention to ourselves by protesting. Whistleblowers recount that all too often what is worse for them is not the way their bosses or the authorities react, it's the way they are shunned by their colleagues.

When life and its rewards are eventually seen as more random than winning the pokies, then life itself becomes meaningless and random. And a major company, Apple, chose exactly that word for its advertising campaign for the iPod: "Life is random".

A SENIOR lecturer in applied psychology told me a couple of years ago that, in the past, young women came for counselling because of problems caused by guilt. Now, it's because they have narcissism issues. There's a problem though: the patients don't realise the problems they're having are caused by selfishness and self-centredness. So what about young men, I asked her, are they coming in with problems caused by narcissism, too? "Well," she replied, "they're pretty good at that anyhow because men are taught to be self-sufficient."

I always wondered what forty years of feminism in a prospering world might have achieved, and now I know: women have claimed the right to grow up as focused on themselves as men are.

In May 2006, Sir Edmund Hillary was openly disgusted with the behaviour of forty mountaineers who'd virtually stepped over a dying man as they climbed Mount Everest. "He's a human being and we would regard it as our duty to get him back to safety," he said of the stricken climber who had run out of oxygen. The man, David Sharp, died later in an ice cave. "I think the whole attitude toward climbing Mount Everest has become rather horrifying," said Sir Edmund. "The people just want to get to the top."

Others, including those who had walked past the dying man, disputed that, saying there was nothing that could have been done for the climber. Within days, experienced climbers were writing in to the newspapers to say that if the mountaineers had had enough oxygen and supplies to get themselves to the top, then it stood to reason they also would have had enough to help Sharp down instead.

An academic at one of Sydney's best graduate schools of management remembers talking to one of his young male students about his future role as a business leader, his responsibilities, his outlook. "I'm not interested in any of that," said the young thug. "Just wanna make money."

A University of Adelaide study of aspirations in teenagers, released in 2004, showed that Generation Y boys in Years 11 and 12, had the kinds of fantasies that inspired Hugh Hefner to get his Playboy empire off the ground in Fifties America. They dreamed of wealth, fast cars and sport, with a beautiful and sexy young wife as the finishing touch.

Researcher Terry Lyons is looking into the reasons fewer kids want to study maths and science these days. It's a worldwide problem and Lyons is busy developing solutions that involve much grassroots research among kids, to whom he is hugely sympathetic. When he investigated why high-school students weren't choosing physics or chemistry, he found many didn't think it was "personally relevant". It turns out that it's not just the difficulty of the subjects; the students object to the focus on content in the courses, rather than *their* relationship to that content.

Totally

"'All he wanted to do was have a laugh,' said one of the neighbours ... 'He was sound as a pound.' Yeah, right. If these four young men were perfectly normal Yorkshiremen, then what the hell is happening to this country?"
MP AND *SPECTATOR* EDITOR BORIS JOHNSON REACTS TO COMMENTS ON THE FOUR YOUNG HOMEGROWN TERRORISTS WHO KILLED 52 PEOPLE IN LONDON IN 2005.

He pondered, too, the kinds of influences the kids were picking up, how "girly" some of the girls were. He added that this was not research-based, just his own observations, but said worriedly, "It's all about being a pop princess on MTV, being blonde ... I don't get it. What social message are they picking up? I suppose it's always easier to conform, and I guess there's this role-modelling ..."

And what do the boys want to study instead of science? When a Norwegian delegate asked that question at a conference on the subject in Poland Lyons attended in July 2004, there came an anguished cry from the audience: "How to be chefs!" That, says Lyons, turned out to be the correct answer. The boys were training to be chefs or going into the hospitality industry. Even Lyons has two nephews who want to be chefs, not scientists. "You have to look at the influence of the media," he says. "All the cooking shows and articles about food. There are no realistic portrayals of scientists on TV apart from forensics and doctors. It's *My Restaurant Rules!* You don't see *My Laboratory Rules!*" Lyons, who works for the National Centre of Science, Information and Communication Technology and Mathematics Education for Rural and Regional Australia, also says of the choices of study, "What 'personally irrelevant' really meant was that there weren't enough immediate advantages."

The preoccupation of the moment is with Gen Y, the group born between 1978 and 1994. Characterised as being confident, impatient, demanding, selfish, used to having multiple choices and phobic about commitment of any kind, they are taken very seriously indeed, given their spending power, their clout in the workforce and their eventual electoral numbers. We survey them, we focus-group them. I want more precise explanations though. I want to know why if they're in a supermarket and standing plonk in the centre of an aisle, they can't hear five escalating sets of "Excuse me" when anyone tries to get past them. And why do they think it's okay to hold up a Gloria Jean's cafe queue for five minutes because they each want to pay for their coffee and cake with a credit or Eftpos card. (Exactly how much forward planning does buying a coffee with cash take?)

Books are published, articles are written and consultants make money by advising employers on this generation's quirks, which, supposedly, are as much a part of them as the colour of their eyes and hair. Every now and then though, a contradictory little paragraph will appear, often in one of the careers sections of the newspapers. It'll be someone trying to put up their hand to plead that really, truly, there's not much difference between any of the generations so long as they're handled the same way. People don't change; it's what we do to them, how we bring them up and how we reward them that make the difference. I was going to write "reward or punish" in that last sentence, but I've yet to hear a parent of today tell me about punishing a teenager under his or her roof, no matter what the aggravation, and if more formal teachers do take a stand, they cop it. Parents are the new school bullies, according to *The Sun-Herald*, which editorialised, "In the past, if a child slipped academically, didn't make a sporting team or failed to get a part in the school play, it was chalked up to experience ... Now, it seems, there is a widespread assumption that, for even the slightest setback, someone is to blame – but never the student, and certainly not the parent. The teacher becomes the target."[6]

No wonder Gen Y goes on as it does, annoying the hell out of everybody else but behaving exactly as you would if you had been taught always that you're not only the centre of the universe but that that is the only place to be. Older generations always criticise younger generations and vice versa. It's the expected way of things, which is why everyone over forty-five was so polite to Ryan Heath when he wrote his diatribe against baby boomers, *Please Just F*** Off, It's Our Turn Now*.[7] The young ones dish it out; and the older ones, from Socrates onwards, have dished it out in return. But there are differences this time around.

Raj Persaud, consultant psychiatrist at Maudsley Hospital in South London and Gresham professor for public understanding of psychiatry, has talked often on the subject of motivation. A regular on a high-rating breakfast programme on British television, he is that country's most visible and sometimes controversial expert on mental health. He has noted a phenomenon of our times to do with whether we are internally or externally focused. The division helps explain how you view your life and what happens to you. Internals believe that ultimately they control their own destiny; that in the end, whatever happens, their success or failure is pretty much down to them. If they fail, they can reach into themselves to come back. If they succeed, they believe they have helped bring that about. Externals believe the opposite: that destiny is something that happens to them because of outside forces such as chance or luck or the way the cards are stacked.

"Now, whether you're an internal or an external has dramatic implications on your behaviour," Persaud said in one address.[8] "Internals tend to vote. Externals tend not to vote, because externals don't believe that can have much impact on the world ... Externals tend to commit more crime, because externals don't believe in the benefits of hard work. They like to take short cuts. Externals are more prone to a variety of psychological problems ... internal people are more motivated than externals."

He believes we are now seeing declining levels of motivation and thinks one possible cause of this is a general shift from internality to externality. Since the concept was first developed in the early Sixties, psychologists have been measuring the population. Persaud cites findings that show a dramatic shift towards externality. "So much so," he puts it, "that the average young person alive today aged between 18 and 21 is more external in orientation than 80 percent of young people of the same age alive in the early Sixties."[9]

He attributes the shift to a number of factors, ranging from lawyers insisting that someone is always to blame for anything that has happened to you, to the helping professions which encourage people to think their bad behaviour is caused by their upbringing or a fierce teacher or their hormones or their genes. He said, "This rise of explanation may be squeezing out personal responsibility at a dangerous level." Another psychiatrist, Professor Ian Hickie, of the Brain and Mind Research Institute at the University of Sydney, has commented on the explosion in multiple personality syndrome. He says what this means, conveniently, is that such people will blame their child side; they will be able to distance themselves from themselves.

Our focus on individuality and the right of everyone to their own "journey", whatever the cost to the people around them, has not led to a super-race of strong, self-motivated, happy people taking responsibility for their actions. Instead, it has produced people who are so focused on "me" that they don't have the wherewithal to understand how "me" has to fit in with "you" if "me" is to survive at all. Unless you want to sign up as a Trappist monk, and even if you agree that "hell is other people", it's not possible to escape other people altogether and nor do human beings want to do that. In every study of happiness, the key factor turns out to be our ability to have good relationships with people close to us and in our community. That ability requires old-fashioned traits, though, such as empathy and unselfishness, at least at times. Fitting into a healthy community also requires that you contribute to it, too, in the best way you can, and that demands even more traditional qualities.

The man who has focused the world's attention on happiness, Martin Seligman, conducted his study[10] of self-discipline with another researcher, Angela Duckworth. One of their strong conclusions was that America's children had trouble making choices that would require them to sacrifice short-term pleasure for long-term gain, such has been the power of the instant gratification message pumped to them since they were born. One journal reporting the research summarised this as a lack of grit, noting "perseverance has come to seem like quaint lip service against the tide of interest in talent and aptitude, flashier gifts that nature, or genes, seem to inarguably confer".[11] But it's the ones with grit who apparently do well at school, work and elsewhere.

Psychologist K. Anders Ericsson's *Cambridge Handbook of Expertise and Expert Performance*,[12] with its carefully researched essays and

Like, whatever

A Missouri woman whose chihuahua puppy died, pushed into the house of the breeder to try to get another one, *Associated Press* reported. When the breeder objected, the woman hit her over the head several times with the dead chihuahua and then drove off, yelling threats and waving the puppy out through the sunroof.

observations from the world's experts, introduces me to a new concept – automatisation. Whenever we learn a new skill, like driving a car or playing the piano, it is natural to eventually go onto automatic pilot so the body and mind can operate with minimal effort. Truly expert performers – concert pianists, racing car drivers – don't allow that to happen though; they are always aware of what they are doing at each tiny stage so they can push themselves further. They develop habits and attitudes that mean they monitor themselves. Nothing comes easily. They compare themselves with others who perform better. Ericsson also notes that expert performers will have accurate and detailed memories of what they did during a competition long after it has occurred. Feedback is essential for that to happen. And also essential, he agrees when I put it to him, is a certain healthy insecurity or concern about your talents.

But what's between the covers of Ericsson's book is not what our children and young people are encouraged to do, because today's environment insists that no-one should have self-doubts. Instead, the mantra is that this is your "journey" and it's your right to go on that journey to find your fulfilment – even if it means holding up an entire aisle at Woolworth's while you decide between shampoos.

As with much of the twenty-first century, the devil is in the juxtaposition. At the very time more are growing up to be externals fixated on the idea that we are all creatures of circumstance and life is what happens to us, life is turning out to be tougher and rougher. Externals now live in a world where the ordinary person in the street is treated with calculation or, worse, disrespect, by almost every other layer of society.

Nobody in business thinks twice about asking people paying for a service to actually perform most of that service themselves; the average person's time is treated as being of no account. Downsizing means constant queuing, which used to be something the rest of the world thought only the British did. It is now an accepted way of life either in reality or because you're waiting on the phone to talk to someone in a call centre. Computerised tills, for stock and revenue control, also mean there is now no such thing as the quick transaction for a customer. Sometimes, I've been tempted to clamber over a counter and study the computer screen myself to find out why an assistant has spent five minutes worriedly punching in figures so I can buy a $15 tin of paint. Media and entertainment producers and executives talk regularly of the "punter", by which they seem to mean anyone voracious enough to devour whatever cost-saving dross they might dream up to capture him or her.

As for politicians, now that we've reached the age of "small government" and, supposedly, less government intervention in our lives, their eyes are all too often fixed on just two goals. First, how to stay in power or get into power, and second, how to line up a lucrative job once they've left politics. Lance Price revealed in *The Spin Doctor's Diary* that British Prime Minister Tony Blair and his spin team often made up policies on the hoof, sometimes minutes before appearing on television. Another spinner for the Blair government even seized on 9/11, emailing the transport minister as the Twin Towers burst into flames that it would be a very good day to bury any bad news.

Here in Australia, politicians are able to glide easily and quickly into high-paying jobs in the private sector later on. It makes me think it must be like telling a bunch of foxes that they have a choice between guarding chickens and the chickens' rights carefully, and so go hungry, perhaps forever; or they can herd chickens into the mouths of other foxes, who will later reward them with chickens, too. What's a fox to do?

The truth is that the main purpose of most of us, according to those in power either in politics or business, is first, to be gulled and wooed, and then to be bullied or coerced into giving them our money, our labour and our tacit agreement that what they are doing to us is acceptable. No wonder then that, increasingly, people who have been brought up in this climate, look around them, look up, look down, have a bit of a think and decide that if this is the way it is, then they'd rather be the ones doing the bullying and gulling than the ones on the receiving end. Who wants to be a chicken when you can be a well-fed fox?

Economist Lord Richard Layard, debating Persaud at the London School of Economics in August 2005, quoted a World Health Organisation survey which asked young people aged eleven to fifteen: "Do you agree with the statement that 'most of the students in my classes are kind and helpful'?" At least 75 percent of the fifteen-year-old children in Portugal, Sweden, Macedonia and Switzerland happily agreed. In the United States, about 50 percent said yes, and in England, about 40 percent. As a revealing comparison, the other country to score low was Russia with 44 percent.[13] Layard, who was speaking on social values and happiness, added that when people were asked if they thought most people could be trusted, the Scandinavians again said yes in very high numbers. But the numbers saying yes in

Britain and the United States had halved in the last forty years. He put that decline down to the growth of individualism in those countries.

In such suspicious and unkind societies, having ethics can seem dangerously close to deciding to walk into a brigands' cave wearing nothing but your wallet.

N ONSENSE begets nonsense. Airheadedness begets airheadedness. A headmistress, talking of her students absorbing glossy magazines and television shows like *Big Brother*, calls it the "garbage-in, garbage-out" equation. But this is more than kids being fed on an intellectual diet the equivalent of sugared popcorn and then popping out platitudes. This is about us stopping them from using their own commonsense and innate sense of right and wrong. What are we doing to all those young brains? Is there any escape or refuge for them?

British children, we now learn, struggle to answer questions they could have answered thirty years ago. A professor of education and a psychology professor assessed 25,000 eleven-year-olds in public and private schools in 2004 and found them alarmingly lacking in commonsense about basics. For instance, they could not work out that a tall thin container held the same amount of water as a short, fat container even though they had watched the thin container being emptied into the fat container and then refilled. Asked if the containers now held the same amount of water, the children were baffled. Another experiment involved two blocks made of the same size but of different materials. One was brass, the other Plasticine.

Ohmigod

"More than half of all young drivers on the roads regularly read and write text messages on their mobile phones while behind the wheel ... 58 percent of 17- to 29-year-olds regularly read text messages while driving."
THE AUSTRALIAN,
JUNE 10, 2004.

Asked which would displace the most water if dropped into a beaker, fewer than 20 percent of today's kids got the answer right.

Thirty years ago when these experiments were first conducted, more than 25 percent of the kids tested scored highly overall. Now, that's dropped to 5 percent. These results reveal that cognition levels in eleven-year-olds are now about three years behind what might have been expected three decades ago. In the report, published in *The Sunday Times*,[14] the researchers claimed the results showed the kids had lower general intelligence and also lacked basic bedrock scientific and mathematical knowledge. The real problem was that the kids didn't seem to know how to handle new and difficult ideas. The story put forward various theories. Maybe the kids didn't get their hands dirty enough playing in sandpits so they lacked familiarity with physical properties. Maybe there should be more Plasticine and Meccano and less xBox, and maybe the constant testing and drilling at school meant kids weren't encouraged to think things through for themselves.

Terry Lyons, who used to be a science teacher, describes how difficult it is for kids to get practical experience with experiments at school. "If teachers think the kids might not behave, they'll either suggest watching a video or they'll do the experiment themselves. You can't send a kid who's misbehaving out of class these days unless he or she can go to a supervised classroom. The other problem is to do with occupational health and safety issues. In New South Wales, and it's likely the same everywhere, teachers have to undertake risk assessments for every experiment they do and that has to be signed off by the science co-ordinator. If no-one else has done the experiment before, you have to get in an expert to show you how to do it. And the real problem, of course, is that kids *love* doing the practical work." I came across two Scottish girls recently who'd studied animal welfare for three years at an Aberdeen university. In the entire course, they'd got their hands on a live animal only once when they were permitted to put a thermometer up a rabbit's bottom. During exams, they'd had to test their bandaging skills on soft toys.

Here's the question to which I finally came: are we losing our minds, or just making sure that more and more of us grow up mindless? I had wondered if something more profound and troubling than celebrity worship and iPod mania was afoot ever since I read a quote from an Australian neurologist in an article about changes in brain behaviour.[15] Associate professor Dr John Watson, from the University of Sydney, and at that time director of the Neuropsychology Unit at the

Royal Prince Alfred Hospital, said we might see signs of the impact of the way we structure learning, work and leisure sooner than we think. Connections between neurons in the brain, especially the frontal lobe, continue to develop from birth to the mid-teenage years and later. If connections are used, they are reinforced while those used less often may be lost. "You could make a strong argument," he told journalist Wendy Tuohy, "but purely speculative, that we are bringing up infants and children and teenagers who are only really asked to attend to something for a few minutes at a time ... it could have some influence on the development of the connections within their frontal lobe, and from the frontal lobe to other parts of the brain – to our detriment."

It led me to wonder if we were literally creating airheads. What if young brains were simply not getting the stimulation and experiences that had shaped brains for centuries? What if the radical overhaul of technology, teaching, values and culture of the last two decades meant we had done the equivalent of early settlers going to a new land and insisting on planting new crops instead of what had prospered there before?

What if the old methods – making kids learn their multiplication tables, teaching grammar – had developed over thousands of years because those methods triggered not just learning, but changes in the brain that actually *allowed* the brain to keep on learning? What if we were also creating kids who had a kind of learned selfishness and lack of regard for others?

And so I ventured into the world of neuroscience.

The area that is commanding attention and excitement at the moment is something called "cerebral plasticity". Richard Webster, a pediatrician who works in neurology at the Children's Hospital at Westmead in Sydney, is fascinated by current research into how our brains grow and develop. The notion of plasticity is reasonably new. We used to think that the brain was pretty much formed by the time children were five or six. Then a process called MRI, or magnetic resonance imaging, was developed late last century. It meant 2D or 3D scans or pictures of the brain structure could be taken. Until scanning, the only way to get information about the brain was by studying cadavers. Functional MRI meant activity in the living brain could be spotted and measured on the scans because the activity is accompanied by increased blood flow in that part of the brain. The MRIs showed that there were changes in the brain until the late teens and early twenties. It's true that the parts of the brain that control sensory perception and motor function develop early, but it's the prefrontal cortex – what scientists call the executive centre – that develops last. This is where we plan, weigh up choices, check impulses and think about consequences.[16] Once this was discovered, a range of teenage activity – risk-taking, drug experimentation, fast driving, early pregnancy – was suddenly a lot more explicable. It's even been discovered that, in teenagers, the bit of the brain, the *nucleus accumbens*, that looks for rewards isn't fully developed and so they either go for things with a high excitement factor or which don't require much effort. Kids automatically go for quick gratification.

There are other areas of the brain that take time to mature: the part that helps prioritise information, the bit that processes emotional input and also the fibres that connect both sides of the brain and which thicken in teenagehood so that information is processed faster.

What shapes the brain is not just about growth either but a complex pruning of nerve cells or neurons, which affects connections between them. This may be why children can learn other languages easily, but with age, unless the facility is used and the language(s) learned, it drops away. Webster's young daughter grew up in Montreal, where he was working at the Neurological Institute, and her French accent is perfect. "But," says her father, "if you don't get the accent right at that age, it will be very unlikely you'll pick it up beautifully later on because you just lose the ability to distinguish so precisely between the sounds."

As the brain grows and develops through childhood and into the teens, it keeps what it believes is functionally relevant and prunes the rest.

Huh?

Almost half the population of Britain had never heard of the death camp Auschwitz, a 2004 survey by the BBC suggests. The figure for women and people aged under 35 was even higher, at 60 percent.

That is what plasticity is about. As *Scientific American* put it in 1992, it's "the tendency of synapses [the contact points between nerve cells] and neuronal circuits to change as a result of activity". It's a quality our brains are supposed to keep all our lives which is why it is theoretically possible to learn the cello at sixty, but it is much more difficult because the neural connections that might have developed if we'd learned at ten, haven't been developed at all. It's also why babies need stimulation.

The scientists I interview are careful not to make grand claims for how different activities might shape the average child and teenager's brain, given the importance of genetics, but "use it or lose it" is a phrase that comes up at times, as it does in literature on the subject. There are famous studies about brainpower like the one about the London cabbies who have to remember all the city's streets and who have an extra-large hippocampus, the bit involved in memory. Another way to look at it, though, is this: did those with a big hippocampus become cabbies because it was easier for them? But then another famous study looked at a group of villagers in Portugal, some of them literate and some not. MRI scans showed there was significantly more volume of nerve fibre in the readers' brains and particularly in those bits of the brain to do with reading. "And so," says Webster, "there is some evidence that environmental exposure can make a difference."

Tomás Paus, chair in developmental cognitive neuroscience at the Brain and Body Centre at the University of Nottingham in England, is about to do a series of experiments on brain development. He says the field, still in its infancy, has begun to realise that it's not just a genetic master plan that gives you a particular brain structure, and that environment and experience can affect it, too. He talks of violinists whose auditory cortex is slightly larger. "It could be self-selection but it's unlikely," he says. "In one German study, students had to juggle three balls. After a couple of months and when they had reached a certain level, there was a change in the cortex for processing visual motion." The students were in their early twenties. Paus says that in other studies, they have even seen changes, driven by experience, in subjects aged forty-five.

When I ask Webster if cellular biology, and changes in it like those in nerve fibre, might determine how we function cognitively, he replies, with candour but also with a sense of excited wonder, "We don't know." It's a frontier science. "It would be risky to make the leap that we might be changing kids biologically," he says of the modern influences on kids – mobiles, television, iPods, video games, texting, emailing, multi-skilling and so on – but he does wonder about the way no-one spends much time reflecting any more. "I love this space," he says later, gesturing vigorously to the hospital's wide-open walkways that link the floors and corridors as he shows me out. "It's not really used but it gives you time to think." He has already asked earlier, "What impact will it have on our society if children don't grow up with reflection time and knowing how to reflect?" Given how many kids live with music and information input all the time, functioning autonomously, he wonders if their connection to society must be affected.

This leads to another contentious area: the importance of mastering the basics so you can live and work in a community, so you can fully grasp what is going on around you. In a world of graphics, calculators and computer algebra systems, for instance, does it matter if children are never taught to do sums and equations in their heads? Does learning have an existence of its own?

Webster says that there do seem to be critical windows in development where if you don't *get* something – "language, maybe maths, probably lots of other areas" – you can't get it later perhaps because of the pruning. John Watson asks rhetorically: "Is it important to know Euclid and know how to do fundamental theorems, even if you will never be an architect or surveyor? Was learning the fundamental classics in Latin and ancient Greek, like studying Virgil, Homer and Horace, a way of learning *how* to learn and *how* to think?"

He strongly suspects yes. In the same way, classicists will argue that learning Latin grammar by rote sets off complex procedures in the brain that make the grammar easier to master in the end.

Then there's the question I want answered. If kids are encouraged to learn only what's relevant to them and to never develop curiosity; if they veer away from the difficult and from complex argument, will they ever learn how to venture into the unknown and deal with it? Will they ever know how to reason and to question if they've never practised and developed those neural pathways properly? Paus is in the midst of studies of social cognition during adolescence that target abilities such as empathy and resistance to peer pressure.

Two neurobiologists, writing in *Scientific American* in 1992 about the biological basis of individuality and learning, stressed that "learning is a major vehicle for behavioural adaptation and a powerful force for social progress".[17]

Cognitive scientist Max Coltheart, who was so instrumental in getting the federal government's inquiry into teaching literacy started, says of course we retain our plasticity all our lives. "If a child hasn't learned to read seriously when young, he or she won't have developed the neural pathways to do that, although they could be developed later on. But the question would be, given the early unpleasant emotional response to reading – would he or she ever bother?'

The same may apply to complex thought. Thinking about serious things. Reading books that challenge what's happening in society. Working out what makes a country a democracy. (In one extraordinary 2004 study, for the National Youth Affairs Research Scheme, fewer than 54 percent of 800 young people surveyed agreed that Australia was a democracy. That wasn't brain plasticity at work, of course, but a lack of education in civics – but still the question remains: what if that ignorance persisted all their lives; what if they never came to grips with what a democracy really is? How difficult would it be to understand the concept much later in life?)

Webster points out something else: that the computerised era has introduced new challenges because the requirements for processing large amounts of information are greater. "Survival skills will be different from fifty years ago. It's not necessarily about competence; it's about how quickly you can decide something. That's the skill that's needed."

American futurist Ray Kurzweil doesn't believe the human brain is up to what we will soon be demanding of it. In interviews, he has talked of the brain's ability to compute per second being tiny compared with the electronic circuits that power computers.[18] His futuristic solution is that we'll soon be downloading and implanting what we need to speed us up.

In the meantime, though, it's just us, our brains and what we put them through.

THIS CENTURY is doing its best to turn the young into thoughtless, selfish airheads as fast as their heads pop up over the primary school parapet. An economic rationalist friend brushes away all my talk of overpaid CEOs, money traders and the like taking more than their fair share of the huge wealth washing around the world. "Compared to the amount of money going to people who were previously poor, those sums are immaterial," he protests. Well, hardly, when the United Nation's Human Development Report for 2005 showed that the world's 500 richest individuals have a combined income greater than that of the poorest 460 million.[19]

There has to be an impact on how we think and behave. Late in 2005, a survey of 2,500 British children revealed that, as far as they were concerned, being rich and being famous were the best things in life.[20]

Anecdotally, though, there is hope. Young minds, at least for a while, do try to do it differently as their brains keep developing. Sydney University's Barry Spurr talks of the "deprived constituency", that is, the teenagers who have never been exposed to rigorous study of either grammar or the Western canon. He believes that eventually, once they realise what they have missed out on, they will turn upon their "self-righteous persecutors and inhibitors", the various authorities and teachers who have insisted that it's for their own good that they study websites instead of Yeats. He says, "In a mild way, we are encountering this already, at the university where students come to us after the miseries of New South Wales HSC English syllabus (not to mention what has gone before it, over those twelve years of school so-called education) and say that, now, they want 'to read the classics'."

As for those kids who weren't sure if Australia was a democracy, they still told the survey interviewers they wanted the opportunity to get involved. They just didn't think governments would be interested in them.[21]

"Modern Western societies are sacrificing young people," says David Bennett, who heads the NSW Centre for the Advancement of Adolescent Health at The Children's Hospital at Westmead. "We have to see them as much more than a consumer market." In Australia, nearly one in four adolescents has a significant mental health problem. An obesity epidemic affects 25 percent of

Like, whatever

"'Mood-stabilising drugs – the breakfast of champions – that's what's still stigmatised,' says a fashion publicist. 'Something like bipolar or, God forbid, schizophrenia, those are very taboo because they're *real*. It's still cool to be sane. You're just supposed to be sane and medicated.'"
ARIEL LEVY WRITING ABOUT THE NEW PILL CULTURE IN *NEW YORK* MAGAZINE, JUNE 9, 2003.

young people. "These problems bugger up their adolescence," says Bennett, who, with Dr Leanne Rowe, published *You Can't Make Me: Seven Simple Rules For Parenting Teenagers* in 2005. "We say they'll grow out of it, but a lot of behaviours like depression, drug-taking and smoking will continue into adulthood. The vast majority of adolescent health problems are preventable."

He also believes that, over time, parents have lost confidence. "There is this sense that you don't say 'no' to your child. It's to do with moral relativism and a reluctance to take a stand on things. But if you want to be a friend to your child, you're failing them. It's okay to have high expectations of kids if it's done with warmth and support."

Bennett is passionate about the need for initiatives, not just with young children, but also with teenagers and their parents. "If you have a difficult time in childhood, adolescence is the time to put things to rights. It's a period of second chances because of the openness to ideas that the teenager naturally has. They can also build resilience then, just through making the effort to stay connected with people. We're squandering this opportunity. Kids can now go to university and get a degree without ever taking time — or having time — for reflection."

Human beings have survived for thousands of years not just because of survival of the fittest. It's the ones who can adapt who survive. When you're vulnerable, you copy the prevailing codes of whoever is dominant. That's how you get acceptance. You camouflage yourself. That's how you survive.

Que?

Virgin Atlantic launched an investigation into flight attendant behaviour after reports that one of its crew had panicked when a plane dropped thousands of metres in seconds. The attendant repeatedly shouted, "We're crashing!" as passengers looked to her for calm and help. One told *The Independent*, "I just thought: 'It's over, if an air hostess is telling us we are crashing … She screamed every time the plane dropped, and when she screamed the whole of the back of the plane screamed."

Unfortunately, adaptation right now means turning into an airhead. In that at least, the supporters of *Big Brother* have it right about why teenagers need the show. It tells them what kind of behaviour is rewarded in the twenty-first century. It tells them what they need to know to get ahead, too.

CHAPTER 12

A Sense of the Ridiculous

"*Men occasionally stumble over the truth but most of them pick themselves up and hurry off as if nothing ever happened.*"

BRITISH STATESMAN SIR WINSTON CHURCHILL

"*The truth is that many of the people who throw around terms like 'loopy conspiracy theories' are lazy bullies who ... want to 'confer instant illegitimacy on any argument with which they disagree'. Instead of facing up to hard questions, they try to suggest that anyone who asks those questions is crazy.*"

PAUL KRUGMAN, *THE NEW YORK TIMES*, MAY 8, 2006

Fifteen years ago, a 97-year-old Arkansas woman sued an American supermarket tabloid, the *Sun*, because it had published her photograph beside a headline that read "World's Oldest Newspaper Carrier, 101, Quits Because She's Pregnant". The tabloid had plucked her picture from its files, assuming she was dead. American political journal *Harper's Magazine* published an extract from the defamation trial,[1] including testimony from witness Manny Silver, a *Sun* reporter:

Plaintiff's lawyer: "What information did you use to write it?"

Silver: "It's total fiction. I made it all up."

Lawyer: "Just off the top of your head?"

Silver: "That's right. I'd say about 90 percent of my stories are off the top of my head."

Lawyer: "Just created out of whole cloth?"

Silver: "That's right."

Then Silver's lawyer started.

Lawyer: "Let me read you some more of these stories, Mr Silver. Let's go to 'Road Kill Cannibal': 'A man who is a self-confessed cannibal refuses to break the law by killing people, so he feasts on the bodies of accident victims left by the side of the road. Hitler Sharon, 38, has eaten human flesh all his life and can't live without it. But ... in an attempt to keep everything kosher, the hungry sicko has asked the government to allow him to eat the bodies of car crash victims.' Now sir, do you believe that?"

Silver: "Not at all."

Given the offhand way with which so many people treat reality these days, Manny Silver's firm

Like, whatever

During Britain's 2005 general election campaign, Prime Minister's wife Cherie Blair paid her hairdresser £275 a day to keep her hair looking good. Total cost for the month-long campaign: £7,700.

fix on it is refreshing. Here is the final exchange that day in the Arkansas courtroom. Silver had written about a farmer who kills himself by breathing in cow gas:

Lawyer: "Do you believe that?"

Silver: "No."

Lawyer: "Do you think that a reasonable person would believe that?"

Silver: "I don't see how."

It would be good to see Manny Silver handling a press conference for some of Australia's corporates or politicians.

In May 2005, Queenslander David Velu tried to open a cheque account for a non-profit company with the Commonwealth Bank. As he wrote to *The Australian* the next month, "It took me eight telephone calls, waiting for promised return calls that never did eventuate and three personal visits to the bank … Waste of time, waste of energy. The bank could not deliver. I ended up going to a competitor bank and opened the account in half an hour."

Mr Velu had just been reading of the appointment of the bank's new chief executive and his desire to improve customer service. The previous CEO was about to retire, in late 2005, with a massive payout, that being the new reality to which we have become resigned.

Meanwhile, Telstra head Sol Trujillo is on a package worth a possible $10 million a year. In 2006, he received $2.6 million in bonuses, on top of his fixed $3 million pay, despite the company's dull performance. Trujillo is sympathetic to just how complicated technology has made our lives: "Too many buttons, too many menus, too many steps, too many screens …"[2] His mantra is the one-click, one-screen system. Sounds good. About the time he said all this, Telstra took it into its head to start sending my Sydney-based publisher's BigPond bills to an address in Queensland. Naturally enough, given the bills were not reaching the publisher, Telstra was soon sending him threatening hand-written messages as well. Mysteriously, these messages turned up at the correct address. As the publisher tried to sort the matter out, Sol's mission statement was fresh in his ears. It went: "Telstra's vision is to know our customers and meet their needs better than anyone else and our mission is to do for customers what no-one else has done: create a world of one click, one touch, one button, one screen, one step solutions that are simple, easy and valued by individuals, businesses, enterprises and government."

It took my publisher 97 clicks to rectify his Telstra-created problem. This won't affect Sol's package, though, nor the fluency of his vision and mission statements. The publisher's Telstra experience and Trujillo's spin exist in parallel universes. (Indeed, as a result of his troubles and complaints, a market research company, hired by Telstra, presumably at some expense, has now contacted the publisher. It wants to know if BigPond's support service met his needs ... Sound of a gunshot offstage.)

President George W. Bush is not the only one who creates his own reality. As a result of all these "realities" colliding with true reality, we now have a kind of institutionalised nuttiness to which we are all becoming accustomed.

In Sydney, the summer sunshine used to pour down on the City Bowling Club, a neat view of green and white resting under the august apricot twirls of St Mary's Cathedral opposite Hyde Park. Men and women in white gathered there to roll their balls across the flattened grass as the city traffic flew past on the opposite side of a low fence.

Sometimes people rented the clubhouse for social occasions. Judith Curr, now a publisher in New York for Simon & Schuster, had her wedding there on a late autumn Sunday in 1996. The cathedral bells pealed in the background and a marquee for the service was set up on one of the greens. The bowling club walls were draped with calico and festooned with flowers, and waiters served French Champagne.

But with the Sydney 2000 Olympics on the way and a city council anxious to put on its most impressive clothes to show off to the guests, St Mary's finally got the two 35-metre spires it had been waiting for since 1868, and the bowling club, opened in 1881, was razed. It was replaced by a giant underground swimming pool, cafe and gym complex.

On top, where city workers used to hang over the fence to watch City Masters tournaments, there is now a barren expanse of grey concrete blocks. Skateboarders use it to practise their kickflips and jumps. The bowling club used to be a green brushstroke of eccentricity in a skyscraper city that mostly hustles and huffs and gleams. Now, what we have, beneath the business towers, is nothing but more hardness, a vast empty space used by few but the skateboarders and occasional pedestrians making a hurried shortcut in the wind.

On the corner of this blank space, there is a sign. It says: Cook and Phillip Park. Pretty funny kind of park. But this is the way in the new age of the airhead. Something looks like one thing but then we're persuaded into thinking it's another. Something bad happens and we are told it's good. No wonder most of us have an

Que?

In early 2006, President Bush rehearsed his State of the Union address for friends, *The Age* reported. One aside referred to his contentious decision to allow security authorities to wire-tap without court approval. He said to his audience: "You know, you can't please some people no matter what you do. Half the time they say I'm isolated and don't listen. Then when I do listen, they say I need a warrant."

increasingly shaky grip on reality. I should know – I'm the one who sent her cat out to work. The truth is that we in the media hardly know what "real" means any more. Too often, the buck has come to matter far more than the reader, which is why some broadsheet newspapers now come with little sticky tags advertising insurance and medical funds on their front pages. You have to remove the sticker before you can read the page one news splash. That should give you a sense of where management's priorities lie. The other day, a young friend had to brief the editor of a magazine on the fitness story she was writing. The magazine is pitched at "real" people, but this is reality with an airbrush. One of my friend's interviewees was to be photographed with a dog. "Is the dog attractive?" asked the editor, worriedly. "It has to be attractive."

When the media loses its grip on reality, you know that we're on the slippery slope that leads to ... oh, of course, back to the unstoppable rise of Paris Hilton. The latest wheeze is that Paris Hilton is secretly, you know, like, very clever. Even *The New York Times* says so: "In the past it has been all too easy to write off Ms Hilton as a publicity-hungry heirhead given to inane pronouncements like 'that's hot', but increasingly people in the business world are taking her seriously …"[3] *Of course* they're taking her seriously, I wanted to shout at the *Times*'s editors. The business world would take Brer Rabbit seriously if it thought it could make a buck out of his briar patch. And there are many bucks to be made out of Ms Hilton's name, her licensing deals and her silliness. As for the idea, typical of our money-obsessed times, that she *must* be clever because she made $US7 million in the year to June 2006, this is a woman who charges $150,000 to $500,000 to turn up to a party. She told interviewers she was paid a million dollars in May 2006 to appear in Austria at the launch of a canned sparkling wine. With that kind of income from brief appearances, you have to wonder what she's been doing with the rest of her time if her annual haul still hasn't made it into double-digit millions.

Apropos of silliness, did you know that the smartest thing for today's fashionable young woman to take out and about is a miniature iron? No, I didn't either, but the style page of a leading broadsheet has just told me this is true. It sounds like the start of a comedy sketch. The journalist responsible had loopily described the Tefal Minute Iron as "creating such excitement among the glossy mag folk that it demands attention". She wasn't being sarcastic, nor even trendily ironic. Her final tip was that "the iron fits snugly into the season's big handbags … the ideal device for whipping out on humid days to smooth the frizz out of a 'do gone pear-shaped", a conclusion which at first seemed to indicate that, somewhere between the first word and the ninety-ninth of this brief par, the reporter's attention had wandered so even she didn't know if she was writing about a clothes iron or a hair-straightening iron. (It's the former. "Well, I *suppose* you could iron your hair with it," said a Tefal spokesman, trying to be helpful. The reporter herself told me enthusiastically that she thought women could take the iron along when they went clubbing and it would be fine for straightening their hair as long as they used it carefully.)

So here we are, heading towards late 2006, and a major newspaper feels it is not beyond the bounds of possibility to suggest that women may sit down for dinner with their dates, notice a crease or an unwanted curl, and hop off to the ladies for a spot of instant ironing, so they can then return to the table crisp and neatly pressed. It's a strange universe, isn't it, this new one of ours?

Even as I was trying to picture this, Queenslanders were readying for their September 2006 state election. Liberal leader Bruce Flegg referred innocently enough to a few of his campaigning slip-ups as him having a bit of a "blonde moment". Next minute, his female chief of staff, a blonde, allegedly resigned in outrage, although she was soon back. Two other blonde staff members were also angry, it was reported. (It's not surprising that on the same day this flicker of a news story was being fanned along, I heard a report that child-care experts had decreed parents who used the words "no" and "don't" on their children were stunting their growth.)

Reality now has as much to do with what is put in front of our eyes as the much promoted muesli bar has to do with wholesome nutrition, and investment banks and management consultancies have to do with keeping the economy on the straight and narrow. Even that fashionable stampede of bright young graduates into CBDs around the world comes with its own reality filter. It isn't about getting out into the real world. The grads head not into business per se, but into jobs where they get to *advise* business, using theory and hypothesis and analysis. God forbid they should actually work in the business of business, with real people, real problems, real results, real products.

Odd.

Or maybe not so odd.

Most of us have forgotten the full story of *The Emperor's New Clothes*. We remember the vain, clothes-obsessed emperor and the little boy, but not the scam. This is how it went. Two artful weavers, intent on making their fortune, came to the court of the emperor and let it be known that they could produce a magical cloth that would sort the dunces from the deserving. The fabric, when woven, would be invisible to anyone who was either unpardonably stupid or unfit for his or her position. The emperor immediately set the weavers up with looms, supplied precious gold thread and silk, and they pretended to work, day after day. The emperor wanted to check their work but was a little uneasy; maybe, just maybe, by some unimaginable chance, the cloth would be invisible to him. By now, everyone in his court knew of the weavers, their cloth with its magical properties and how it could pick who was fitting and who wasn't.

The emperor decided to send one of his oldest ministers instead, reckoning that he, of all people, would be able to see the fabric. Of course, the old man turned up at the looms and could see nothing – but was he going to tell anyone that? The swindlers invited him to admire the delicacy of the weaving, the pattern and the colours. Secretly horrified that he was obviously so inadequate that the cloth was invisible to his eyes, the old man enthused about its wonders and then went back to the emperor to describe its beauty. More gold thread, silk and money were sent to the weavers. And so it went, day after day, until all the senior court ministers had visited the weavers, been confronted by the sight of nothing, feared for their positions or being thought stupid and, so, marvelled at the non-existent material. Soon everyone had agreed with the weavers that what they were producing was truly splendid. People gossiped to each other about its exquisiteness.

The emperor could wait no longer. He rushed to the looms with his most trusted confidants at his side. As they enthusiastically pointed out the cloth's details – for they each imagined the others could see it for real – the emperor saw nothing. At once, he realised the horror of his situation. He was either stupid or unfit to be emperor, or both. That could never be, and so he, too, believing he alone could not see the cloth, gave in to expressions of joy and delight.

The tricksters were home and hosed. The invisible cloth was made into invisible clothes that were invisibly stitched together; a procession was planned; the emperor dressed by his courtiers in his new non-existent finery. As the swindlers crept off with their sacks of gold, silk and money, the emperor strutted out of the palace to parade in front of his people, only to be exposed – finally – by the one little boy who had nothing to fear and who knew what reality looked like.

But how many of us still have that luxury? This is the age of spin, short-sightedness, short-term memory and keeping your mouth shut. I have a set of newspaper clippings with similar opening paragraphs: "The customs service has threatened staff with 'serious consequences' if they co-operate with a parliamentary inquiry into aviation security" and "Public servants who provided the federal government with evidence that its higher education policies were hurting poorer and older students will be the subject of a formal inquiry".

The best way to withstand entrenched airheadedness is to have a clear eye and a grounded

---

Huh?

"This new security environment of the twenty-first century is so distinctly different that it's going to take time for people to get comfortable with it, to understand it, to realise what it means ... What was normal and seemed right in the last century may not be normal or right at all in this century."
US DEFENCE SECRETARY DONALD RUMSFELD, SPEAKING AT THE ELEVENTH ANNUAL SALUTE TO FREEDOM EVENT HONOURING ARMED FORCES PERSONNEL, FEBRUARY 14, 2003.

set of values so it's easy to see through the smoke-and-mirror tricks practised in front of us every day. There's the rub though. Who wants us to see clearly? Who is teaching the basic values? Not the market. Not the postmoderns. No wonder Paris Hilton manages to slither between to reign triumphant. The other day I even saw her called a "postmodern Marie Antoinette", a description that captures our confused and giddy era exactly.

AT THE same time, historian Mark Peel, author of the haunting book *The Lowest Rung: Voices of Australian Poverty*,[4] says our language about the poor is starting to sound extreme. He means powerful people openly using phrases such as "dole bludgers", "no-hopers" and "people who don't count". The political speech of today mirrors the way people talked in the Twenties, he says. "There was this suspicion of the poor, and you can see that in the social workers' case files of the time. There was this idea that it was about finding the liar, finding the fraud. They didn't see poverty as being to do with disaster or vulnerability." Peel, who is working on a book about social work and charity in the Twenties and Thirties, says that often, it was only as the Depression intensified and poverty started to affect the case workers, too, that they realised the truth. When they lost their own jobs, they understood the indecency of poverty.

Social researcher Hugh Mackay tells me a story which echoes an anecdote another friend had told me. Mackay was in a conversation with a group of very wealthy people when he happened to praise a professor who had done interesting work. Much to his surprise, his companions scoffed. Says Mackay, "This man was absolutely denigrated and when I pointed out all the things he had achieved, they dismissed it with 'he's a loser'. They meant that this senior academic hadn't made any 'real' money. At that level, that was all that mattered."

My friend, who is in television, remembers hearing the pretend Caesars running his TV network dismissing people in the same way with the disparaging phrase: "Hasn't got any money".

In August 2006, as one large discount retailer said that higher petrol prices and interest rates had badly affected customer spending at his end of the market, the sleek and chic David Jones reported a surge in sales. Its customers were spending freely; the rises weren't an issue. A newspaper headline captured it: "DJs Result Confirms Rich Are Different".

It was Clive Hamilton, an economist and director of the think-tank The Australia Institute, who pointed out in his bestseller *Growth Fetish*[5] that the world needs less growth, not more. He wrote of the comfortably off being engulfed in shopping mania and materialism, and reported data that proved material things really don't buy happiness. Hamilton speculated that "a society in which no-one cared for others would be a type of hell".

His concern for human beings is uncharacteristic of economists. Theirs is usually a darker view. In January 2004, *The Boston Globe* newspaper ran a story about how people make moral choices.[6] It cited Cornell University economist Robert H. Frank's wish to examine self-interest and trust. Frank, who wrote *Luxury Fever* and *What Price The Moral High Ground?*, devised a complicated experiment in which people had to make a decision after weighing up self-interest, the interests of another person and the combined good. Surprisingly but gratifyingly, most people, 75 percent, chose to act co-operatively even though it meant they could end up with less. But guess what, reported *The Boston Globe*. There was one group of people in the test who proved to be exceptions and they were Frank's own peers. Economists. The very people who have had so much say in the last fifteen years about how our society and corporations work or should work. Sixty percent of economics students, operating on the basis that humans would be rational and therefore must be selfish, opted *not* to behave co-operatively.

Their view of humanity turns out not only to be unpleasant, it has little to do with understanding how people really behave. Peel is concerned about the education of our politicians and heads of bureaucracies when so many of them have come up through either economics or law. "They don't do history or philosophy or the broad social sciences ... They are scarily limited," he says.

Most of the rest of us get what's going on with this disjunct. When Prime Minister John Howard joined with the NSW Chief Justice in early 2006 to lament the erosion of good manners, letter writers to newspapers were quick to point out the flaw in his argument. Jonathan Barry, of Paddington, wrote to *The Australian*:[7] "What a pity Howard's policies of the past ten years have helped create a society where people are only looking after number one ... Howard has built a workplace where people can no longer stand together to defend their mates who have been sacked unfairly. He has created a fearful environment where people stay at their desks as long as possible to stay in good with the boss. The other day I was driving behind a

Really?

"Why of course the *people* don't want war. Why would some poor slob on a farm want to risk his life in a war when the best that he can get out of it is to come back to his farm in one piece ... But after all, it is the *leaders* of the country who determine the policy, and it's always a simple matter to drag the people along whether it's a democracy, a fascist dictatorship, or a parliament, or a communist dictatorship ... Voice or no voice, the people can always be brought to the bidding of the leaders. That is easy. All you have to do is tell them they are being attacked, and denounce the pacifists for lack of patriotism, and exposing the country to danger. It works the same way in any country."

NAZI REICHSMARSCHALL AND LUFTWAFFE CHIEF HERMANN GOERING, SPEAKING TO HIS INTELLIGENCE OFFICER/PSYCHOLOGIST IN HIS CELL AT THE NUREMBERG TRIALS IN APRIL 1946.

bus which displayed an ad for a private health insurer that said: 'Don't pay for someone else's hip replacement.' ... the look-after-yourself rule of thumb is all-pervading."

Mackay tells me he has, for the first time since he started his intensive social research fieldwork in 1979, noticed a sense of entitlement among those in the top third of Australian society. He picked it up in 2004 and it has become stronger since, showing up most clearly in the young and affluent, those pretty much born to their status. "That seems to me to give a sense of an early warning signal," he says, his tone showing his concern. "That's the beginning of the institutionalising of these differences." In the last few years, Mackay, who now writes a weekly column on moral dilemmas in *The Sun-Herald*, has focused his writing on the jaggedness and unfairness of our deregulated society.

Meanwhile, over in the land of the long white Cadillac, Steven Rattner, head of a private investment firm and former deputy chairman of an investment bank, has written of the emergence of a second gilded age "in which the fruits of economic success have gone not to the broad populace but to a slim sliver at the top".[8] Rattner, once a reporter for *The New York Times*, now a multi-millionaire courtesy of his career switch, continued: "For this handful, life is a sweet mélange of megafortunes, grand houses and massive yachts." Shame, he wrote, on all of us who have been passive witnesses to this return to another Roaring Twenties.

This is what historian Peel was alluding to when he ended a book review with this question: "When the people of the future come to write the histories of the early twenty-first century, they will note the discussions of increasing inequality and the evidence of division and they will ask: who stood and spoke against this?"[9]

Well, not Paris Hilton for a start.

Finance columnist Michael West told an intriguing story about reality and the privileged in May 2006. An artist at News Limited had done a drawing of Macquarie Bank CEO Allan Moss and it had run on the opening pages of *The Weekend Australian*'s business section. Someone from the bank rang the artist to ask about buying the original artwork. The artist, not knowing or even caring who Moss was, named his standard fee: $500. The caller baulked at the price. It's worth remembering that Allan Moss is the man whose annual earnings are so high that even the Australian treasurer was baffled one person could be worth so much. And that was when Moss was on $18 million a year. The following year, he was up to $21 million. Remember also that Macquarie Bank's nickname is the millionaires' factory. But apparently, $500 was beyond the budget.

The bank went back and forth on offers. The artist dropped his price to $350. That wasn't low enough either. Apparently, $150 or $200 was as far as the Macquarie bank staffer wanted to go. The artist kept the illustration.

This is not a simple ooh-ah fable about a bunch of Scrooge McDucks. It's about entitlement and exclusion. In the world of investment banking, business people earn massive amounts of money and that is expected and approved by everyone in that world. They don't flinch at a lawyer charging $5,000 to draft a series of letters; lawyers are part of the business world and it is expected they will charge mightily. That's how the business world goes on spinning happily and sending rewards in all the approved directions. But a newspaper artist – what kind of being is that? A staffer in the bank's media office said it was likely that the offer to buy the Moss illustration had come, not from Moss himself, but from someone in the bank's archives or library. "We're always buying up illustrations and cartoons for people's anniversaries or presentations," she said, adding, "If a newspaper artist wants to make themselves rich, they should concentrate on Macquarie Bank people." Yessum! At $200 a pop! *Tout de suite* and right away, and let's not spend it all at once.

There are huge amounts of commonsense, kindness and intelligence in our community – just read the letters pages in our newspapers – but we could do with a bit more of it in key places. This book does not argue that we should go back to the Fifties and Sixties; nor that globalisation be stopped and the free market banished. But it would be good to think that, faced with all the opportunity of this century, our leaders in business and politics, education and society might act with some foresight, and with generosity and concern for others, too.

Do we really have to go into the future like a tribe of baboons performing in an economic field study for Charles Darwin? Do we always have to choose our politics, economics and behaviour from one of two extremes? When the little bowling club disappeared, it was replaced with charmless concrete. If the club had to go because it was no longer financially viable and it occupied valuable land, couldn't someone have created a greener, friendlier place, one that recalled the club's gentle humanity while still allowing the pool complex to be built? Many people in Sydney fought hard for the club and then for a restful park to replace it. It's as if they had never spoken.

It's the same with so much now. The winners take all, while the middle ground continues to disappear, and rationality, sane debate and accommodation between people vanish along with it.

The famous Harvester judgment of 1907, delivered in the Australian Commonwealth Court of Conciliation and Arbitration, is derided by economic rationalists and IR reformers. Feminist historians object to its assumption that women were supported by fathers or husbands. I still feel proud of my country, though, when I read those humane and far-sighted words of Henry Bournes Higgins, a justice of the High Court and the arbitration court's president. In determining the case, which put a large manufacturer of agricultural machinery against the union representing its employees, Higgins set down as the reasonable basis for fair remuneration "the normal needs of an average employee regarded as a human being in a civilised community". He made his calculations based on the budgetary needs of a family of five, if that family was to have decent shelter, fresh air, enough wholesome food, and he made extra allowance for the purchase of such household items as "sewing machine, mangle, school requisites, amusements and holidays, intoxicating liquors …" He also allowed for loss of employment, sickness and death. Even though the manufacturer went on to successfully appeal Higgins's judgment, the ruling led to the establishment of the basic wage. That notion underpinned the stability of Australian social and domestic life during most of the twentieth century. People could afford to get married, to have children and a family life. They could afford to bring up their families, who mostly went on to have productive lives.

Now if you mention the Harvester judgment to someone who believes instead in the efficacy of the free market to set wages and prices, you'll get the same reaction you would if you idly experimented with dipping a cat's tail in kerosene. But is it so hard to appreciate one key point in Higgins's thinking: that workers have lives apart from their work and that it is important for a civilised country's future and, yes, its economy, that they have those full lives? It's odd to think that some might now consider such a moderate sentiment radical.

Extremism breeds intolerance; it pushes people to polarise so that the moderate looks extreme. I listen to business leaders now, talking about the responsibilities of companies. According to them, there is only one and that is to shareholders. Thus, they argue, whatever drives up the share price, must take precedence.

The self-serving glibness of that argument has to make you wonder where the referee has gone. We have agencies to control baboons. They're called governments and, in a representative democracy, they're supposed to govern in the interests of the voters (*all* voters, not only the rich and powerful ones; and not only the ones who voted the government in either). Australia has a population of just over 20 million and three well-staffed and well-supported layers of government chewing through millions of dollars each year. You'd think with that, and all our wealth and history of stability, we'd be able to look after the welfare of all our small population. But no, it seems not. Mark Peel says that what we have today is a crisis of compassion. I'd also call it a crisis of commonsense.

Ohmigod

A Christian charity is sending a film about the Christmas story to every primary school in Britain, the Press Association reported in October 2005, after hearing of a boy who asked his teacher why Mary and Joseph had named their baby after a swear word.

Totally

"At 7 am yesterday I read in various on-line newspapers and journals that the Americans are about to bomb or even nuke Iran; that Venezuela is preparing for a possible attack by the US; and that Iraq, led by a democratically elected leader who is not to Washington's liking, has descended into civil war. Moreover, Indonesia threatens to withdraw its love from Australia. At 8 am, I took a stroll down the leafy avenue where I live and heard the birds singing, stroked a neighbour's cat, saw the council had emptied my garbage bin with its usual efficiency, felt the sun on my face and returned the smile given to me by my local baker as I munched into one of her delicious croissants. Therefore, in this self-serving and hedonistic, neo-liberal world, all my mornings shall in future begin at 8 am."

STEPHEN FOX, IN A LETTER TO *THE AUSTRALIAN*, APRIL 11, 2006.

We are always being told that history is a matter of a pendulum swinging back and forth. If the Sixties swung too far towards radicalism, then now we are in an age of conservatism. We may live in selfish, airheaded times, the argument goes, but it doesn't really matter because soon we'll go back to being serious, thoughtful and compassionate. Spray-on tans will be out. Guppies will go back to living in fish tanks.

But every age is created by the age before it and is therefore unique. What is current is always shaped by what has gone before. Sometimes there are such profound changes, such undermining of basic structures and beliefs, that the world goes dark before our eyes. It's all about the choices we make.

An assistant professor of English at a small American Midwestern college wrote a gentle piece about books and university libraries in 2005.[10] He was a true book-lover and concerned at the way more and more universities were switching to digital on-line libraries. He talked of how his habit of slowly scanning shelves had led to wonderful discoveries and how scribbled references in a margin of a book had sent him off on even more rewarding explorations. Some of the card catalogues he consulted had helpful notations from scholars dating back more than a century. But print libraries take up huge amounts of space and it's only the wealthy universities such as Harvard which are proving less enthusiastic about dumping print for digital. They have the funds to have both. For, as the University of Sydney's librarian said in a newspaper interview in August 2005 announcing plans for a digital-era library: "We can't afford that."[11]

(*Why* can't it be afforded? As ABC-Radio's Virginia Trioli keeps asking generally of our new economic prosperity: where's all the money gone?)

The Midwest academic pondered why American campuses no longer have much room for books when they have so much for coffee bars, sports facilities and other expensive, space-consuming amenities. He realised that, often, there *is* enough money and space. However, the universities, and perhaps their students, wish to use those two commodities differently. Maybe there is more interest in amenities than education. As for the digital book versus the printed one that can be held in your hands, the one that lasts for generations, he asked sharply, "Who will profit most from the transformation now and in the future as fees and updates for new technologies continue indefinitely?" He also worried about wholesale digital changes: "I do not want to see libraries – institutions that I treasure – embark on some kind of drastic transformation that cannot be undone."

There are many of us who feel the same way about the other sweeping and airheaded transformations we're seeing. Maybe the only way to hang on to reality is to hang on to a sense of the ridiculous as well. When I did my interviews for this book, I would introduce myself, saying that I was writing about the shaping of popular culture. As indeed I was and am. It was only when the interviewees and I had talked for some time and I had established my credentials that I would tell them the book's title. Very, very often, they would snigger. Then they would laugh. These people are academics, doctors, mid-ranking journalists, scientists, students, researchers, shop staff, teachers, lawyers, mid-level business people, all apparently used, in some degree, to seeing the rise of airheads in our midst …

But sometimes I would find myself talking to someone much, much higher up the ladder and, when I told them the book's title, the reaction would be strikingly different. It was as if I had just sneezed all over their BlackBerry.

It reminds me of Hans Christian Andersen and his naked emperor again. The emperor, even when he was clothed, didn't have much of a sense of humour, let alone a firm grip on reality. When the little boy cries out and the crowd starts rustling and passing along the message – "he's not wearing any clothes, he's not wearing any clothes" – the emperor doesn't falter or run for cover, even though he suspects that the little boy is right. Instead, he draws himself up tall, naked bottom and all. He continues to parade.

His courtiers continue to hold up his non-existent train.

ACKNOWLEDGEMENTS

*A*nyone who writes a book depends upon the kindness of friends and strangers. I am grateful again to Sharon McGrath for her inspired design, to Carol Cromie, who edited and shaped this book with her usual insight, precision and humour, and to Marion von Adlerstein and Jane Gleeson-White, who were early readers and whose suggestions were spot-on. Thanks, too, to Barry Spurr, Catherine Runcie, John Vallance, Terry Lyons, George Megalogenis, John Murphy and Rebecca Ling for their particular help and insights; to Bruce Guthrie, who published the initial essay on airheads in *The Weekend Australian Magazine* and so gave the idea lift, and to Rachel Skinner and Jeanne Ryckmans, who were early enthusiasts. My thanks to all the interviewees, from economists and management experts to neurologists and magazine editors, who were so generous with their time, listened patiently to my ideas and helped me explore them further. And thanks, of course, to Stephen Balme, Craig Osment and Philip Gore at Park Street Press, who must be the only publishers in the world relaxed enough to allow a writer to keep fretting and working away until the last possible minute. I think it must be the lunches.

Below is a list of books which, along with those footnoted, helped my research and/or which I would recommend if you are interested in the questions raised here:

The Angel & the Octopus by Simon Leys, Duffy & Snellgrove, 1999
Brave New Workplace: How individual contracts are changing our jobs by David Peetz, Allen & Unwin, 2006
Catholic Values and Australian Realities by James Franklin, Connor Court Publishing, 2006
The Closing of the American Mind by Allan Bloom, Simon & Schuster, 1987
Conspiracy of Fools by Kurt Eichenwald, Broadway Books, 2005
The End of Poverty: How we can make it happen in our lifetime by Jeffrey Sachs, Penguin, 2005
Fragmented Futures: New challenges in working life by Ian Watson, John Buchanan, Iain Campbell and Chris Briggs, The Federation Press, 2003
Gangs of America: The rise of corporate power and the disabling of democracy by Ted Nace,

Berrett-Koehler, 2005

How Mumbo-Jumbo Conquered the World by Francis Wheen, Harper Perennial, 2004

Lend Me Your Ears: Great speeches in history edited by William Safire, revised edition, Norton, 1997

The Longest Decade by George Megalogenis, Scribe, 2006

One Market Under God: Extreme capitalism, market populism and the end of economic democracy by Thomas Frank, Doubleday, 2000

The Overspent American: Upscaling, downshifting and the new consumer by Juliet B. Schor, Basic Books, 1998

Other People's Money by Andrew Main, HarperCollins, 2003, updated, 2005

The View from the Bridge: The 1996 Boyer Lectures by Pierre Ryckmans, ABC Books, 1996

The Voice of Liberal Learning: Michael Oakeshott on education edited by Timothy Fuller, Yale University Press, 1989

ENDNOTES

CHAPTER 1, PAGES 13-25

1 These two terms will appear often in this book. I'm using the word "postmodern" as a general term to cover the "isms", from deconstructionism to relativism, which have come to dominate cultural and social thinking and literary theory and which had their origins in the philosophy that came out of France in the late Sixties, formulated by Jacques Derrida, Michel Foucault, and Roland Barthes, among others. These are the notions that there are no such things as truth or objective reality; that all texts contain hidden meanings, which have to be revealed; and that to talk of "foundations" or "a canon" is to make assumptions, which may reveal post-colonial, sexist or racist bias. Unfortunately, many of the most fervent exponents of postmodernism have pushed it on to areas such as primary and secondary education where it has bred nonsense, an insistence on a particular kind of individualism and a brand of well-schooled ignorance. "Economic rationalism" is used in Australia to describe the belief that market forces when left to themselves will nearly always give the best economic outcome for a society, that the individual should be free to pursue his or her economic interests and that state intervention is to be resisted. Elsewhere, it is called neo-liberalism. I have yet to meet a poor economic rationalist although there are very many rich ones.

2 *The Sydney Morning Herald*, July 21, 2005. "Luxury-lite is yesterday's trick, says style guru" by Julian Lee.

3 *The Deluxe Election-Edition, Bushisms* by Jacob Weisberg. A Fireside Book, published by Simon & Schuster, 2004.

4 In March 2006, Paul Omodei successfully challenged Matt Birney for the leadership. Just before the challenge, Simon Adams, dean of arts at the University of Notre Dame, summed up modern politics, and Birney's appeal, for ABC-Radio: "You know, we really do live in an age – and I think this is not just about Western Australia, this is about, you know, politics in Australia, politics in any Western democracy – we really do live in an age where image sometimes overwhelms substance, where personality politics that everybody talks about, you know, how good you look when you're kissing the babies, you know, whether you say 'mate'. These sorts of things actually really count a lot. So I think on that level, I think Matt Birney's actually performed pretty well. There's a whole other level though, in which he probably hasn't performed very well. He obviously, as far as his party colleagues or a substantial number of them are concerned, he hasn't been very good as an opposition leader, he hasn't been very good as a party colleague."

5 *The Economist*, December 20, 2005. "Inconspicuous consumption", quoting the World Wealth Report 2005 by Merrill Lynch and Capgemini.

6 Survey for ipac Securities; research conducted by Brandmanagement, 2005.

7 *The Sydney Morning Herald*, July 4, 2005. "How financial risk is being heaped on households" by Matt Wade.

CHAPTER 2, PAGES 27-43

1 www.bigbrother.3mobile.com.au, July 24, 2005. Day 77, 20.35pm. "Christie gets crunched".

2 *The Powers That Be* by David Halberstam. First published by Alfred A. Knopf, 1979.

3 *The Age*, May 26, 2005. "Informative, educative and entertaining? Not your B-list ABC" by Gay Alcorn.

4 Simon Doonan, creative director of New York store Barney's, was widely reported. He felt the celebrity's show lowered standards.

5 www.fuel4arts.com. Case Study, July 2004. "Art Gallery of NSW: Art After Hours" by Liz Gibson and Katie Russell.

6 ibid.

7 *Fahrenheit 451* by Ray Bradbury. First published by Ballantine, 1953. This 50th anniversary edition, published by Voyager, HarperCollins, 2004.

8 *BusinessWeek*, June 15, 2005. "A course on the green" by Francesca Di Meglio.

9 ibid.

CHAPTER 3, PAGES 45-63

1 *The Man Who Was Vogue: The Life and Times of Condé Nast* by Caroline Seebohm, Weidenfeld & Nicolson, 1982.

2 *The New Yorker*, September 22, 2003.

3 *Louis XV* by G.P. Gooch, Longmans, Green and Company, 1956.

4 *The Times*, February 23, 2005. "Heady odour of the last French Queen set to roll on to market" by Adam Sage.

5 *Time Magazine*, February 10, 2002. "How Fastow helped Enron fall" by Bill Saporito.

6 The World Wealth Report 2006, figures based on 2005 surveys, compiled by Merrill Lynch and Capgemini.

7 *Journal of Australian Political Economy*, No 56, December 2005, "Setting the double standard" by John Shields. Chief executives surveyed belonged to the Business Council of Australia.

8 *The Sydney Morning Herald*, May 23, 2006. "Executive plunder – super rich are back" by John

Garnaut. Garnaut cites several studies including Shields's above, "The distribution of top incomes in Australia" by Anthony Atkinson and Andrew Leigh for the Centre for Economic Policy Research, from which the 98-times figure comes, and "Where did the productivity growth go?" by Ian Dew-Becker and Robert Gordon for the US National Bureau of Economic Research.

9 *The Sydney Morning Herald*, August 25, 2005. "BHP hits jackpot of a lifetime" by Matt Wade and Jamie Freed.

10 *The Sydney Morning Herald*, August 24, 2006. "Economy surfs in BHP wake" by Matt Wade and Jamie Freed.

11 *The New York Times*, September 1, 2005. "Waiting for a leader".

12 *The Australian*, September 2, 2005. "New Orleans to be abandoned as Katrina's death toll tipped to climb into the thousands" by Geoff Elliott.

13 Znet Commentary, September 3, 2005. "How the free market killed New Orleans" by Michael Parenti.

14 ABC-Radio, *PM* programme. September 2, 2005.

15 *The New York Times*, September 2, 2005. "They saw it coming" by Mark Fischetti.

16 *Good Morning America*, ABC Television, United States. September 1, 2005. Bush later tried to clarify his statement, saying what he really meant was that, at first, officials thought the levees had escaped hurricane damage. It was an explanation that didn't gain traction.

17 *The Sydney Morning Herald*, September 10-11, 2005. "A superpower humbled by bungling bureaucrats" by Gerard Wright.

18 *The New York Times*, September 9, 2005. "Political issues snarled plans for troop aid" by Eric Lipton, Eric Schmitt and Thom Shanker.

19 The videotape of a video-conference involving President Bush and other officials the day before Katrina struck helped Mike Brown's reputation to some extent, showing him warning of the size of the hurricane. Brown later talked of a "fog of bureaucracy". The President did not ask questions during the conference.

20 *The Australian*, July 6, 2005. "Water board warning 26 years ago" by John Lehmann. Sydney Water was corporatised in 1995.

21 *The Sydney Morning Herald*, August 27-28, 2005. "What's mined is yours" by Matt Wade.

22 *Merchants of Cool*, produced by Barak Goodman and Rachel Dretzin, first screened on *Frontline*, on PBS, February 27, 2001. The speaker here is Robert McChessney, communications professor at the University of Illinois.

23 *The Times*, February 4, 2004. "No-one saves for a rainy day now" by Amrit Dhillon.

24 Archives of Paediatrics and Adolescent Medicine, Volume 160, No.5, May 2006. "Estimate of the commercial value of underage drinking and adult abusive and dependent drinking to the alcohol industry". Thanks to crikey.com.au for highlighting.

25 "Young people and alcohol: Taste perceptions, attitudes and experiences", Technical Report 241, a study conducted for the National Drug and Alcohol Research Centre by J. Copeland, P. Gates, D. Stevenson and P. Dillon, 2006.

26 *The Sydney Morning Herald*, October 13, 2005. "Record Apple result strikes the wrong note" by Garry Barker.

CHAPTER 4, PAGES 65-82

1 The World Wealth Report 2006, compiled by Merrill Lynch and Capgemini. In the 2001 report, Australia had just 100,000 such millionaires.

2 *Sydney Central Courier*, July 27, 2005. "Finnish phone fandango".

3 *The Australian*, September 6, 2005. "Nation's rich pay only 25pc tax" by George Megalogenis, citing Melbourne Institute research.

4 *The Financial Times*, January 22, 2006. "Incoming Nokia chief fined for minor tax fraud" by Paivi Munter.

5 *The Sydney Morning Herald*, December 19, 2005. "Tax cuts not the only option" by Ross Gittins.

6 *The New York Times*, January 29, 2006. "Corporate wealth share rises for top-income Americans" by David Cay Johnston.

7 "The distribution of top incomes in Australia" by A.B. Atkinson and Andrew Leigh. Discussion paper No 514, March 2006, for the Centre for Economic Policy Research, Australian National University.

8 *The Australian*, September 8, 2005. "CEOs are overpaid, say directors" by Geoffrey Newman.

9 *Journal of Australian Political Economy*, No 56, December 2005, "Setting the double standard" by John Shields. Chief executives surveyed belonged to the Business Council of Australia.

10 *The Sydney Morning Herald*, September 25, 2003. "Bond: Lest we forget" by Miranda Devine.

11 *Manhattan,Inc.* April, 1987. The editor and founder of the magazine, Jane Amsterdam, who had once worked for Watergate's Bob Woodward at *The Washington Post*, resigned soon after, although not as a result of this issue. She cited differences with her publisher over issues of editorial control. She later edited *The New York Post* and also worked for Knopf and the television network ABC. I tracked her down to upstate New York where she now lives in Westchester and still dreams up ideas for whichever friends are still practising journalism.

12 *The Australian*, May 19, 2005. "Faithful flock to the sage of Omaha" by Geoff Pritchard.

13 CNN *Money*, May 2, 2005. "The oracle speaks" by Jason Zweig.

14 *The New Yorker*, October 18 & 25, 1999. "The kids in the conference room" by Nicholas Lemann.

15 2006 Universum Survey, American MBA edition.

16 *The Sydney Morning Herald*, January 29-30, 2005. "Economics graduates do the best sums" by Ross Gittins.

17 The Institution of Engineers submission to the Department of Education, Science and Training, September 2002, in response to the paper "Varieties of excellence: diversity, specialisation and regional engagement".

18 "Do the mathematical sciences have a future in Australia?" Submission 108 to the Department of Education, Science and Training, June 27, 2002, by J. Hyam Rubinstein in response to the paper "Higher education at the crossroads".

19 The Institution of Engineers submission to the Department of Education, Science and Training, September 2002, in response to the paper "Varieties of excellence: diversity, specialisation and regional engagement".

20 Professor George Cooney, of Macquarie University's Australian Centre for Educational Studies, was advising on the study conducted by Madeline Raison. He was quoted in *The Australian*, April 12, 2006, "Science shunned for money" by Brendan O'Keefe.

21 *The Financial Times*, December 23, 2005. "Make that two Ferraris" by Julie Earle-Levine.

22 *The Sydney Morning Herald*, August 19, 2005. "Magpies get fat as pollies slice cake" by Mike Seccombe.

23 *American Theocracy: The peril and politics of radical religion, oil, and borrowed money in the twenty-first century* by Kevin Phillips, Viking, 2006. Also noted, a review of the book in *The New York Times Book Review*, "Clear and present dangers" by Alan Brinkley.

24 *The Wall Street Journal*, December 6, 2005. "From Australia, money chases roads, airports around globe" by Patrick Barta and Mary Kissel.

25 *The Weekend Australian Financial Review*, February 4-5, 2006. "Nameless army has world domination in sight" by Deirdre Macken.

26 *The Sun-Herald*, January 22, 2006. "Airport 'one of the worst'" by Alex Mitchell and Daniel Dasey.

27 *The Sydney Morning Herald*, January 31, 2006. "MacBank shamed: fined over sham deal" by Lisa Murray.

28 *A Distant Mirror* by Barbara Tuchman, 1985. First published by Alfred A. Knopf, 1978.

29 *The Praise of Folly* by Desiderius Erasmus, translated with an introduction and commentary by Clarence H. Miller, Yale University Press, 1979.

30 *The Australian Financial Review*, July 7, 2005. "DJs still in contract talks with McInnes" by Sue

Mitchell.

31 *The Sydney Morning Herald*, October 17, 2005. "Fairfax CEO goes back to university" by Linda Doherty.

32 *Respect in a World of Inequality: The formation of character in a world of inequality* by Richard Sennett, W.W. Norton, 2003.

33 Published by Cambridge University Press, 2003.

CHAPTER 5, PAGES 83-99

1 *The Australian*, November 11, 2005. "Last word in sinful delight" by Georgina Safe.

2 First published by Putnam, 2005.

3 *Vanity Fair*, August 2004. "Girl meets fame" by Krista Smith.

4 Published by Scribe, 2004.

5 Forbes.com, June 15, 2005. Edited by Peter Kafka. "Special report: The celebrity 100".

6 Colloquium, State Library of New South Wales, May 16-17, 2002. "Creating lives: the role of the State Library of New South Wales in the creative process of biography" by Jacqueline Kent.

7 *The Sydney Morning Herald*, September 10-11, 2005. "Too much S&M" by Deirdre Bair, biographer of Samuel Beckett, Simone de Beauvoir and Carl Jung.

CHAPTER 6, PAGES 101-124

1 *A Good Life* by Ben Bradlee, Simon & Schuster, 1995.

2 PBS *Frontline – The Persuaders*. November 9, 2004. "Neuromarketing: Is it coming to a lab near you?" reported by Mary Carmichael.

3 *The Sydney Morning Herald*, October 17, 2005. "No sex, no politics, just ads for shoppers" by Julian Lee.

4 *American Theocracy: The peril and politics of radical religion, oil, and borrowed money in the twenty-first century* by Kevin Phillips, Viking, 2006.

5 *The New York Times*, February 20, 2006. "After $12,000, there's even room to park the car" by David Kocieniewski.

6 See *Hypermodern Times* by Gilles Lipovetsky and Sebastien Charles. British edition, Polity Press, 2005.

7 "Worldwide trends in childhood overweight and obesity" by Youfa Wang and Tim Lobstein, for the International Obesity Taskforce, 2006.

8 *The Sydney Morning Herald*, April 24, 2006. "Fat chance of getting the obesity epidemic on the talkfest circuit" by Neer Korn, a director of social and market research company Heartbeat Trends.

9 *The Newcastle Herald*, October 15, 2002. "Letting it all hang out" by Jeff Corbett.

10 Nine Network, *Sixty Minutes*, July 11, 2004. "It's only natural" reported by Charles Wooley.

CHAPTER 7, PAGES 125-152

1 *The Australian Financial Review*, January 27, 2006. "So much for that theory" by Luke Slattery.

2 *Academe*, January-February 2005. " 'Believing in yourself' as classroom culture" by Susan Ostrov Weisser.

3 *The New York Times Magazine*, October 17, 2004. "Without a doubt" by Ron Suskind.

4 www.funderstanding.com/constructivism.cfm

5 Donnelly was chief of staff to federal workplace minister Kevin Andrews, for 2004, and classifies himself as being close to the Liberals.

6 Published by Pluto Press, 2004.

7 *The Weekend Australian*, November 12-13, 2005. "Wanted: graduates who can teach children to read" by Samantha Maiden.

8 Learning Disabilities Association of America website Idanatl.org "Why reading is not a natural process" by G. Reid Lyon, LDA Newsbriefs, January/February 2000, Vol 38, No 4. G. Reid Lyon is chief of the Child Development and Behavior Branch of the National Institute of Child Health and Human Development, National Institutes of Health, US Department of Health and Human Services.

9 *The Australian Financial Review*, November 29, 2005. "Education's simple – judge for yourself" by Peter Ruehl.

10 *The Daily Telegraph*, August 30, 2005. "Hiding ignorance behind low standards" by Ryszard Linkiewicz.

11 *The Australian*, September 15, 2005. "Students 'let down' by English education" by Elizabeth Gosch and Lisa Macnamara.

12 *The Australian*, October 21, 2005. "Literacy lagging behind" by Kevin Donnelly.

13 *The Australian*, January 24, 2006. Letter from Jennifer Page Lefroy.

14 The survey was compiled for The Nuffield Foundation, a British charity established in 1943 by Lord Nuffield, founder of Morris Motors, to "advance social well-being".

15 *The Daily Mail*, February 9, 2006. "The Oxbridge students who can't spell or do their sums" by Sarah Harris.

16 *The Times Higher Education Supplement*, February 10, 2006. "Tutors in despair at illiterate freshers" by Jessica Shepherd.

17 *The Sydney Morning Herald*, November 8, 2005.

18 Political philosopher Michael Oakeshott puts this idea in his 1972 essay, "Education: the

engagement and its frustration", collected in *The Voice of Liberal Learning*, a series of his essays on education, Yale University Press, 1989.

19 "The Idea of a University" by Michael Oakeshott, first published in *The Listener*, XLIII, 1950. Also collected in *The Voice of Liberal Learning*, see above. This essay adds to themes expressed in 1852 and 1854 in a series of lectures by Cardinal Newman titled "The Idea of a University".

20 This essay, "On the University: Asian studies, liberal studies, literary studies" was published in *Quadrant*, March 1994, and reprinted in *The Angel and the Octopus: Collected Essays 1983-1998* by Simon Leys, Duffy & Snellgrove, 1999.

21 "Changes in academic work – Implications for universities of the changing age distribution and work roles of academic staff" by Don Anderson, Richard Johnson and Lawrence Saha, Commonwealth of Australia, 2002.

22 "Performance Indicators in Australian Universities: Establishment, Development and Issues" by James Guthrie and Ruth Neumann, presented to the European Institute for Advanced Studies in Management, 2nd Workshop on the Process of Reform of University Systems, Venice, June 2006.

23 In New South Wales, the state rail manufacturing and maintenance workshops in Chullora were run down, and eventually closed in the late 1990s, with the loss of several thousand jobs. They had also been a key source of highly trained apprentices. This happened under the state Labor government of Bob Carr although the process was started under the Labor government of Barrie Unsworth and continued under the Liberal governments of Nick Greiner and John Fahey, under the stewardship of then transport minister Bruce Baird. (Both Carr and Greiner now work for private enterprise; Baird is a federal politician.) A management paper published in 1995 in *International Journal of Manpower* by Vincent Smith, Amrik Sohal and Brian D'Netto boasted how successful were initial changes in the public transit system between 1988 and 1992, so that it became a "commercially focused organisation with a clear vision of the future" and how it had finally returned a dividend to the government. Less than 10 years later, Sydney's train system was in crisis and, in mid-2005, a report from the New South Wales auditor-general criticised a decade of under-investment. By 2005, there was a national skills shortage crisis, recognised at state and federal level. Anyone wishing to see a snapshot of short-sighted politics at work should access the debate in the New South Wales legislative assembly on September 3, 1992 at http://www.parliament.nsw.gov.au/prod/parlment/hansart.nsf/V3Key/LA19920903026. Neither Bruce Baird nor former NSW Labor MP Peter Nagle wished to comment in retrospect on this debate.

24 *Academe*, January-February, 2005. "'Believing in yourself' as classroom culture" by Susan Ostrov Weisser.

25 The Australian Association for the Teaching of English response to "Teaching Reading", media

release, December 8, 2005 – www.aate.org.au

26 *The Sydney Morning Herald*, May 1, 2006. "HSC English is tougher and smarter, not dumb and dumber" by Melina Marchetta. (I was keen to talk about this point with Ms Marchetta but several emails sent via *The Sydney Morning Herald* netted no response.)

27 *Psychological Science*, Vol 16, No 12, December 2005. "Self-discipline outdoes IQ in predicting academic performance of adolescents" by Angela Duckworth and Martin Seligman.

28 The Curriculum Corporation is a company whose members are the various government education ministers in Australia and New Zealand. It was set up to enact collaboration on national agreements and to avoid duplication in developing education resources. There is a lot more on www.curriculum.edu.au although not much that gives any more clues than the above. The corporation was heavily involved in the promotion of outcomes-based education in the Nineties. From my interviews, it appears most parents aren't aware of its existence, despite its impact on children's education.

CHAPTER 8, PAGES 153-180

1 Data found on www.humanresourcesmagazine.com.au in Archives: facts and figures.

2 National Bureau of Economic Research, working paper 11416. "Happiness and the human development index: the paradox of Australia" by David G. Blanchflower and Andrew J. Oswald, June, 2005. Their findings on happiness in Australia were disputed, in mid-2006, in a paper for the bureau by Andrew Leigh and Justin Wolfers, but levels of job dissatisfaction were not disputed.

3 "The growth of psychometric testing for selection" by Alison Wolf and Andrew Jenkins, published by the Centre for the Economics of Education, London School of Economics and Political Science, June 2002.

4 *Human Resource Management Journal*, Vol 16, No 2, 2006. "Explaining greater test use for selection: the role of HR professionals in a world of expanding regulation" by Alison Wolf and Andrew Jenkins.

5 *Watson's Dictionary of Weasel Words, Contemporary Clichés, Cant & Management Jargon* by Don Watson, Knopf, 2004.

6 Very early on, LaRouche was married to one-time US presidential candidate from the extreme Right, Lyndon LaRouche, whom she left in the Sixties, taking with her their young son. They met when both were members of the Socialist Workers' Party. In her introduction, she writes of this period and its influence on what she did next as: "My marriage had broken up some years before, when my son was still a baby, and thereafter I had been responsible not only for his care, but also for supporting the two of us." She went on to learn business management not through theory but through practice. "Bit by bit, I learned to negotiate, to be assertive and, gradually, to be independent …"

7 ABC-Radio, *The Media Report*, May 25, 2006. "Meet the ABC's new managing director", interview by Gerald Tooth.

8 "Investigation into foreign exchange losses at the National Australia Bank". Report by PricewaterhouseCoopers, sent to the bank, March 12, 2004.

9 johnquiggin.com "Word for Wednesday: Managerialism (definition)", posted July 2, 2003.

10 *The Weekend Australian*, August 27-28, 2005. "Captain Kirk's paper chase" by John Lehmann.

11 *The Daily Telegraph*, September 1, 2005. "Magician helps taxpayers' money to disappear" by Saffron Howden.

12 *The Sydney Morning Herald*, November 3, 2005. "Axed: CSIRO to cut 200 research jobs" by Damien Murphy.

13 Commonwealth of Australia, Senate estimates, Employment, workplace relations and education legislation committee, May 31, 2006.

14 *The Age*, February 21, 2006. "A culture of fear builds at the CSIRO" by Michael Borgas and Pauline Gallagher.

15 Commonwealth of Australia, Senate estimates, Employment, workplace relations and education legislation committee, February 16, 2005. Labor senator Kim Carr described the decision to not supply Pockley with information as "peculiar". He also called it "blackballing".

16 *The Age*, February 21, 2006. "A culture of fear builds at the CSIRO" by Michael Borgas and Pauline Gallagher.

17 At the time of that speech, Commonwealth Bank customer satisfaction levels stood at 65 percent, according to Norris. By May 2006, levels had risen to 72 percent, although that was still the lowest of the big four banks, and that survey, conducted by Nielsen Media Research, reported that customer satisfaction with all four in the first quarter of 2006 was at its lowest since the beginning of 2003. Reasons given were high fees followed by poor service. Nielsen said the banks were reporting record interim profits. Ex-building society St George had levels of 88.4 percent. Interestingly for this chapter, St George's CEO, Gail Kelly, has an MBA and spent several years in banking HR in South Africa. It can work. See comments from Jo Mithen later in this chapter.

18 Nine Network, *Sunday* programme, November 20, 2005. "John Howard's industrial revolution" reported by Sarah Ferguson, researched by Jo Townsend and produced by Nick Rushworth.

19 "Restoring trust in the human resource management profession" by Thomas A. Kochan, presented at the University of Sydney's celebration of 50 years of industrial relations teaching and research, November 2003.

20 *Asia Pacific Journal of Human Resources*, 2004/42(2). "Broadening the horizons of HRM: Lessons for Australia from the US experience" by Russell D. Lansbury and Marian Baird.

21 ibid.

22 For two examples, see *Pay without performance: The unfulfilled promise of executive compensation* by Lucian Bebchuk and Jesse Fried, Harvard University Press, 2004. Also, "Setting the double standard: chief executive pay the BCA way" by John Shields, published in the *Journal of Australian Political Economy*, Issue 56, December 2005.

CHAPTER 9, PAGES 181-208

1 ABC-TV, *Enough Rope* with Andrew Denton. November 3, 2003.

2 *The Australian Financial Review* Rear Window, November 24, 2005 "Murdoch repetitive over memory lapses".

3 The author of this book was founding editor of *The Australian's Review of Books*.

4 www.tomdispatch.com, posted February 26, 2006. "Mark Danner on Bush's state of exception".

5 *The Nation*, July 4, 2005. "Sins and the Citi" by William Greider.

6 *Journal of Australian Political Economy*, No 56, December 2005. "Setting the double standard: chief executive pay the BCA way" by John Shields. Shields's survey covered the 51 Australian Stock Exchange-listed companies whose CEOs are BCA members.

7 John Shields's research into the rise in average salaries between 1990 and 2005 gives an inflation-adjusted figure of 1.4 percent per year. Later in this chapter, see footnote 9, Stephen Jackson, at the Workplace Research Centre, says real (that is, inflation-adjusted) average salaries went up 3.6 percent between 1998 and 2004, a rise of 0.6 percent each year. The reason for the discrepancy is that Shields's data included managers while Jackson's data omitted all managers. If Shields's figures were also applied to the six-year period 1998-2004, they would show an average rise of 8.4 percent, but only because of the managerial component.

8 *The Age*, February 21, 2006. "A culture of fear builds at the CSIRO" by Michael Borgas and Pauline Gallagher.

9 The Prime Minister and the Workplace Research Centre were using different data. The PM cited 1996-2005 national account figures from the Australian Bureau of Statistics, which accounted for all workers, including managers. Centre researcher Stephen Jackson says the centre worked from ABS employer survey data of non-managerial employees, 1998-2004. He also says that the PM's office's other argument against the research, that these findings were drawn from the 1997-2001 period, is wrong. Meanwhile, by mid-2006, government ministers were saying the average wage had risen by 16 percent since 1996. (See also footnote 7 in this chapter.)

10 *The Weekend Australian*, June 4-5, 2005. "Hollowing out the backbone" by George Megalogenis.
11 *The Australian Financial Review*, July 11, 2005. "ACTU scare campaign on shaky ground" by Michael Baume.
12 The two years of growth to mid-2006 shifted that figure, but Sue Richardson maintains the accuracy of the long-term trend.
13 Published by Scribe, 2006.
14 *The Weekend Australian*, June 10-11, 2006. "The old and the poor left behind in queue" by George Megalogenis.
15 For more data and information on this trend, see *No Time to Lose: The wellbeing of Australia's children* edited by Sue Richardson and Margot Prior, published by Melbourne University Press, 2005.
16 The Australian Family Association's 2004 report, "Men and Women Apart", is drawn from whole-population data from the 1986, 1996 and 2001 censuses.
17 Published by Random House, 2005.
18 *The Weekend Australian*, March 11-12, 2006. "Mao film's soft focus may shock his critics" by Mary-Anne Toy.
19 ABC-Radio, *PM* programme, May 12, 2006. "Australian workers passed over for imported labour", reported by Stephen Long.
20 *The New York Times*, May 28, 2006. "The other legacy of Enron" by Alex Berenson.
21 *American Journalism Review*, March 1999. "What do readers really want" by Charles Layton. The piece referred to a German poll conducted in 1995 and reported in *Public Opinion Quarterly*.
22 "How vital is motivation in our lives?" Address by Professor Raj Persaud delivered at Gresham College, London, October 6, 2005.
23 *The Sydney Morning Herald*, January 26, 2006. "Too many off to university – abroad" by Joy Thompson.

CHAPTER 10, PAGES 209-233

1 *The Sydney Morning Herald*, January 5, 2006. "Talks to ignore emissions targets" by Stephanie Peatling. In a news story a month earlier, Campbell had warned of the world's possible "hot death" but maintained that tackling global warming shouldn't be allowed to harm economic growth.
2 *New York*, April 3, 2006. "I want your text" by Em & Lo.
3 Published by Wakefield Press.
4 *Leverage Points*, Issue 54, a subscriber e-letter. "A new capitalism we can live by: an interview with Danah Zohar".
5 *Personnel Today*, December 6, 2005. "The spirit of enterprise" by Noel O'Reilly.

6 In the interview "The spirit of enterprise", published in British magazine *Personnel Today* on December 6, 2005, SQ founder Danah Zohar is described as working with the McKinsey consultancy's new global spiritual intelligence training initiative. McKinsey however denies there is any formal agreement with Zohar or any such initiative, although Michael Rennie, a McKinsey director, was happy to confirm separately that "she had helped us [McKinsey] develop our thinking on spiritual intelligence and its impact on organisational values in the twenty-first century". A follow-up email to McKinsey's spokesman requesting clarification led nowhere. Odd.

7 *The McKinsey Quarterly*, Number Two, 1997.

8 *The Wall Street Journal*, January 17, 2002. "McKinsey's close relationship with Enron raises question of consultancy's liability" by Suein Hwang and Rachel Emma Silverman.

9 Note: EBIDTA stands for earnings before interest, depreciation, taxes and amortisation.

10 *Forbes*, July 1, 2005. "Paradigm for a fleecing" by Tatiana Serafin.

11 *BusinessWeek*, July 8, 2002. "Inside McKinsey" by John A. Byrne.

12 *Rip off! The Scandalous Inside Story of the Management Consultancy Money Machine* by David Craig (real name, Neil Glass), Original Book Company, 2005. Other reports describe Birt's insistence that the BBC develop an "internal market". That is, that departments, from libraries to graphics to sound recording, had to start billing each other for services rendered rather than those services being provided as below-the-line costs. Apart from being a bureaucratic catastrophe, it had some extraordinary effects. The Record Library started charging so much to lend out recordings that producers found it cheaper to buy them at the record shop over the road. A story in *The Guardian*, from July 19, 1993, reported that "if a record is popular, 20 different departments or stations now purchase their own copy – a method of money-saving which Lewis Carroll would have adored".

13 Simplyfamily.com "Consulting: The 21st century's $40 billion industry" by Gary Younge.

14 *Fast Company*, November, 2001. "Tom Peters' true confessions" by Tom Peters.

15 *The Sydney Morning Herald*, April 24, 2006. "HSC English is trapped in a straitjacket" by Daniel Brass.

16 Australian census of women executive managers, 2006, conducted by the Equal Opportunity for Women in the Workplace Agency (EOWA). Figures based on the companies listed on the ASX 200 index of the Australian Stock Exchange.

17 Salary figures are from a CommSec survey of wage figures released in November 2005.

18 National Science Foundation, Infobrief, November 2005.

19 UNESCO's Innovations in Science and Technology Education, Vol VIII, 2003. "Science and Technology Education: Current Challenges and Possible Solutions" by Svein Sjøberg.

20 *The Demon-Haunted World: Science as a candle in the dark* by Carl Sagan and Ann Druyan,

Random House, 1996.

21 *The Australian*, May 3, 2006. "Media management spins out of control" by Leigh Dayton.

22 *The Sydney Morning Herald*, January 13, 2006. "Heart cry of a generation as young Christians jump for Jesus" by Linda Morris.

23 *Academe*, January-February 2005. " 'Believing in yourself' as classroom culture" by Susan Ostrov Weisser.

CHAPTER 11, PAGES 235-261

1 *The Sydney Morning Herald*, August 31, 2005. "What the gossip mags say" by Jacqueline Maley.

2 In an interview with Iain Shedden of *The Australian*, June 6, 2006, Gittoes muses on another follow-up film if his protégé gets into a studio. He says, "It could be interesting to see him getting out of one frying pan into a different kind of fire … If I have made him into a star, then that's an incredible thing."

3 "Perceptions of the prevalence and seriousness of academic dishonesty in Australian universities" by Mark Brimble and Peta Stevenson-Clarke, Griffith University, 2005.

4 "Managing academic dishonesty in Australian universities: Implications for teaching, learning and scholarship" by Mark Brimble and Peta Stevenson-Clarke, Griffith University, 2006.

5 *Newsweek*, August 29, 2005. "Of criminals and CEOs" by Tara Pepper.

6 *The Sun-Herald*, July 2, 2006. Editorial: "Don't let parents become the new school bullies."

7 Published by Pluto Press, 2006.

8 "How vital is motivation in our lives?" Address by Professor Raj Persaud delivered at Gresham College, London, October 6, 2005.

9 ibid

10 *Psychological Science*, Vol 16, No 12, December 2005. "Self-discipline outdoes IQ in predicting academic performance of adolescents" by Angela Duckworth and Martin Seligman.

11 *Psychology Today*, November/December 2005. "The winning edge" by Peter Doskoch.

12 *The Cambridge Handbook of Expertise and Expert Performance* edited by K. Anders Ericsson, published by Cambridge University Press, 2006.

13 Figures from World Health Organisation report, "Young people's health in context", from the Health Behaviour in School-aged Children 2001/2002 survey, the latest available. Australia was not included in the survey.

14 *The Sunday Times*, January 29, 2006. "Failing to teach them how to handle real life" by Sian Griffiths. The story reported on research conducted by professors Philip Adey and Michael Shayer.

15 *Sunday Life*, January 20, 2002. "The runaway brain" by Wendy Tuohy.

16 *Time Magazine*, May 10, 2004. The cover story "Secrets of the Teen Brain" provides a readable and authoritative analysis of this maturation of the brain.

17 *Scientific American*, September 1992. "The biological basis of learning and individuality" by Eric R. Kandel and Robert D. Hawkins.

18 *The Guardian*, July 7, 2005. "New lease of life" by Clint Witchalls.

19 *The Sydney Morning Herald*, September 10-11, 2005. "Wake up and smell the roses" by Matt Wade.

20 National survey of 2,520 British children under 10 years, conducted by Luton First for National Kids' Day in the UK, 2005.

21 *The Sydney Morning Herald*, August 21-22, 2004. "Young feel remote from decision-makers" by Andrew Stevenson.

CHAPTER 12, PAGES 263-279

1 *Harper's Magazine*, December 1992. "Tabloid Journalism 101".

2 Address to Future in Review conference by Sol Trujillo, San Diego, May 15, 2006.

3 *The New York Times*, May 2, 2005. "Paris Inc." by Lola Ogunnaike.

4 Published by Cambridge University Press, 2003.

5 Published by Allen & Unwin, 2003.

6 *The Boston Globe*, January 18, 2004. "Researchers ask if Americans are cheating more often – and what can be done about it" by Laura Secor.

7 *The Australian*, February 2, 2006.

8 *BusinessWeek*, August 8, 2005. "The rich get (much) richer" by Steven Rattner.

9 *The Australian Review of Public Affairs*, February 6, 2006. "Arguing for a fairer Australia" by Mark Peel, a review of two books: *The Poverty Wars* by Peter Saunders and *Australia Fair* by Hugh Stretton, both published by UNSW Press.

10 *The Chronicle of Higher Education*, July 18, 2005. "Stacks' appeal" by Thomas H. Benton, a pseudonym.

11 *The Australian,* August 10, 2005. "Digital future at Fisher" by Bernard Lane.